THE GREATEST
PHILLIES
CLUBS
OF ALL TIME

KEN BINGHAM

Camino Books, Inc.

Philadelphia

Manufactured in the United States of America

1 2 3 4 5   14 13 12

Library of Congress Cataloging-in-Publication Data

Bingham, Ken.
 The greatest Phillies clubs of all time / Ken Bingham.
     p. cm.
 ISBN 978-1-933822-37-2 (alk. paper)
 1. Philadelphia Phillies (Baseball team)—History. I. Title.
 GV875.P45B58 2012
 796.357'640974811—dc23   2011043212

Interior and cover design: Jerilyn Bockorick

This book is available at a special discount on bulk purchases for
promotional, business, and educational use.

Publisher
Camino Books. Inc
P.O. Box 59026
Philadelphia, PA 19102

www.caminobooks.com

This book is dedicated to my wife, Sally,
who still makes me ecstatic
every time she walks into a room.

From *The Philly Fan*

a play by Bruce Graham

Tell ya the truth...I'm not sure why we boo alla time. I mean, sometimes it's not our fault—it's the TV and newspapers. They bring up that Santa Claus thing one more time—I swear...I was at that game. Didn't keep the ticket stub. So it's 'round Christmas and at half-time they bring out Santa Claus. This guy's out there, right, doin' his ho-ho-ho bit and we get a good look at him.

Typical Iggles, they went cheap. Poor guy looked like some wino—he was about 12 pounds and had this crappy costume. Beard half hangin' off—it was a joke. So we booed 'im. But we weren't booin' Santa Claus, for Christ's sake.

Well, what I'm sayin' is...what's the word? It's kinda' ingrained, that it? I mean, I was a kid ya just booed when ya didn't like somethin'. Say what ya will about us, ya always know where we stand.

Phillies Memory

Michael A. Ginsberg, Longtime Fan

My in-laws live a short drive from Cooperstown. As any fan of the first team to lose 10,000 games will tell you, the Hall of Fame is far from a shrine to Phillies glory. That's okay. Anyone can be a Yankees fan, walking through the sacred halls and finding something honoring the Evil Empire seemingly around every corner.

Being a Phillies fan requires you to hunt for your heroes floor after floor, finding the plaques of Schmidt, Bowa, Carlton and others, holding my daughter's hand with tears in my eyes as I touch each one and tell her what those guys mean to me.

I love going through the part where they keep the memorabilia from World Series winners, and going past case after case after case after case until we get to 1980 and it feels like I've lived the desperation of waiting for that series win all over again.

Contents

Acknowledgments

There isn't any possible way to acknowledge everyone who took part in putting this book together. There's my father, whom I would sit beside, wide-eyed and open-eared, as we listened to the games on radio when I was a kid; my mom, who is so passionate about the team that she can't bear to watch them unless they're in the lead; and my family, from my sister and my brother to my nephews and nieces, who are so rabid about the sport that watching a game beside them in front of the TV is as thrilling as being at the ballpark. And, of course, to all my friends, who have put up with me through the ups and downs of Philly sports. If I named one, I'd have to name several hundred, so let's just say en masse, "Sorry. I'll replace that. I guess I got too excited." To Jacqui Harper, who helped produce the photos you'll find within these pages. Also to John Cunningham and John Andelfinger, as well as to Brad Fisher of Camino Books, who helped me edit this piece. And, finally, to Camino's publisher, Edward Jutkowitz, who thought this book worthy of baseball's greatest fans.

To one and all.

Introduction

Pleasure.

Pain.

Pleasure. Pain.

Pleasure. Pain. Pain. Pain.

That's the life of a Phillies fan. Or at least it's been my life with them. From the very beginning, which for me came as early as 1964, I continuously set myself up for disappointment. I can't help myself. I just believe in them so much. And I mean really, REALLY believe. I think that every single season is going to be remarkable.

No. Scratch that.

I think that every single game is going to be remarkable, to the tune of going undefeated: 162 and 0. Okay, perhaps 161 and 0. I can understand the occasional rainout.

This kind of belief system is the only rationalization I have for how upset I get with every loss that the team suffers.

Scratch that again.

I get upset every time we walk a batter, let in a run, strike out with a runner in scoring position. Sometimes, we don't even have to make a mistake for me to go into agony. All it takes is Brad Lidge to stroll onto the field with a one-run lead, a bad call at first base, a two-strike count. Hell, I've been known to come unglued when we've got the bases loaded, nobody out.

Sometimes Ryan Howard will connect with that long drive to deep right field, and sometimes we get the strikeout, popout, long flyout scenario.

Every Phillies fan knows what bases loaded, no one out means. Strikeout, popout, long, long flyout.

Pleasure. Pain. Pleasure. Pain. Pleasure. Pain.

I learned it from my father. A diehard Phillies fan.

My first Phillies memory is inextricably tied to him. It was 1964 (I'm sure any true-blooded Phillies fan just shuddered—sorry). I was only four years old and swimming my little arms and legs off at a lake in Montgomery County Park. At one point,

I stopped thrashing about and looked around me. What I saw was frightening. Just moments ago, I'd been surrounded by fellow bathers. Now the lake stood empty.

Did everyone disappear? Had I crossed some dimensional time barrier?

I swiveled my head and found that everyone was up on the beach, huddled around their transistor radios. I quickly transitioned from fear to curiosity, and moved on out to find them listening to the melodious sounds of By Saam as he called Jim Bunning's perfect game.

Now, mind you, I had no idea what a perfect game was. But I understood emotion. I could read the tension, feel the excitement, could sense it building until it exploded into the joyous elation of baseball glory. "These aren't just any Phillies club," my father told me on the way home. "These are the 1964 Phils. And they're going to do something special this year."

Most of you know how this turned out. You wouldn't have even casually thumbed through this book and gotten this far without knowing how this turned out.

After the heartache of that season, my father sat me on his knee and apologized. That's right, apologized. He wanted to tell me he was sorry for bringing me up as a Phillies fan. This team would tear my heart out.

My next clear recollection of the Phillies came on a soft summer's night in 1971. I was hanging out at my cousin Louie's house, all of 11 years old and excited about staying up late now that school was out. We'd just come in from a game of kick the wickie (same as kick the can, only without the can), and found the dining room empty.

When we'd gone outside, my family, his family, a cousin's family, and a neighbor's family had been hunkered around the kitchen table, drinking shots of Sambuca and eating my grandmother's fried pizza. They'd been laughing about things we couldn't understand, telling stories about events we didn't even want to understand, and, more than anything else, having a great time.

We found them huddled around my grandmom's 12-inch black-and-white, taking in Rick Wise's no-hit bid. I sat beside them and watched a club that had languished in the cellar for the past seven years suddenly become national news, thanks to this hero who strapped on the cape and was willing to carry the entire city on his broad shoulders.

I begged my father to buy me a Rick Wise jersey, a Rick Wise hat, a Rick Wise ball, bat and glove. And, of course, a Rick Wise cape. Less than a year after the greatest pitching performance I had ever seen, the Phillies jettisoned their star to the St. Louis Cardinals.

Pleasure. Pain. Pleasure. Pain.

I wasn't happy. How could I be? Who the hell was this Steve Carlton, and how the hell could he ever dethrone Rick The Man?

The next year was probably the most stunning of my Phillies life. I can distinctly remember sitting on the edge of the bed in my brother's room, where we had the best radio reception, listening to each and every pitch that Steve Carlton threw. When he pitched for these last-place Phillies, they suddenly became a major league contender. And the national press started paying attention. The Phils had landed.

Only three years later, Dave Cash arrived and after he helped turn a game-winning double play, fervently announced, "Yes we can!" Larry Bowa asked him, "Who you talking to, man?" To which Cash responded, "Anyone who'll listen, man. Anyone who'll listen."

Well, I listened, every single night, as the Phils continued to get better and better until, come the summer of 1977, they really did seem like the best team on the planet. Spirits were high in Philadelphia that summer. The Red & Blue were everywhere. People wore caps, jerseys, and smiles. They spent money freely. They spoke well of their city. Our economy went up. Way up.

And then it happened.

With a large, ninth-inning lead at home against the Dodgers, the Phils found a way to turn the pages back to 1964. I still cringe, as I'm sure many of you do, when I think back on Black Friday. It was the first time I ever questioned the existence of God. And, from what happened to the state of the Philadelphia Spirit, God had indeed left town.

Pleasure. Pain. Pleasure. Pain. Pain pain pain pain.

We won the division for the third year in a row the next season, but the city's heart wasn't in it, and, after a lackluster defeat to the improved Dodgers in the playoffs, no one was shocked. The surprising thing was actually watching Tug Mc-

Graw cry after the final defeat. Hadn't he known before the last pitch? Hadn't he known before the season?

This was Philadelphia. You don't win in Philadelphia.

Finally, 1980 came to wash all those tears away, but for me it was just another reminder that the Phillies hated me. Personally. That was the year I moved to Florida, the Phillies won, had a parade, and mocked me from two thousand miles away.

Pleasure. PAIN!

For me, 1983 was a footnote. Yes, we won the division again. And, yes, we made it to the World Series, but the team was made up of several players from the Big Red Machine, our rivals through the mid-seventies.

The Phillies, more than anything else, had been a family. We loved them. And we cheered adamantly against anyone who pledged to defeat them. Now we had to open up our arms to our enemies? We did, and we cheered, but it wasn't with the same fervor.

In contrast, we welcomed the 1993 team as immediate members of the family. In many ways, this made manager Jim Fregosi's decision to bring Mitch Williams into the deciding game of the World Series pardonable. He'd been our man for the ninth the entire year; he was the one who had gotten us this far, and though he might lose the game, you don't humiliate him in front of the entire baseball world by sitting him down. Better he lose it by his own hand.

We all know the rest. Mitchie Poo let up a three-run homer and the Phils went to the showers again.

Pleasure. Pain.

Years later, with my son, a strapping lad of six, I watched as the 2006 Phils barely missed a Wild Card bid for the second year running. My boy put his head down and began to well up. I stroked his back as he kept saying, "But we looked so good all year," and "How could it be over just like that?" and some other such idioms the likes of which many Phillies fans have repeated over and again. I lifted his chin, looked him in the eye and, like my father before me, apologized to him for the very fact that I'd doomed him to grow up a Phillies fan. Nothing but pleasure, then pain.

Then something very strange happened. In 2007, the Fightin' Phils forgot the playbook. They actually turned around the 1964 curse when they marched back from a seven-game deficit with only 17 to play. Okay, they lost in the division series afterward, but we all felt it: this was the dawn of a new era.

The very next year, they actually took the World Series title, and as I put my son to bed that night, he told me I was wrong.

I didn't understand.

He kissed me on the cheek and said that there was nothing to be sorry about. There never was. Being a Phillies fan is great. And, perhaps for the first time since I ambled up onto that beach back in 1964 to listen to Jim Bunning toss those last few pitches in that Father's Day perfect game, I knew he was right.

This book, which collects and compares the greatest teams in all the vast history of our fair Phillies town, is set to celebrate that fact. However, it certainly doesn't claim to be all-inclusive. I for one hope it becomes incomplete within the very next year. In fact, I already know this to be true. I've crunched all the stats, done the comparisons and contrasts, run the numbers against the Pythagorean formula, and come to the undeniable statistical conclusion that the Phillies are going to go 162 and 0 this season.

I have absolutely no doubt.

THE PAST

THE PAST

1

1915: Of Souses, Series, and Sovereigns

1915 National League Standings

Team	Wins	Losses	WP	GB
Philadelphia Phillies	90	62	.592	0
Boston Braves	83	69	.546	7
Brooklyn Robins	80	72	.526	10
Chicago Cubs	73	80	.477	17.5
Pittsburgh Pirates	73	81	.474	18
St. Louis Cardinals	72	81	.471	18.5
Cincinnati Reds	71	83	.461	20
New York Giants	69	83	.454	21

WORLD SERIES: BOSTON RED SOX 4; PHILLIES 1

Preseason

I love old-time baseball—the image of players standing on a dirt field, pulling some flimsy piece of leather over their bruised knuckles, playing for little salary, more like playing for the true heart and love of the game. Yeah, I know that's bullshit. Baseball was always a business, but the images make me think of why I fell in love with the game to begin with, hanging out with my friends during endless summer afternoons, tugging my brother's worn old glove over my hand, and running out to left field. No one was paying me, but every pitch meant the world to me.

The game was about pride above all. Whose town was better than the other? Who got to hold your head up in the end? If your club was having troubles, you couldn't just purchase the top pitcher in the free agent market, throw in a speedy leadoff hitter and the last year's winner of the RBI crown. For the most part, you had to play with what you had.

The problem was, the 1915 Phillies didn't look to have a whole lot, especially because they'd already built up a reputation of being just that: the Phillies. They joined the National League as the Philadelphia Quakers back in 1883, and, after finishing dead last at 17-81, quickly established Philadelphia baseball tradition. In the 32 years prior to 1915, they'd never won the pennant and were just coming off a sixth-place finish in 1914, a full 20^1/$_2$ games behind the Boston Braves. Adding insult to injury, the Braves won the World Series that year in only their third year of existence.

Still, there was reason to be optimistic about the coming year. Sure, they may have had only one player that hit over .300: outfielder Beals Becker at .325. They may have had only two players that topped the .400 mark in slugging percentage: Becker again at .446 and outfielder Gavvy Cravath at .499. They may have had only two players that hit over 10 homers: Cravath at 19 and first basemen Fred Luderus at 12.

You've got to remember, though, that this was the Dead Ball era. Their .263 team batting average was third best in the league, trailing the league-leading Trolley Dodgers by only .006. Their team slugging percentage of .361 was actually the best in the league. They had more home runs than any other team by a long shot, outdistancing the second-place Cubbies, 62-42. It would be like a team of today hitting 180 homers and leading the second-place team by 60.

The pitching staff looked to be the problem. Even though they had men like Grover Cleveland (Pete) Alexander (27-15, 2.38), Erskine Mayer (21 wins, 2.58), and Ben Tincup (2.61), their staff ERA of 3.06, which might look good to us today, was good enough only for a last-place finish in the eight-team league. That's right. A 3.06 ERA was laughably bad in those days.

Naturally, the club felt no need to act on Alexander and Mayer. They would keep Tincup, but would never again give him a starting assignment; Rube Marshall, who started 17 games in 1914, went on to Buffalo, while Joe Oeschger, who started 12 games in 1914, would be relegated to relief.

The Phillies took a big risk by sending the 1911 MVP, third baseman Hans Lobert, to the New York Giants for the unproven duo of third baseman Milt Stock and pitcher Al Demaree. The 30-year-old Demaree had just come off a 10-17 season with one of those bloated 3.09 ERAs. Stock was an untested 20-year-old kid who'd done quite well in his first season in the majors, but did not have the pedigree of Lobert.

The club promoted 23-year-old Eppa Rixey to a full-time starter, even though he'd gone 2-11 the year before. They'd done the same with George Chalmers, who'd only seen action in three games in 1914; for relief they would rely on 19-year-old Stan Baumgartner, a sophomore who had seen only limited action.

Even though they had arguably the best offense in baseball, the Phils were not willing to stand pat there either. They removed their entire middle infield, in Lobert and shortstop Jack Martin, who, after only two years in pro ball, promptly retired at the age of 27.

The Phillies would sign 24-year-old rookie Davey Bancroft to start at short, move Bobby Byrne from second to third, and trade player-manager Red Dooin to Cincinnati for second baseman Bertie J. Niehoff. Niehoff was a sure-handed youngster coming off a rookie season where'd he'd hit .240 for the Red Legs.

Finally, the Phils would call in their player-to-be-named-later deal with the Boston Braves by taking outfielder Possum Whitted. Whitted was a 25-year-old journeyman in his sixth year, playing now for his fifth team. He seemed destined for an early retirement.

Manager

Pat Moran had been a prominent name in major league baseball for 14 years; a catcher by trade, he started his career with the Boston Braves, then moved on to the Cubbies, before landing with the Phillies in 1910. Once with the Phils, he ceased his starting catcher responsibilities and became a player-coach under Red Dooin.

Moran is credited with the grooming of one of the greatest pitchers who has ever played the game—Grover Cleveland Alexander. During his first year as manager of the Phils, he would see Old Pete enjoy the best season of his career. Moran would lead the Phils to their first-ever pennant, and then manage the Cincinnati Reds to their first world championship during the infamous 1919 World Series against the Chicago Black Sox.

The Starting Lineup

Leading Off:
Third Baseman Milt Stock, .260; Bobby Byrne, .206

Mostly a singles hitter, Milt Stock was quick on the bases, and could unnerve a pitcher with his constant movement. He became the Phils regular during the final stretch run and throughout the World Series.

Stock would later play a pivotal role in another landmark year for the Phils—1950. While serving as the third-base coach for the Brooklyn Dodgers, he made the error of waving home Cal Abrams in the ninth inning of a tie game. If Abrams had scored, the Dodgers would have finished the season tied with the Whiz Kids and forced a three-game playoff. As it happened, center fielder Richie Ashburn burned Abrams at the plate with ease, giving the Phils the opportunity to win the game and the pennant in the 10th.

During much of the season, Stock platooned with Bobby Byrne, who had seen some excellent years at bat, most notably when he hit .296 and led the league in hits and doubles when playing for Pittsburgh in 1910. Though his batting average dipped measurably low in 1915 (.209), he was a stalwart in the field, with great range and an accurate arm.

Batting Second:
Shortstop Davey Bancroft, .254

Though not a great hitter for average, Davey Bancroft knew how to make his hits count, scoring 85 times (third in the league). He would always try to force something to happen on the base paths. This habit had the unfortunate result of getting him thrown out a league-leading 27 times, but it always kept the pitcher on his toes, which many account for the immense success of the batters that followed him.

Considered one of the surest hands not only in Phillies but in all of baseball history, Bancroft would have a brilliant career that would take him from Philly to the Giants and Braves. After retiring as an active player in 1930, he would return to baseball as a manager in the All-American Girls Professional League from 1948 to 1950.

Batting Third:
Right Fielder Dode Paskert, .244; Beals Becker, .246, 11 HR

Veteran Dode Paskert would play a stunning role for the club both at bat and in the field. J.C. Kofoed of *Baseball* magazine said of his play in 1915, "It is no exaggeration to say that Paskert is one of the greatest judges of a fly ball in the game today. Those who have seen him circle, hawk-like, turn his back and speed outward, and then make a daring leap, with the spoiling of a three-bagger at the end of it, know how true that statement is."

Though Paskert hit only .248, he was a very patient hitter who ran deep into pitch counts, allowing not only the men on base to maneuver, but the men who came after to study the pitches that would be coming their way.

Paskert shared his position with Beals Becker, who had just come off a year where he'd hit .325 for the Phils with 66 RBI and nine homers. He'd already been a part of two World Series clubs, both with the Giants, one in 1911 and another in 1912. Becker would club a personal record 11 homers in 1915, then abruptly retire at the ripe old age of 28. Reportedly, he could never adjust to the raucous Philadelphia fans who would ride him when he hit a slump. It seems we've always been able to unnerve ballplayers. And here I thought it was only Bert Hooton.

Batting Cleanup:
Left Fielder Gavvy Cravath, .285, 24 HR, 115 RBI

Cactus Gavvy Cravath put together one of the greatest offensive performances for a Phillies player to date. He would lead the league in home runs (24), runs scored (89), RBI (115), walks (86), on-base percentage (.393), slugging percentage (.510), total bases (266), and extra base hits (62).

This came in the middle of six excellent years that saw Cravath lead the league in homers five times, RBI twice, and hits once. Cravath began his career with the Boston Red Sox in 1907, but on his third team in as many years, he was sent to the rival-league American Association Minneapolis Millers, where he put together two more extraordinary years.

No one made it easy to return to the MLB at that time. Reportedly, Cravath managed his way back thanks to a clerical error in which the Millers forgot to put the word "not" beside the word "available." As a consequence, the Phillies picked the man up in 1912, and history was made.

Cravath would win the home run title six times—a record until Ralph Kiner broke it in 1952. Only Mike Schmidt, with eight, has led the league more. His 119 career homers would be the MLB's best until George Herman Ruth came along to topple him.

After retiring in 1919, Cravath returned to manage the Phils in 1920; however, after a lukewarm season in which he was criticized by the press for being way too easygoing, he left the majors to return to the Millers where he finished his career.

Batting Fifth:
First Baseman Fred Luderus, .315

Veteran Fred Luderus led the club in batting average with a .315 (second in the league). It would be the highest batting average of Ludy's career and come dead center in a spate of 10 very strong seasons for the Phillies, which would see him earn 99 RBI in 1911 and bat .293 in 1919, his last full season with the club before retiring in 1920.

Luderus distinguished himself as an iron man, once playing in 533 consecutive games, and was never once lifted for a pinch hitter. He proved to be the only strong hitter in the Phillies' first-ever World Series appearance.

Batting Sixth:
Center Fielder Possum Whitted, .287

Possum Whitted was just coming off a season with the "Miracle Braves" of 1914, who had managed to come back from floundering in last on July Fourth to an improbable upset over the heavily favored Philadelphia Athletics of Connie Mack.

Whitted was traded to the Phillies in 1915, but didn't miss a beat, helping to take his team to the World Series as well. Whitted would star with the Phillies for the next two seasons before signing up for the war effort in 1917. He would retire in 1919, still at the top of his game.

Batting Seventh:
Second Baseman Bertie J. Niehoff, .238

Bertie Niehoff was a sure-handed, sure-footed fielder who would hit only .238 in 1915, but could make things happen on the base paths, stealing 21 bases—second on the club only to Whitted's 24. His 61 runs scored came in third behind Cravath and Bancroft. That's really quite a remarkable feat for a man at the bottom of the order who didn't get on base much.

Niehoff would steadily improve at the plate over the next two seasons, leading the league in doubles in 1916, but would be traded at the end of the 1917 season, and retire at its conclusion from the Giants. He would return to baseball as the manager of the South Bend Blue Sox of the All-American Girls Professional Baseball League.

Batting Eighth:
Catcher Reindeer Bill Killefer, .238; Catcher Ed Burns, .241

Killefer and Burns had comparable offensive stats, were hard outs, and could move a runner along, as can be seen in Niehoff's scoring percentage. Both handled their pitchers extremely well, thanks to the excellent instruction of manager Pat Moran.

Killefer would see his best batting average in 1917 when he clubbed a .274, but be rewarded in a remarkable trade that sent him and Pete Alexander to the Chicago Cubs for the likes of Pickles Dillhoeffer.

As for Burns, he would see his average and playing time steadily decline over the next three years until he retired at the end of the 1918 season.

The Pines

While many championship teams of the Dead Ball era would depend on a starting eight while using few men off the bench, the Phils regularly platooned three players, so at any one time they might turn to the likes of Beals Becker or Dode Paskert for power, to Bobby Byrne or Mile Stock for singles and speed, or to Bill Killefer or Ed Burns for patience and contact.

The Starting Staff

The Ace:
Right-Hander Grover Cleveland "Pete" Alexander,
31-10, 1.22 ERA, 241 K

Grover Cleveland Alexander enjoyed the best season of his il-
lustrious career in 1915, leading the league in wins (31), winning
percentage (.756), ERA (1.22), complete games (36 out of 42!),
shutouts (12), innings pitched (376.1), and strikeouts (241).

Alexander had led the league in wins while a rookie in 1911
with 28, a record for a rookie still. From 1912 to 1920, he led the
league in ERA five times (1915, 1916, 1917, 1919, and 1920),
wins five times (1914–1917 and 1920), innings six times (1912,
1914–1917, and 1920), strikeouts six times (1912, 1914–1917, and
1920), complete games five times (1914–1917 and 1920),
shutouts four times (1915, 1916, 1917, and 1919), and would take
the Triple Crown in 1915, 1916, and 1920.

Astonishingly, Pete would be shipped along with his favorite
receiver, Reindeer Bill Killefer, to the Cubs in 1918, where he
would continue to dominate. And what did the Phillies get in return? Some cash, a pitcher named Mike Pendergast who would
last only a season, and the one and only Pickles Dillhoeffer.

Go get 'em, Pickles.

Alexander suffered from shell shock while stationed in France
during World War I, and though already a drinker, he became a
man who depended on alcohol in order to dampen the physical
demons he soon had to battle. He would enjoy a last hurrah with
the Cardinal organization, where he was traded in 1926. After
throwing complete game victories in Games Two and Six of the
World Series, he went out on the town. Knowing he wouldn't be
pitching again until spring, there was nothing holding him back
from drinking long into the night, then into the morning.

Teammates say Alexander was still feeling the effects of the
alcohol when the Cards took the field for Game Seven against
the Yankees. Things seemed well in hand with the Cards leading 3-2 in the seventh; however, they called on Pete with the
bases loaded, two outs, and the feared slugger Tony Lazzeri
striding to the plate. Pete went on to strike out Lazzeri, throw
two more shutout frames to win the Series, then win 21 more
the very next season.

As for Pickles? He would retire in 1921, back with the Cardinals after enjoying a career that saw a total of no homers and a composite .223 batting average.

Second in the Order:
Right-Hander Erskine Mayer, 21-15, 2.36 ERA, 114 K

Erskine Mayer prospered in 1915, winning 21 games (third in the majors), while posting a 2.36 ERA, and 20 complete games (sixth). This marked his second consecutive 20-win season, a mark he would never reach again. Mayer would be traded to Pittsburgh during the 1918 season, and end his career with the historic 1919 Black Sox, pitching six games for them during the season, and throwing one inning of shutout ball in the World Series.

Third in the Order:
Right-Hander Al Demaree, 14-11, 3.05 ERA

Al Demaree provided a strong third arm for the club. At 30 years old, he notched his third consecutive double-figured win count, though his ERA by league standards was fairly robust. His best season would be reserved for 1916, however, when he'd win 19 while posting a 2.62. Demaree would be traded prior to the 1917 season, and retire at age 34 from the 1919 Boston Braves.

Fourth in the Order:
Left-Hander Eppa Rixey, 11-12, 2.39;
Right-Hander George Chalmers, 8-9, 2.48 ERA

Alexander, Mayer, and Demaree would be ably supported by Eppa Rixey, who earned 11 wins in his 20 starts while recording a 2.39 ERA, and George Chalmers, who racked up another eight with a 2.48. An eventual Hall of Famer, Rixey would blossom under the tutelage of Pat Moran to win 22 games the next year, and become one of the most dominant pitchers in the game when he followed Moran to Cincinnati. Chalmers, however, would see only eight more starts and one victory before retiring after the 1916 season.

The Pen

During the Dead Ball era, starting pitchers would provide most of the relief, the Phils' top five making 34 relief appearances. Other than them, the Phils' go-to men were George McQuillan, who threw 63 innings of ball while garnering a 2.12 ERA; Stan Baumgartner, 2.42 in 16 appearances; and Joe Oeschger, 3.42 in six.

Phillies Memory

Jim Monitor, Center Fielder and Insurance Salesman

I still get a thrill when I look over the 1915 Phillies lineup: Stock, Burns and Byrne. Cravath. Grover Cleveland Alexander. Eppa Jeptha. These are people I grew up with, an indelible part of my youth.

No, I'm not over a hundred years old. I got to know these guys playing APBA Baseball, a baseball board game. So many hot summer afternoons, I would sit out with my friends on the family porch. We all had our favorite teams. I had the '15 Phils. Rich had the '27 YankMEES. Terry loved the '31 A's.

We would play full 154-game seasons with 10 clubs in all. Kept all the stats, relived some games late at night. When we went away to college, we took the packs with our teams with us, vowing to play every time we got together. Of course, life gets in the way sometimes, and those "every times" never really got to happen.

I only won once in the seven seasons that we played, but my God, I remember that final battle, when Grover Cleveland Alexander struck out Babe Ruth in the last game of a four-game sweep. I can still feel my heart beating like it did when I was a kid.

I suppose that's what baseball does for you, what it does for every little boy and adult alike. It makes you remember that inside of us all, we're still little kids and the world is full of popcorn, hot dogs, and cotton candy. And, every now and then, Grover Cleveland Alexander can strike out the sides for your club and give you a memory to last a lifetime.

The Season

The Phillies were in a tight race for most of the year. August would see them in first place, but only three and a half games from the sixth-place New York Giants. It would still be a three-team race in early September when the Phils gained a one-game lead on the Dodgers and three on the Braves, but then the club would slowly pull away to a six-and-a-half-game lead over the second-place Braves, 18? over the sixth-place Cardinals, and 21? over the once-in-the-hunt Giants.

They were like a python that ever-so-slowly ingests its food. They allowed most of the National League to think they might be able to pull it off before winning 37 games in their last month and a half of play, finishing the year with a 90-62 record.

THE 1915 WORLD SERIES

The Phillies would run into a buzz saw in 1915 as they met the American League Champion Boston Red Sox. On their way to taking the Fall Classic in three of the next four years, the Bosox had won 101 that season to beat out Ty Cobb's Tigers by two and a half games. Their team ERA of 2.39 was second best only to the fourth-place Senators. Babe Ruth, then a hard-throwing pitcher, clocked in with 18-8 record and a 2.44 ERA—and he was the lowest man on the totem pole; Ernie Shore won 19 with a 1.64 ERA (third in the league); Rube Foster added another 19 with a 2.11 ERA (seventh); Dutch Leonard chalked up 15 with a 2.36; while the league leader Smoky Joe Wood posted a 1.49. And if that weren't enough, this club could flat-out hit. Their .260 average was second only to the Tigers, while their .339 slugging was second only to the White Sox. Tris Speaker (.322, 69 RBI, 108 runs scored) and Duffy Lewis (.291, 76 RBI) led the bashers, while the fleet-footed Harry Hooper (90 runs scored) and Larry Gardner (51) held down the top of the order.

Though the Phillies would manage to take the opener at the Baker Bowl behind Grover Cleveland Alexander's complete game performance, they would lose the next four thanks to the stellar Bosox arm corps. Each game, however, was a tight one. Though the Phils could manage only three hits against second game starter Rube Foster, they would enter the ninth inning tied at 1, before Erskine Mayer allowed a two-out, game-winning single to Foster himself.

Game Three saw pretty much the same scenario. The Phils again managed only three hits, this time against Bosox starter Dutch Leonard; nonetheless, they entered the ninth with the game knotted at one. This time it was Alexander who let it go, allowing a two-out, game-winning single to Duffy Lewis.

In Game Four, they found themselves on the short end of an Ernie Shore masterpiece, trailing 2-0 in the eighth. Gavvy Cravath kicked off a two-out rally with a triple and came around to score on a Fred Luderus single, but could get no closer.

Returning to Philadelphia, the team found themselves in a two-game hole for the first time all season. Now was the time when they could find out what they were made of. And they didn't hesitate.

Rube Foster hit Milt Stock to start the game, then allowed an infield single to Davey Bancroft, before Dode Paskert bunted to load the bases for Cactus Gavvy. Cravath was only 2 for 13 thus far in the postseason, with six strikeouts. He stared down Foster to the thrill of the crowd, worked the count full, and then promptly hit a sharp grounder to the pitcher, who turned a home-to-first double play. Suddenly, the Phils were in danger of not scoring at all.

On an 0-2 count, however, Freddy Luderus doubled to right center to bring both runners home. Two runs! No team in the previous games had needed more to nail down a victory. Things looked good. The only problem was that Erskine Mayer did not. With two outs and nobody on in the top of the second, Duffy Lewis tripled to the left center, then came home on a Jack Berry single. The Sox would tie the game in the very next frame, when right fielder Harry Hooper led off with a homer. After Tris Speaker stroked a one-out single, Pat Moran had seen enough, and removed Mayer for Eppa Rixey.

While Rixey held them down, Luderus smashed a home run to right in the fourth, and with two outs, Bertie Niehoff smacked a single to center, sprinted to third on an Ed Burns single, then scored on an error. The Phils had taken the lead.

Fans started dreaming of a 3-2 Series, and Eppa Rixey looked more than up to the task. He glided into the eighth having only allowed an infield single. The fact that Del Gainer led off the inning with a bloop single over third didn't seem much of a concern. Duffy Lewis, however, pounded the next pitch deep over the center field wall to tie the game at four. The crowd went silent while Moran went out to talk to Rixey.

He decided to keep him in. It would prove to be an unfortunate decision. Harry Hooper promptly hit his second homer of the game to give the Sox what would prove to be the winning run for the game and for the Series.

The Phils' bats, which had proven so lethal during the season, fell nearly silent in their first Series. They hit only .182 as a team and scored only 10 runs, 40 percent of them coming in their final losing effort. The great Gavvy Cravath would manage only two hits and a .125 performance; only Fred Luderus offered much to cheer about, hitting at .438 with two doubles, a homer, and a full six of the 10 runs batted in for the club.

The Phils didn't sulk, however. They were a strong team and knew that if they continued to work hard, they'd be back the very next season. As most know already, "next season" wouldn't come around for another 35 years.

THE AFTERMATH

The Phillies would indeed remain strong for the next couple of seasons. They actually improved on their record in the 1916 season with 91 wins, the franchise record at that point. No team would win more until the 1964 club, but we don't need to go into that right now, do we?

Alexander won 33 in 1916, Rixey won 22, and Demaree 19. Mayer would unfortunately fall to 7-7. The Brooklyn Robins proved too much for them, as they earned 94 victories. The Phils would be within a game on October 2, but dropped three of their last four against the Boston Braves to see their pennant hopes slip away. The Robins would go on to lose the World Series to those Sox again, by a familiar 4-1 drubbing.

The Fightin's would notch up another 87 in 1917, but trail the first-place Giants by a full 10 games. The bottom would fall out in 1918, as the Phils lost a good deal of their stars either to the war or to bad trades. Cravath remained on the club, but his star had ceased to shine, as he turned in a .232 performance. Only Erskine Mayer remained from the stalwart 1915 staff, but he would serve up only a 7-4 record. The club itself finished with only 65 wins, good enough for sixth place.

Things would be black for Philadelphia baseball for a long time to come. They would have only one more winning record over the next 39 years, before Richie Ashburn, Robin Roberts, and those Whiz Kids took to the Shibe Park diamond.

1950: One with Whiz!

1950 National League Standings

Team	Wins	Losses	WP	GB
Philadelphia Phillies	91	63	.591	0
Brooklyn Dodgers	89	65	.578	2
New York Giants	86	68	.558	5
Boston Braves	83	71	.539	8
St. Louis Cardinals	78	75	.510	12.5
Cincinnati Reds	66	87	.431	24.5
Chicago Cubs	64	89	.418	26.5
Pittsburgh Pirates	57	96	.373	33.5

WORLD SERIES: NEW YORK YANKEES 4; PHILLIES 0

Preseason

For the first time in over a third of a century, fans had reason to feel optimistic as the 1949 club had just completed their first winning season in 32 years. Sure, they'd finished in third place, their first time in the top of the division in 14 years. Incoming manager Eddie Sawyer and his belief in the youth movement seemed to make the difference.

Center fielder Richie Ashburn was only 23, right fielder Del Ennis, 24; third baseman Willie Jones, 24; shortstop Granny Hamner, 22; second baseman Mike Goliat, 24; catcher Stan Lopata, 24; right-handed starter Bubba Church, 24; right-handed starter Bob Miller, 23; utility infielder Putsy Caballero, 22; outfielder Jack Mayo, 23: left-handed starter Curt Simmons, 20; and right-handed starter Robin Roberts, 23. The wizened veterans on the club were catcher Andy Seminick, 29, and first baseman Eddie Waitkus, also 29.

Hence their nickname: the Whiz Kids.

These Phils were too young to know, and perhaps too foolish to understand, that they weren't supposed to win a pennant. They didn't know that the National League just kept them around to help tune up the other clubs so that they could lose to the Yankees.

They'd climbed to the top half of the division in 1949, thanks to their pitching. Their team 3.89 ERA was good enough for fourth, and they were a club that prided itself on control; no team had walked less of the opposition and only one allowed fewer home runs.

Left-hander Ken Heintzelman had turned around a losing career at 33, when he finished 17-10 (fourth in the league) with a 3.02 ERA (fifth); he led the league with nine shutouts and only three others allowed fewer walks. In only his second season, Robin Roberts won 15 games (fourth) and posted a 3.89 ERA. Right-hander Russ Meyer had put together 17 wins (fourth), a .680 winning percentage (fourth), and 14 complete games (10th). Meanwhile, Jim Konstanty had been given the newly designed closer's job, and he had done remarkably well. Appearing in 53 games, he threw 97 innings for a 3.25 ERA.

The offense, however, still failed to click. They finished with the lowest team batting average, and produced the third fewest runs in the league; their 122 homers might have been good enough to place them in fourth, but only one team drew fewer walks, and no team struck out more.

Still, they did have some men with more than a little promise. Richie Ashburn hit .284 from the leadoff position where he'd scored 84 runs, this following his rookie season where he'd hit .333. Philly native Del Ennis hit .302 (ninth) with 25 homers (sixth) and 110 RBI (fifth). Still just a kid of 22, Ennis had put together four consecutive solid seasons and seemed like a poised leader in the outfield.

First baseman Dick Sisler, in his second year as a Phillie, hit a then career-best .289, while striking out only 38 times in 446 appearances. The team also had some pop, both from catcher Andy Seminick, who clubbed 24 long balls (seventh), and from third baseman Willie "Puddin' Head" Jones, who posted 19 round-trippers and 77 RBI in his first full season as a starter in the majors.

In addition, 1950 would see the return of first baseman Eddie Waitkus, who had been shot the year before by an obsessed fan. This would allow Sisler to move to the outfield, and return the weak-hitting Bill Nicholson to the bench.

The Manager

Eddie Sawyer had come up through the Yankees organization as a player-manager, making his mark in 1939 when he took the Amsterdam Rugmakers (gotta love that name) to first place while hitting .369 with 103 RBI. He joined the Phillies farm system in 1944, and would replace Ben Chapman at the helm in 1948.

Sawyer would win Manager of the Year in 1950, but his light wouldn't shine for long. The club's fortunes fell quickly, leading to his removal in 1952. He would return as manager, replacing Mayo Smith, in midseason 1958, but not be able to help turn around their poor play. After they dropped their Opening Day game 9-4 in 1960, Sawyer stepped down, claiming, "I'm 49 years old and I want to live to be 50."

The Starting Lineup

Leadoff:
First Baseman Eddie Waitkus, .284, 102 R

Eddie Waitkus would return strong for the club in the leadoff role. He was a huge fan favorite, which really was the problem. While with the Cubs for his first three years in the majors, he developed a fine fan base. One fan in particular, Ruth Ann Steinhagen, became particularly obsessed with him.

It wasn't dangerous, apparently, while Waitkus played for the Cubs. However, once he went to the Phils, Steinhagen felt betrayed, and decided to kill the young first baseman. She checked into the hotel where he was staying, using the name of an old high school friend of his, then left a note asking that he stop by her room. Ruth Ann would be waiting for him with a rifle. She shot him in the chest, just missing his heart, then took her own life. Bernard Malamud used the Waitkus tale as inspiration for *The Natural*, which in turn was made into the classic Barry Levinson film starring Robert Redford.

Waitkus would not disappoint the fans on his return. Batting .284 with 182 hits (fifth) and 32 doubles (ninth), he would score 102 runs (sixth) to ignite the team at their home, Shibe Park. He was also sure in the field, with his .933 fielding percentage second in the league.

Batting Second:
Center Fielder Richie Ashburn, .302, 14 Triples, 14 SB

Left-hander Richie Ashburn led the league in triples with 14, while stealing 14 bases (fifth) and never getting caught. A singles hitter, Ashburn could strike the ball to all fields. Ashburn was known for his terrific glove and fine arm, leading the league in putouts for every season but one from 1949 through 1958; he would consistently place first in outfield assists as well.

Nearing the end of his career, Ashburn was drafted by the expansion New York Mets for their infamous inaugural 1962 season. Strong right up to the end, he became one of that club's only bright spots, hitting .306 in his last year of play.

Ashburn returned to Philly in 1963 to begin broadcasting games and was joined by his great friend, Harry Kalas, in 1976. The two had an on-air relationship unlike any other. During the difficult years—and there were many—it was a joy just to sit back and listen to them have fun on the air. Ashburn was inducted into the Hall of Fame by the Veterans Committee in 1976.

Batting Third:
Left Fielder Dick Sisler, .296, 13 HR, 83 RBI

Returning to the outfield after a year of filling in for Waitkus at first, Dick Sisler saw his offensive production go up across the board. He hit .296, rapped 29 doubles, 13 homers, knocked in 83 and scored another 79. It was good enough to earn him his only All-Star team nomination.

Ernest Hemingway immortalized Sisler in *The Old Man and the Sea*, when one character said of him that "[Sisler] hits the longest ball I've ever seen."

Sisler originally joined the Phils in a trade with St. Louis in 1948, and would remain here through the 1951 season, when the Phils packed him and Andy Seminick off to Cincinnati for the promising youngster, Smoky Burgess. Sisler would retire in 1953, but he returned to coach in the Cincinnati organization, eventually becoming manager in 1964.

Batting Cleanup:
Right Fielder Del Ennis, .311, 126 RBI, 31 HR

Del Ennis would have the best season of his career in 1950, leading the league in RBI with 126, to go along with career highs in batting average (.311, fourth in the league), runs scored (92), homers (31, fifth), total bases (538, second), and a .531 slugging percentage (seventh). A product of the Philly farm system, Ennis would become the first winner of the *Sporting News* Rookie of the Year. He would also be the first rookie to win a spot on the All-Star team.

Ennis would put in another six years with the Philadelphia club, all of them profitable. He'd hit over 100 RBI in four of them, and blast over 20 homers in each, before being traded to the Cardinals. He would have yet another productive year in 1957, earning another 105 RBI to go with 24 homers, before sliding in '58 and retiring as a part-time player for the White Sox in '59.

During his playing career, only Stan "The Man" Musial had more RBI, and Ennis would hold the Phillies team home run record of 259 until one Michael Jack broke it in 1980.

Batting Fifth:
Third Baseman Willie "Puddin' Head" Jones, .267,
25 HR, 88 RBI, 100 R

Willie Jones would prove that his breakout season of 1949 was no fluke, as he slugged 25 round-trippers (10th) to get himself 88 RBI and scored 100 times (10th). He was well known around the majors as the best third baseman in the game. He led the league in fielding percentage five times, in putouts seven times, and in assists and double plays twice. Jones would stay with the Phillies until late in 1959, and finish his career with the Cincinnati Reds in 1962.

Batting Sixth:
Shortstop Granny Hamner, .270, 82 RBI, 78 R

Although Granny Hamner's offensive numbers weren't alarming by any means, he earned himself a sixth-place finish in MVP voting mostly because of his remarkable range at short and his incredible leadership abilities. Eddie Sawyer named him team captain in 1952.

Hamner would have a solid career with Philadelphia, having his best season in 1954 when he would hit .299, with 89 RBI and 83 runs scored; he would make the All-Star team three times in his career. He was traded to Cleveland in 1959, but hit only .164 for the club before stepping down.

Granny did not step away, however. He actually worked on his pitching game, went into the Kansas City organization, and came up to throw three games for the club in 1962. He produced a 9.00 ERA and promptly left the field for good as a player at the end of the season. Hamner would manage in the Phillies farm system in the '70s and '80s.

Batting Seventh:
Catcher Andy Seminick, .288, 24 HR

Andy Seminick was lethal from the seventh position, as he enjoyed career bests in batting average (.288), home runs (24), RBI (68), and runs scored (55). He would finish in 14th in MVP voting.

Seminick was a true fan favorite in Philadelphia, the epitome of the hard worker: constantly training, always optimistic, and always persevering. It's amazing that he had been able to keep his easygoing nature and good humor in his first years of the game, where he served as manager Ben Chapman's whipping boy.

His offensive numbers would slip in a big way in 1951, causing the club to trade him along with Dick Sisler for catcher Smoky Burgess; ironically, he would be traded back for Smoky Burgess after the 1955 season. He'd play a limited role for three years for the Phils before retiring after 1958. Managing in the minor league system from 1959 to 1973, Seminick churned out prospects that would put Philadelphia back on the baseball map in the '70s.

Batting Eighth:
Second Baseman Mike Goliat, .234, 13 HR

Mike Goliat had the best batting average of his career in 1950; the fact that it was only .234 says a whole lot. His real value to the team came in his fielding. Needing a middle infielder, Eddie Sawyer threw Goliat in at second just prior to the season, even though he was a first and third basemen by trade. Goliat didn't let him down. He led all second basemen in putouts, and ranked third in assists.

New York Giants manager Leo Durocher had this to say about Mike Goliat: "He doesn't look like a major leaguer. But all I know is that I haven't seen him make an error yet, and every time I look up he's making a double play to take us out of a rally."

Hitting only .225 with 15 RBI and a total of eight extra base hits, the Phillies put Goliat on waivers in 1951. Claimed by the St. Louis Browns, he would gain only two more hits in the 15 times he stepped to the plate through 1952 when he hung up his major league spikes for good.

Mike Goliat wasn't done with baseball, however, and continued to play in the minors until 1961. He would see some good offensive numbers for the Toronto Maple Leafs, where he spent most of his minor league career. Goliat would hit in double figures in homers most of the time, and took home MVP honors for the International League in 1956 when he led the Leafs to the pennant.

The Pines

Stan Lopata served a good deal of time as backup catcher and first baseman. He didn't hit for much (.209, one home run), but was cool and steady both at the plate and behind it. He learned his famous squat stance from Rogers Hornsby, not a bad hitter himself. When the Phils finally gave him a full-season starting job in 1956, he made it pay off with 95 RBI (sixth), 32 homers (sixth), 95 runs scored (seventh), and 33 doubles (second); he made the All-Star team and received votes for MVP. Even though Lopata didn't have the eye in 1950, he certainly had the swagger and confidence—something that influenced the club whether he was on the bench or the field.

Dick Whitman, a reserve outfielder who had just been purchased from the Dodgers for the season, was a singles hitter with little pop. He had an excellent eye, however, and could work the pitchers into deep counts.

Outfielder Bill "Swish" Nicholson had seen his glory days with the Cubs in the '40s. A four-time All-Star, he'd twice led the league in homers and RBI. Even though he'd managed only 10 RBI and three homers in his part-time role here, he was still a feared hitter who could make things happen at any time.

The Starting Staff

The Ace:
Right-Hander Robin Roberts, 20-11, 3.02, 146 K

Robin Roberts made good on the promise he displayed in his sophomore year by turning in his first of six consecutive 20-win seasons. He led the staff with a 20-11 record (second in wins), the first Philly to win 20 games since Grover Cleveland Alexander won 30 in 1917. He recorded a 3.02 ERA (fourth) and led the league with five shutouts; he struck out 146 (fourth), threw 21 complete games (fourth), and even saved a game. He would make the All-Star team for the first of seven consecutive years.

Roberts was a throwback in this era where relief pitchers were now regularly used. He once threw 28 consecutive complete games. To repeat, that's 28 consecutive complete games! By comparison, Roy Halladay led the majors the last three years, with nine in 2010 and 2009, and seven in 2008. You have to go back almost a third of a century, to 1980, to find a pitcher like Rick Langford of the A's, who could even record 28 complete games in a season.

Roberts won more games than any other pitcher in four consecutive years, starting in 1952, when he went 28-7. He led the league in complete games and innings pitched five times. He was primarily known as a power pitcher who had great control. Though Robin was susceptible to the long ball, as many power pitchers are, he rarely got hurt when the game was on the line. Roberts started to develop shoulder problems in 1956 when he went 19-18, his consecutive 20-win streak finally coming to an end.

Roberts' numbers continued to fall in Philadelphia until, after going 1-10 for the club in 1961, he left to sign with the Orioles. It was there that he ceased depending on his power and began to develop his craft. He turned in three consecutive winning seasons before being traded to Houston, finally finishing his major league career with a disappointing 2-3, 6.14 record with the '66 Cubbies. Roberts was elected to the Hall of Fame in 1976 in his fourth year of eligibility.

Second in the Order:
Left-Hander Curt Simmons, 17-8, 2.82, 146 K

After a brief and bright journey, Curt Simmons came into his own in 1950. Just a few years before, Phils owner Bob Carpenter had been so impressed with this high school fastballer that he arranged for an exhibition between the Phillies regulars and an All-Star high school team led by Simmons. Curt proceeded to strike out 11 Phillies as the high school team battled the major league club to a 4-4 tie.

Simmons had battled control problems in his first couple of years on the mound, but manager Eddie Sawyer had seen enough to give him a full starting assignment for 1950. Curt responded with 17 wins against eight losses (fourth in win/loss percentage), and would surely have won 20 had he not been called to the Korean War in early September.

Simmons would not return to major league baseball until 1952, when he notched a 14-8 record with a league-leading six shutouts and a 2.82 ERA (ninth). He was sporadic after that, able to turn in an incredible game, but at times seeming to succumb to his early wildness. Curt went 72-71 in his next five years as a Phillie, with bests of 16 in '53 and 15 in '56; then he developed arm trouble in 1959, after a 7-14 season the year before, and was summarily released.

Simmons was signed by the Cardinals in 1960, and became a breaking ball pitcher. After a couple of years working on the pitch, he saw his career blossom once again. Ironically, Curt became a Phillies killer in 1964, when he went 18-9 for the team that would oust the Phils at the wire in one of the greatest comebacks (or greatest collapses) in baseball history. Simmons' star began to fall in 1965 when he went 9-15, and he would retire after the next season.

Third in the Order:
Right-Hander Bob Miller, 11-6, 3.57

In many ways, the story of Bob Miller is the story of the 1950 Phillies in miniature. Like almost all of the Whiz Kids, Miller was a young, promising player who looked like he had a fabulous future ahead of him. Though not considered to be of incredible potential, Miller, like his team, exploded onto the 1950 scene. He outdueled Vern Bickford of the Braves 2-1 in his first start, shut out the Pirates in his second, and the Reds in his third. Miller went on to an 8-0 start, and not only looked like an easy vote for Rookie of the Year, but also like the ace of the staff.

Then tragedy struck. While carrying a suitcase to an away game, Miller stumbled. It seemed like no big deal, but it caused a constant sacroiliac problem from which he never recovered. He managed to hold onto a winning record, but by the time he got to the World Series, the Yankees utterly dismantled him.

Miller's back problems kept him from starting more than three games in 1951, and landed him in the minors in '52. He pitched with modest success from the bullpen before retiring in 1958. Someone else should have helped the guy with his suitcase. Perhaps then there would be more great teams from the '50s to write about in this book.

Fourth in the Order:
Right-Hander Russ Meyer, 9-11, 5.30

Russ Meyer followed up his 17-8, 3.02 season in 1949 with some tepid mound stats. However, that didn't mean he didn't have impact on the game and on his team. Hell, Meyer had an impact on everyone. With a bubbling personality and a bizarre temper, Meyer could inflame everyone from his teammates, to the opposition, to the crowd itself. Known as the Mad Monk, Meyer would incur as much wrath as support from those around him. He seemed to relish any reaction as long as it was a reaction.

After regaining his mound savvy in 1951 and '52, Meyer went on to have several fine seasons with the Dodgers. However, like Bob Miller before him, a fall and a resulting back problem derailed his once-promising career. He'd hang around for three more seasons with four other clubs, but would win only three more games.

Fifth in the Order:
Right-Hander Bubba Church, 8-6, 2.73

Bubba Church dazzled in the Phils' minor league system before finding room on the starting major league staff in 1950. At the age of 25, the rookie found himself one of the oldest of the Whiz Kids, and he showed his maturity with his poise on the mound. At midseason, he was 8-6 with a 2.73 ERA, and looked ready to turn in not only an impressive season, but the start of an impressive career.

These 1950 Phils, however, were snakebit. No one asked Church to carry their luggage, but the Reds' Ted Kluszewski did happen to carry a bat, which he used to hit a screaming line drive that smacked off Church's forehead with such ferocity that it caromed into right field on the fly. Church took the mound the next week against the Dodgers, but complained of dizziness after the performance and was forced to set his season aside.

Bubba returned to form and then some in 1951, enjoying his best season with a record of 15-11 to go along with a 3.53 ERA and 104 strikeouts. But after going to Cincinnati in 1952, he never again compiled a winning record.

Sixth in the Order:
Left-Hander Ken Heintzelman, 3-9, 4.09

After posting 17 wins the previous season, Ken Heintzelman returned to the form that had distinguished him both in Pittsburgh and in his early years in Philadelphia. His impact was felt on this team, however, as the 11-year veteran had a great deal to teach the youngsters in the club. He came back to go 6-12 in 1951, then closed his major league career as a reliever in '52.

Relief Core

The Closer:
Right-Hander Jim Konstanty, 16-7, 2.66, 22 Saves

The Phillies soared to an unlikely pennant on the unlikely shoulders of reliever Jim Konstanty, who turned in one of the most remarkable pitching performances in the history of the club. A simple look at his statistics doesn't offer the full view of his uncanny season. Konstanty didn't throw enough innings to qualify for the ERA title; his 22 saves seem modest in comparison with a closer of today, while his 16 wins didn't even put him in the top 10 for the league.

So what was so magical about Konstanty? For one thing, it was the fact that closers were still new at the time. There wasn't even a statistic known as the save. Konstanty was a workhorse who appeared in a league-leading 74 games, and did so with nerves of steel. The last pitcher to appear in more games than Konstanty was the Cincinnati Reds' Bill Hutchinson back in 1892. That's before the Spanish-American War!

In late August, Jim was riding the wave of a 13-game scoreless streak when he faced the Pittsburgh Pirates. He came into a 6-6 game in the bottom of the seventh and held on till the Phils could win in 15. A nine-inning relief performance from a closer? Can you imagine any closer today pulling such a feat? When a closer comes in with an out remaining in the eighth, we consider it stalwart duty. For Jim Konstanty, it was all just part of the gig.

In fact, it was so much a part of the gig that Konstanty did it again two weeks later. Trailing 5-3 against the Reds after eight, Jim proceeded to throw nine innings of shutout ball. He allowed a run in his 10th, but the Phils came back to win in 19. Ho hum—just another 10-inning relief performance. What makes it even more uncanny is that the man didn't show a whole lot of promise when coming up through the minors. In fact, that's putting it mildly. He showed no promise at all.

After graduating from college (an uncommon occurrence to begin with for baseball players in the prewar era), Konstanty became a gym teacher. His love of baseball led him to try out and fail a couple times, but he kept at it until signed by the unaffiliated Springfield Nationals in 1941.

When World War II broke out, the pros began signing players with one arm, players whose feet were too big for regulation army shoes, players who were too young to go to war, and they started leagues of women players in order to keep America interested in the game. Cincinnati, however, put Jim into double A where he posted an unremarkable 5.85 ERA.

Konstanty's career began to turn around when he learned the palm ball and the slider, and he finally made the majors in 1948 with the Phillies. Only an iconoclast like Eddie Sawyer could have looked at this 32-year-old journeyman minor leaguer and said, "That's our closer!"

But just as quickly as his star rose, it began to dim. Konstanty turned in only a fair performance from the bullpen over the next two years, with ERAs of 4.05 and 3.94; then, under new management, he was made a starting pitcher in 1953. Jim pulled in 14 victories, but his ERA was still a bloated 4.43. He was picked up on waivers by the Yankees in '54, and there he played for a couple seasons before retiring at the end of '56.

In the end, Konstanty went 66-48 with 74 saves and a 3.46 ERA. Fine stats—not great, but fine. However, for one glorious season, he was the greatest pitcher who graced a baseball diamond. Not many can say that.

And the Rest

The Phillies starters appeared in 44 games of relief, making up the bulk of the relief core for the club. However, Eddie Sawyer could also turn 32-year-old right-hander Milo Candini, who'd spent his formative years toiling with the Senators; like many of the other Phils, he turned in a career year in 1950, notching up a 2.70 ERA in 18 appearances.

Left-hander Ken Johnson (4-1, 4.01), who was just picked up from the Cardinals in a late-April trade, could be counted on as a spot starter and reliever; while right-hander Blix Donnelly (2-4, 4.29) completed his fifth and final year in the majors with the club.

Okay, none of these guys might look very impressive, but seeing as how the Phils would win the league by only two games, you could make the argument that without any one of these important parts of the overall machine, they wouldn't have had enough wins to do it. More than anything else in 1950, this was a total team effort.

The Season

The 1950 Phillies season really began in 1943 when lumber baron William B. Cox purchased the team. Up until this point in

Phillies history, they had never spent much time working with their minor league system. Cox began a revolution that eventually churned out most of the young stars on this club.

They looked like a juggernaut right from the start, and by late July, they were working well on all engines. Robin Roberts had clearly established himself as the ace of the staff, but just barely, because Curt Simmons was proving that he had finally overcome his wild youth, while rookie Bob Miller was busy shutting down the opposition and starting his major league career at 8-0, and fellow rookie Bubba Church had earned eight wins himself. And, of course, there was Konstanty, who was having the best year of any pitcher in the major leagues.

Then the bottom fell out. First Bob Miller stumbled while carrying his luggage, Bubba Church got beaned by a line drive, and while Curt Simmons never faltered, he had to leave the game the first week of September to join the armed forces in the Korean War.

With 11 games to go in the season, the Phils still looked pretty secure, holding onto a seven-and-a-half-game lead over both the Boston Braves and the Brooklyn Dodgers as late as September 20, but by this time they were working on steam. The Dodgers swept a two-game series to pull to within five and a half. Then, after splitting their next two games against Boston, they dropped a four-game series to the Giants.

Suddenly, they were in deep seas. The Dodgers would host our boys for the final two games of the season, trailing the Kids by only two games. The Phils turned to Bob Miller for the opener, but he was out by the fourth en route to a defeat that would bring the Dodgers to within a game. It was one of those "Oh, dear God, this can't be happening" moments that Phils fans know so well. The whole pleasure-pain bit.

Philadelphia braced itself for the final game of the season that would pit the two staff aces against each other in Roberts and Don Newcombe. Both pitchers looked to be on top of their game as they went through the first five, scattering three weak singles between them.

The game stood tied going into the bottom of the ninth, when all went wrong for the Phils, and then suddenly went right. Roberts walked Cal Abrams to start the inning, only the third Dodger to reach base in the entire game. Pee Wee Reece followed with a looping single to left that sent Abrams to second, before Duke Snider rapped a fastball sharply into center.

It was hit so hard that Ashburn didn't even have to move, playing it on the second bounce. There is no reason for Abrams to have rounded third and tried to score. The Dodgers would have had the bases loaded, no one out, and at least three chances to hit a meager fly ball that would have won the game, tied the Phils, and forced a three-game playoff for the pennant. But our old friend Milt Stock, former third baseman for the 1915 club, was the third base coach, and made the greatest blunder of his coaching career. He proudly waved Abrams home. Ashburn, who was known as having one of the best arms in baseball, threw Abrams out easily. Then, after coaxing Carl Furillo into a lazy pop to first baseman Eddie Waitkus, Gil Hodges lofted a fly to Del Ennis to end the inning.

Clearly tiring, Don Newcombe allowed a single to Roberts himself to lead off the 10th. Eddie Waitkus followed with a line drive single to center and, after Ashburn grounded out, Dick Sisler hit the most dramatic home run of his career. Roberts put the Dodgers out in order in the bottom of the frame, and just that quickly, the Phils had turned around a capsizing pleasure cruise to claim only their second pennant in franchise history.

Thank you, Milt Stock.

Phillies Memory

Dick Rosen, Baseball Historian

I was a true Philadelphia A's fan, thanks to an uncle who taught me about the famous A's teams of '29, '30, and '31. I knew the names and the batting averages of the 1929 Athletics before I knew the names of the kids in my third grade class. However, living in a two-team town allowed me to follow the Phillies as well. As the A's began to falter in '49 and '50, the Phils were on the rise and I followed them closely in 1950. They were ahead in the pennant race in early September and then started a nose dive

Roberts was tapped for the final game against the Dodgers (October 1). He had pitched on September 27 and 28. This would be his fourth start in five days. Without the luxury of TV, we were forced to listen to the game on the

radio that warm Sunday afternoon. I was "helping" my father paint the bedroom as we listened intently. The teams
traded runs in the sixth and the game remained tied into the
ninth. In that inning, Cal Abrams was on second with none
out. Duke Snider hit a single to center and when Ashburn
came up with it and threw home, he cut down Abrams. I did-
n't get to see that play until a few days later, but Gene
Kelly's call sounded great on the radio. Roberts got the
Dodgers out in the ninth and it went to the 10th.

In the 10th, Roberts started the Phillies with a single. Ashburn missed with a sacrifice attempt and then with first and
second occupied, Dick Sisler hit a homer (the Phillies' own
"shot heard around the world") to give the Phils a 4-1 lead, all
against Don Newcombe. My whole family jumped all around
the bedroom, probably spilling half the paint. We were ecstatic but the Dodgers still had their 10th inning. Eddie Sawyer
sent Roberts out to finish; he had a 1-2-3 inning. It was over,
Roberts won his 20th of the season, ending 35 years of frustration in Philly. The Whiz Kids had done it.

THE 1950 WORLD SERIES

After such a grand struggle for the pennant, the Phillies knew
there would be no letup in the Series—the dreaded Yankees
were coming to town. They had won the World Series the year
before and were on their way to winning five in a row; in all they
would make 14 World Series appearances over the next 16 years.

The Yanks had won their league by three games over Detroit
and four over Boston. They ranked second in offense in almost
every category to Boston, but their pitching outdistanced all
save Cleveland, which finished 11 games back.

The offense was led by Yogi Berra, who hit .322 (ninth in the
league) with 28 homers (sixth), 124 RBI (third), and 116 runs
scored (fourth). Joe DiMaggio hit .301 with 32 homers (third),
122 RBI (fifth) and 114 runs scored (fifth). Phil Rizzuto hit .324
(sixth) with 125 runs scored (second), while Hank Bauer turned
in a .320 (10th).

Vic Raschi led the Yankee pitching staff with a 21-8 record
(second in wins) and 155 strikeouts (third). Allie Reynolds
backed him up with another 16 (eighth), a 3.74 ERA (eighth),

and 160 strikeouts (second). Eddie Lopat went 18-8 (fourth) with a 3.47 ERA (fourth); Tommy Byrne went 15-9 (10th); and in his rookie year, Whitey Ford went 9-1 with a 2.81.

This was a formidable team. They were managed by the great Casey Stengel, who in his second year was taking them to the World Series for the second time. All in all, during his 12 years at the helm, they would win 10 pennants and seven World Series.

As for the Phils, they were working with patches. Curt Simmons had been granted special dispensation to attend the World Series; the Phils did not ask that he be allowed to play. Robin Roberts was still at his best, but had just started two of the last three games for the Phils and was coming off a complete game, 10-inning performance.

That left Russ Meyer, who had been roughed up in his last outings; the injured Bubba Church, who they still managed to march out there in the last few games to get brutally knocked around; Bob Miller, who hadn't been the same since his stumble earlier in the season; and Ken Heintzelman, who had lost his mojo after a stunning 1949. Their offense, however, was still at full throttle, and they had the youthful exuberance to not recognize that they should be cowed by the Yanks.

Game One

Wednesday, October 4 (Shibe Park)

True to form, manager Eddie Sawyer made an unconventional choice for the starting pitcher in Game One. He would go with MVP reliever Jim Konstanty, who had not started a game in his entire major league career.

It proved to be a remarkably clear-sighted move. Konstanty would scatter four hits and allow only one run in his eight innings. Unfortunately, it wouldn't be enough as Vic Raschi tossed a complete game, two-hit shutout to give the Yanks the 1-0 opening game win in Philadelphia.

Game Two

Thursday, October 5 (Shibe Park)

No matter how exhausted he might have been, Robin Roberts was pedaled out there for Game Two. He allowed two hits but no runs in the top of the first, then another two hits and a walk, highlighted by a line drive RBI single from Gus Woodling in the second to give the Yanks the early lead. The Phils faithful began to fear that the awesome Roberts had just run out of steam.

For their part, the Phils troubled Yankee starter Allie Reynolds all day. Richie Ashburn had burned a one-out double in the first, but couldn't advance. Granny Hamner struck a one-out triple in the second, but found himself stranded as well. Eddie Waitkus smacked a one-out double in the third, but just as the two before him, could not move up. Hamner tried to force something in the fourth when he drew a two-out walk, promptly stole second to move into scoring position, but was stranded when Andy Seminick struck out. The Phils finally drew blood when Richie Ashburn lofted a sacrifice fly in the fifth that brought home Mike Goliat to tie the game.

The starting pitchers then put the screws on the game. Reynolds would allow only a bunt single to Ashburn through the eighth, while Robin Roberts became...well, he became Robin Roberts, scattering only a handful of hits into the 10th. Unfortunately, he did let one pitch get away from him, and DiMaggio got all of it to lead off that 10th frame, giving Game Two to the Yanks, 2-1.

They'd been hard-fought games, but the Phils had nothing to show for it. Now they had to take the brief trip north to the unfriendly confines of the House That Ruth Built. And they had very little left in the tank.

Game Three

Friday, October 6 (Yankee Stadium)

The Phils went with left-hander Ken Heintzelman to try to shore up a much-needed victory. Somehow, Heintzelman found his 1949 form to hold the Bronx Bombers to four hits through seven innings, allowing only one unearned run. The Phils tied the game in the sixth when Dick Sisler singled home Del Ennis, and would take their first lead in the seventh when Mike Goliat singled home Granny Hamner from second.

Heintzelman looked in control in the bottom of the eighth as he induced Gus Woodling to pop to second to start it off, then Rizzuto to ground meekly to third. Two outs. No one on. A lead. You could start dreaming. But then, just that quickly, Heintzelman began to tire. He walked Jerry Coleman, then walked Yogi Berra, then walked Joe DiMaggio, then walked to the showers.

The Phils called on Jim Konstanty to douse the flames against pinch hitter Bobby Brown. Philadelphia hearts thrilled to the little bouncer that went directly to Granny Hamner a short moment later, then sank when Hamner overthrew Waitkus at first, Coleman scored, and the game was tied.

Things looked promising for the Phils in the top of the ninth, when Granny Hamner led off with a double against reliever Tom Ferrick. Seminick bunted him to third, and then, in a key play, Ferrick intentionally walked Mike Goliat. This set up a force at second and effectively removed the Phils' best pitcher from the game, as Eddie Sawyer was forced to pinch hit for Konstanty, sending Dick Whitman into the game. Whitman hit a soft grounder to first and Hamner took off for home. The play wasn't close.

Russ Meyer came in for the ninth and immediately took down the first two hitters before Gus Woodling hit a bleeder between short and first. Phil Rizzuto followed with a line drive single to send Woodling to second, and Coleman hit a game-winning single to left center to end the game. It was their only earned run.

The Yanks had won another squeaker, this time 3-2. The Phils were down in the Series 3-0, even though their patchwork pitching staff had compiled a team ERA of 1.93.

Game Four

Saturday, October 7 (Yankee Stadium)

The Phillies offense suffered more of the same in the final game of the Series. They proved able to set the table, but were unable to bring home the run. They started to press, which could be clearly seen from an ill-chosen sprint toward home from Eddie Waitkus with one out in the first.

Bob Miller took the mound for the Phils and looked clearly uncomfortable, as he allowed two runs on two hits and left the game after recording only an out. Jim Konstanty, despite the fact that he'd thrown eight innings in the opening game and had just appeared in the game before, came into Game Four basically as the starting pitcher...and held the Yanks at bay. No wonder the guy won MVP in 1950.

In the sixth, with the score still standing at 2-0, things began to slip away. Yogi Berra led off the inning with a homer to deep right; Bobby Brown tripled in Joe DiMaggio one out later, then came around himself on a sacrifice. And that, for all intents and purposes, would be the game.

Trailing 4-0 in the ninth, the Phillies would finally mount a rally, thanks to a two-run error by Hank Bauer, but could manage little more. In the entire series, the Phils scored more than a single digit in only one frame, and neither run was earned.

While their pitching had been outstanding, the offense never got on track. Dick Sisler hit .059; Del Ennis, .143; Richie Ashburn, .176; Andy Seminick, .182; and Mike Goliat, .214. Jim Konstanty himself hit .250. If the Phils could have just followed his lead, perhaps they would have gone further. They could at least find some solace in the fact that they were the "Whiz Kids." They were just beginning.

THE AFTERMATH

It didn't quite work out that way. The Phils fell to fifth place the next year with a 73-81 record, finishing 23^1/$_2$ games behind the New York Giants. Andy Seminick's average dipped to .227; Mike Goliat's bat became so anemic that he was benched for Putsy Caballero, who would hit only .186. Robin Roberts would win 21 games in the season, but would drop 15, and while Bubba Church rebounded with his best season ever (15-11), Bob Miller could only manage three starts and a 6.82 ERA. Jim Konstanty became mediocre, and Curt Simmons remained in Korea.

The 1952 squad didn't fare much better. Seminick was gone; Sisler was gone; Goliat was gone; Caballero was benched. Roberts had an even more extraordinary year than the two before, but Bubba Church and Bob Miller started just two games between them and managed to win neither. Eddie Sawyer was replaced halfway through the season.

The magic had gone. And so had the Whiz.

3

1964: *Titanic,* Meet Iceberg

1964 National League Standings

Team	Wins	Losses	WP	GB
St. Louis Cardinals	93	69	.574	0
Philadelphia Phillies	92	70	.568	1
Cincinnati Reds	92	70	.568	1
San Francisco Giants	90	72	.556	3
Milwaukee Braves	88	74	.543	5
Pittsburgh Pirates	80	82	.494	13
Los Angeles Dodgers	80	82	.494	13
Chicago Cubs	76	86	.469	17
Houston Colt .45s	66	96	.407	27
New York Mets	53	109	.327	40

I've dreaded writing this chapter from the beginning; I tried to talk myself into cutting it completely. Hell, the Phils didn't even win the pennant. But that's the thing, isn't it? They didn't win the pennant—despite the fact that they were a very good team, perhaps even a great team. Some say that their collapse was not the surprise. Some say that the fact that they were in a position

to collapse was the surprise. Some say that the team never collapsed, that it was just how Gene Mauch worked the stretch run
that caused the implosion. Some say the captain of the *Titanic*
knew of the icebergs; some say that the *Titanic*'s engineers simply designed it wrong; some say, oddly enough, that the boat
never sank, that it's all been a big hoax. The *Titanic* Truthers.
Whatever the case, no matter how you look at it, the story of the
1964 season is one that needs to be told so that you can draw
your own conclusions.

Preseason

In 1961, a young manager by the name of Gene Mauch took over
a club that had just finished in last at 59-95, a full 36 games behind the leading Pirates. Mauch quickly made a lot of believers
when the 1962 version of his club stormed to an 81-80 finish.
They continued to improve into 1963, working their way to 87-
75, landing them only 12 games behind the Dodgers of Koufax
and Drysdale.

The Phillies themselves sparkled from the mound, posting a
team ERA of 3.09 (third in the league). Their staff was led by the
likes of rookie right-hander Ray Culp, who went 14-11 with a 2.97
ERA. He was ably backed by Chris Short, who in his fourth full
year with the team had come into his own, finishing with what
was then a career-best 2.95 ERA and 160 strikeouts (10th).

On offense, the Phils looked more than capable. They posted
a team batting average of .252 (third), a .381 slugging percentage (third), and clubbed 126 homers (fifth). The big bopper was
23-year-old Johnny Callison, who knocked 26 homers, while
Tony Gonzalez led the team with a .306 batting average (eighth).

The Phils made a couple big moves before the season kicked
in. They traded hard-hitting Dom Demeter to the Detroit Tigers
for Jim Bunning. Bunning was a 10-year veteran who had led the
league with 20 wins back in 1957, but his career seemed to be
waning.

They also promoted Dick "Don't call me Richie" Allen to
third base; he'd hit .293 while up for a cup of coffee in 1963. First
baseman Roy Sievers was purchased by Washington, making
room for John Herrnstein, who'd proven to be a power hitter
with a good average in his minor league career.

It did seem the Phils had gotten better, and Philadelphians were ready for a fine season. But this was Philadelphia after all. People were realistic. No one seriously believed we had the Koufax-Drysdale Dodgers in our backyard.

The Manager

Gene Mauch. The man who brought us so quickly to rhapsody. The man who thrust us so quickly into the abyss. A saint, a sinner, a devil, a martyr, a crafty tactician, or a mindless blunderer? Take your pick. All of 38 years old in 1964, Mauch quickly distinguished himself in two major areas. First, he was an intense student of the game who played small ball. Gone were the friendly confines of Baker Bowl, which could make today's Citizens Bank Park look expansive, and here instead was the mammoth Connie Mack Stadium. This was perfect for the game Mauch brought, one that depended on contact and patience, speed and sacrifice. Second, Mauch was an intense competitor who had a helluva temper. He would taunt the other team, hassle the umpires, fly off and away at the opposing fans. Mauch treated the game like a war, and didn't much like it when other teams, players, or fans thought they had earned the right to try to beat him.

Mauch would lead the Phillies through 1968, always with a winning record, then move to helm the upstart Montreal Expos. He would reach national prominence once again when he turned around the California Angels of the early '80s from a losing club to one of the best in the majors. He twice led the Angels into the Championship Series, which, like 1964, ended much the same: a breath away from glory, followed by much depression, a temper tantrum or two, and a sideline view of the other club jumping jubilantly into each others' arms to celebrate an astounding upset victory.

Of his fateful career, Mauch could only say, "If it's true you learn from adversity, then I must be the smartest son of a bitch in the world."

The Lineup

Trying to claim that there is a common lineup for the '64 Phils is a bit like saying that the season itself is common. Gene Mauch believed in the platoon system, and did so with a gusto unlike anyone before or since. He mixed and matched, thrust and parried, turned and overturned depending on the hot hand, depending on the opposition, depending on the state of the field, the skies, the temperature, the fans, and his hunches. So, even though I'm going to throw a lineup at you, it certainly wasn't every day, and I'll try to do my best to detail some of Mauch's calibrations.

Leadoff:
Center Fielder Tony Gonzalez, .278, .352 OBP

Cuban-born Tony Gonzalez was the prototypical Mauch leadoff man. He had great patience at the plate, could hit for average, drew a good number of walks, and would be among the league leaders in hit-by-pitchers throughout his career. After a fine stint with the Phils that went through 1968, Gonzalez spent his last three seasons bouncing along three different teams before retiring from the Angels in 1971.

Sometimes Leadoff:
Utility Infielder Cookie Rojas, .291, .334 OBP

You can't even solidly describe Cookie Rojas as an infielder. Mauch used him everywhere. The Phils had so many solid infielders, and Mauch liked Rojas so much, that he frequently put him in the outfield as well. He would eventually settle in at second base in 1965 and become a forceful double-play combination with Bobby Wine, but this year he was a plug-and-play. During his career with the Phils, this incredibly versatile player even took turns at pitcher and catcher.

Cookie was another speedster who hit for average, coming in at .291 in '64, with 58 runs scored. He would hit .303 the next season and make the All-Star team, then see his average steadily fall through his last four years as a Phillie, until the club traded him after a .228 1969 season. Rojas saw a resurgence in his career with the Royals in the early '70s, as he made the All-Star team in four consecutive seasons.

Batting Second:
Second Baseman Tony Taylor, .251, 13 SB

Sometimes it was Rojas who batted second, sometimes it was Gonzalez, sometimes it was a power hitter like Johnny Callison,

John Herrnstein, or Dick Allen. But since I'll get to each one of those in later lineup slots, let's just deal here with Tony Taylor, who would sometimes bat...well, anywhere else in the lineup.

Taylor was universally loved by the fans for his spirited and hard play. He was an exciting and excitable ballplayer whose love for the game was infectious. You could always count on Tony to be there (he started 1,003 consecutive games) and to ignite the team (his six steals of home still ranks second for the Phils).

After a year when he played well enough to receive MVP votes in 1963, Taylor tailed off a bit, his batting average dipping 30 points to .251 and his runs scored falling by 40 to 62, but he was a Mauch guy who did all that he could to get on base. He led the majors in hit-by-pitch with 13, accumulated more walks than the season before, and despite the big drop in batting average, Taylor managed only a 10-point dip in on-base percentage.

Batting Third:
Right Fielder Johnny Callison, .274, 31 HR, 104 RBI, 101 R

You could also plug in Dick Allen here, or Wes Covington, or John Herrnstein, but for the most part it was Johnny Callison who had the most consistent place in the lineup of all Mauch batsmen. Callison responded by making the All-Star team, where he hit the game-winning three-run homer with two on and two out in the ninth, and finishing second in the MVP voting to the Cardinals' Ken Boyer.

Callison mated his fine offensive stats with a terrific arm and glove, leading all outfielders in assists and putouts. "He can run, throw, field, and hit with power," Mauch said. "There's nothing he can't do well on a ballfield."

After another strong season in 1965, when he popped 30 homers and once again made the All-Star team, Callison's power began to recede. He was traded to the Cubs in 1969 before finishing his career as a New York Yankee in 1973.

Batting Cleanup:
Dick Allen, .318, 29 HR, 91 RBI, 125 R

You could find Dick Allen all over the leader boards in 1964. He led the league in triples (13), runs scored (125), extra base hits (80), and total bases (352). He came in third in slugging percentage (.557), fourth in doubles (38), fifth in batting average (.318), and seventh in homers (29). And this was the guy's rookie year!

Gene Mauch loved to use Allen at cleanup where his power could bring the speedsters on home. Then again, he liked to bat him second, to quickly move a runner into scoring position for Callison. At times, he would move him to third, where Allen could move a player along to set up the power behind him.

Baseball historian Bill Jenkinson rates Allen—along with Babe Ruth, Jimmie Foxx, and Mickey Mantle—as one the four greatest long-distance sluggers ever to play the game. Sabermatrician Bill James ranks him as the second most controversial player, behind Rogers Hornsby, ever to put on spikes. He deserves both monikers.

In the turbulent era of the '60s, Dick Allen combated racism, ownership, the fans, and himself. By all accounts a well-adjusted and affable young man, Allen faced a life-changing minor league placement in Little Rock, Arkansas, where he served as the team's first African American ballplayer.

Unlike Jackie Robinson, who was brought to cosmopolitan Montreal, Allen had to face a siege of hecklers at each and every game. Despite his great play, Philadelphia didn't take to him either. He carried an understandable chip on his shoulder and was ready to stand down anyone.

After watching Allen club a baseball deep over the roof of Connie Mack Stadium, Pittsburgh bomber Willie Stargell remarked, "Now I know why they boo Richie all the time. When he hits a home run, there's no souvenir."

Allen made the All-Star squad from 1964 to '67, hit well over .300 each season, led the league in slugging and on-base percentage in '66, and was always in the top 10 in runs scored, hits, doubles, triples, homers, RBI, and total bases. Yet the fans continued to boo him everywhere he went.

One famous incident in 1965 involved teammate Frank Thomas, who struck Allen on the shoulder with a baseball bat. The full story is still not known today, but Thomas was a notorious racist and Allen was well known for not tolerating bigotry. Thomas was fired the very next day, while the rest of the team was forbidden to speak of the incident. The firing made Thomas' side of the story the only one heard, and Allen the scapegoat for the Phils' loss of a much-needed power hitter. Allen was showered with trash, fruit, eggs, even flashlight batteries, every time he took the field. He started wearing his batting helmet at all times, creating the nickname that he would carry for the rest of his life: Crash Allen.

In a storied incident in 1967, Allen purportedly injured himself by pushing his hand through a car headlight while trying to assist a friend in getting a vehicle out of a ditch. There have been numerous and much more colorful accounts of the incident, which involved bars, drinks, wives, illicit relationships, and lots of flying glass and chairs.

In 1969, Allen was suspended indefinitely when he missed a twinight doubleheader against the Mets, owing to the fact that he had driven up to New Jersey in the morning to see a horse race, but got stuck in traffic on the way back. On October 7, 1969, Allen was involved in the most controversial trade in the history of baseball when he was sent to St. Louis for Curt Flood. Flood refused to report to Philadelphia, which led to lawsuits and court cases, anger, hardship, and headaches, finally resulting in the birth of free agency. Allen would eventually land in Chicago in 1972, where he won MVP honors and became an instant hero. Many actually credit him with saving the entire organization, which had been rumored to be on its way to Seattle before his arrival.

Sadly, attitude and controversy derailed Dick Allen again. In 1974, with two weeks to go in the season, he simply stopped playing after a fight with teammate Ron Santo. Since Allen refused even to speak of whether he would ever return to the game, the White Sox sold his contract to Braves. Allen refused to report and promptly announced his retirement.

The Phillies managed to talk Dick back onto the field in 1975, where Allen would play an important but supporting role in carrying the club back toward contention. He would retire quietly from the Oakland Athletics in 1977 at the age of 35.

Dick Allen is still not in the Hall of Fame, despite his high career batting average (.292), slugging percentage (.534), on-base percentage (.378), and the fact that he carried three teams on his strong back toward respectability. Nonetheless, the controversy that Allen carried along with him brought nonvoters out in droves. In 14 years on the ballot, the best Allen ever did was in 1996, when he received 89 of the 353 votes needed for election.

Loved or hated, Crash Allen was an event. And that event hit Philadelphia in 1964. Without him, this chapter could not have been written.

Batting Fifth:
Left Fielder Wes Covington, .280, 13 HR

Say what you will about Gene Mauch, but he was an excellent chess player who made use of all his pieces, shifting them according to field, strength, streak, and optimism. And there's no better way to see how he worked than to look at Wes Covington.

Mauch depended on Covington a great deal, both as a starter (89 games) and a pinch hitter (40 games). You might find him batting cleanup when Allen batted second (sixth when Herrnstein could be trusted to drive in runs from the fifth position), and, because of his speed, he might even be found batting second. As for his position, Covington could often be found in left, but might be found in center or right depending on the situation or the batter.

At 32, Covington was a proven veteran in the last years of his career. Always a journeyman, he had been a consistent starter during his previous seasons with the Milwaukee Braves, but never an everyday player. He was made for a manager like Mauch, who saw in Covington a man who could be plugged in almost anywhere, and who had studied a career based on sporadic use.

Covington practiced such incredible patience at the plate—stepping in and out of the box, fouling off pitch after pitch—that it would drive the opposing pitcher crazy, while at the same time giving the runners every opportunity to make their move, and the coming batters the chance to see what the opposing pitcher had in his arsenal. Once again, perfect for a small ball team.

Covington's 1964 season was one of his best, as he hit .280, with 58 RBI to go along with 13 homers and 18 doubles. He would remain with the Phils through 1965, and would retire as a Dodger at the end of the '66 season.

Batting Fifth, Sixth, or Sometimes Seventh:
First Baseman or Left Fielder John Herrnstein, .234,
.360 SLG

John Herrnstein came along through the Phillies farm system where he established himself as an extra base threat with speed. Once the 26-year-old replaced the established Roy Sievers at first in 1964, he didn't display many flashes of his former promise. He would hit only .234 with six homers and 25 RBI. Sadly, things didn't improve. He would hit only one more career homer and two doubles, while collecting just nine RBI before retiring in 1966 at just 28 years of age.

Also Playing First and Batting Anywhere from Fourth to Seventh:
Roy Sievers, .183

A wizened veteran by 1964, Roy Sievers had spent his formative years in Washington, D.C., and with his skills on the wane and his batting average falling to just .183, he was sent back to the Senators for cash in mid-July. The 10-time All-Star and former Rookie of the Year would be released by the Senators early the next season, forcing him into retirement.

Usually Playing First and Batting Anywhere from Fourth to Seventh:
Frank Thomas, .294, .517 SLG

Having sold 37-year-old former-great-but-still-able-to-sock-a-ball Roy Sievers, the Phils were quick to pick up 35-year-old former-great-but-still-able-to-sock-a-ball Frank Thomas. Thomas filled in well in the 36 games he started at first, where he popped seven homers and collected 26 RBI, but he would be fired after the Allen incident in 1965.

Batting Second, Sixth, or Seventh and Playing Shortstop, First, Second, Third, or Left:
Rubén Amaro, .264

Rubén Amaro really did get around—and mostly as a starter. His incredible versatility made him another perfect fit for Mauch. A rare strikeout victim, Amaro could be counted to get his bat on the ball. He would go to the Yankees in 1965, but an injury incurred during his first week would set off a spate of injuries that plagued him for the rest of his playing career. Amaro would return to the Phillies as a coach for the World Series club of 1980.

Batting Seventh and Sometimes Eighth:
Catcher Clay Dalrymple, .238

Not known for his power or bat speed, Clay Dalrymple was a fine field general for a staff that needed his guidance. Other than Jim Bunning, these were a group of youngsters who suddenly found themselves on the national stage competing for the pennant.

Dalrymple had an especially strong arm, leading the league in runners caught and assists-by-catcher in 1961, '63, and '65. In his career, Dalrymple threw out 49 percent of the runners who tried to take a base against him. He would stay with the Phils through 1968 before joining Earl Weaver and the Orioles for a few seasons. An injury forced him into retirement in 1971.

Batting Seventh and Sometimes Eighth:
Catcher Gus Triandos, .250, .339 OBP

Gus Triandos was a promising catcher who made his bones with the Orioles in the mid-'50s when he made the All-Star team for three years running. With his offensive skills on the wane, he filled in ably for Dalrymple, and proved he still had pop in that old bat. Triandos would be traded to Houston for cash midway through the 1965 season, and would be released only a month thereafter to begin his retirement.

Batting Eighth:
Shortstop and Second Baseman Bobby Wine, .212

A career .215 hitter (the fourth worst of all time for anyone with more than 2,500 at-bats), Bobby Wine was the prototypical no-hit, good-field shortstop in an era when this was perfectly fine. Sharing his position with Rojas, Amaro and Taylor, Wine didn't see a full-time assignment until he was sent to the expansion Montreal Expos in 1969. Wine basked in his position, leading the league in games started by a shortstop and setting a record for 137 turned double plays in 1970. He would retire shortly after the Expos brought along Tim Foli in the '72 season.

The Pines

On a Gene Mauch team, no one was really a bench player. Everyone would get their starts and play vital roles on the club. I'm going to put Danny Cater (RF, LF, CF, 1B, 3B) and Alex Johnson (LF, RF) on this list, but could easily be talked out of it. Both players started more than they relieved. In his rookie season, Cater would hit .296 and be a rare strikeout victim. Alex Johnson, who would go on to an All-Star career with the Angels, hit a crisp .303 in this, his rookie season.

The Starting Staff

The Ace:
Right-Hander Jim Bunning, 19-8, 2.63, 219 K

When Philadelphians consider the name Jim Bunning, they think of him as nothing but a Phillie. However, he spent the bulk of his career in Detroit, and he has made the greatest name for himself as a congressman from Kentucky. All it took was one perfect game, thrown on Father's Day 1964, and Bunning became a permanent denizen.

Bunning won 20 games for the Tigers in 1957, and, though he never again won 20, he clocked in at 19 in '62, '64, '65, and '66. In '67, when he won only 17 games, Bunning set a record for losing a full five 1-0 contests. He made the All-Star team five times in Detroit and three times in Philly, and he threw no-hitters in each league. In his last season as a Tiger, Bunning suffered a 12-13 record while allowing a league-leading 38 homers. Detroit saw the signs of wear on this 31-year-old frame and was quick to send him to the Phils for slugger Don Demeter.

Always his own man, Bunning didn't quite fit with the Gene Mauch design. He would rebel each time Mauch called for a certain pitch from the dugout, not because he didn't agree with the pitch, but because he didn't like to be bothered. The fiery Mauch didn't take this lightly, but it's tough to contend with a man who went 19-8 (fifth in wins), with a 2.63 ERA (fourth), five shutouts (second), 13 complete games (ninth), and 219 strikeouts (fifth). Jim wasn't a great hitter, but at a career .167, he was pretty close to Bobby Wine.

Bunning's last year in Philadelphia certainly offered no indication that he was on the downswing. He'd just won 17, had his best ERA of all time (2.29—second in the league), led the majors with a career-best 253 strikeouts, and finished second in the Cy Young Award voting. However, since Bunning had just turned 35, the Phils felt the need to be proactive. So they traded him to the Pirates for Don Money and Woodie Fryman. After bouncing along a couple of clubs, Jim returned to Philly to finish his career out in 1971 at 39.

Bunning managed in the minor leagues for five years before turning his attentions toward political office. He is noted as being one of the most conservative of conservatives. This usually comes as a surprise to Philly fans. Jim Bunning? He's Philadelphia through and through, and we're not a conservative city. Everyone over a certain age must remember that delivery of his. He had a unique sidearm motion that would end with his gloved hand touching the ground well out in front of his body. Now you tell me what's conservative about that.

For the average Philadelphian, Jim Bunning is still delivering that last pitch with the same motion as on Father's Day 1964. It's eternal.

Second in the Order:
Left-Hander Chris Short, 17-9, 2.20, 1.81

Known ironically as "Style" because of his lack of sartorial skills, Chris Short was a young man who fell in pleasantly with Mauch's managerial style. Always promising but erratic, Style found his path in 1963 when he posted a 2.95 ERA and struck out 160 (10th in the league). The Phillies were modestly hopeful that Short could turn in a like performance the next season. No one was prepared for his 17-9 and 2.20 ERA (third behind Sandy Koufax and Don Drysdale—not too shabby for company), while throwing 12 complete games and four shutouts (sixth). Short enjoyed his best seasons from '64 to '68 before back problems began to curtail his performance. The Phils would release him after the '72 season. Chris Short's 132 Phillies victories rank an all-time fourth for the club, behind Steve Carlton, Robin Roberts, and Grover Cleveland Alexander.

Third in the Order:
Left-Hander Dennis Bennett, 12-14, 3.68

For a while, it looked like Dennis Bennett could have been one of the great ones. After a lightning-strike minor league career, he stormed through his 1962 rookie season with nine wins, a 3.81 ERA, and 149 strikeouts. In comparison, Chris Short had gone 6-9 with a 3.94 his rookie year, while Bunning went 3-5,

6.35 coming up as a Tiger. The Phils were predicting big things for Bennett, but then tragedy struck. While vacationing in Puerto Rico, Bennett got into an auto accident from which many say he never fully recovered. He still threw with promise in 1963, going 9-5 with a 2.64, but he was clearly laboring at times.

Bennett's problems became more acute in '64, causing the Phils to trade him to the Red Sox at the conclusion of the season. After bouncing from Boston to the Mets to the Angels, Bennett found a home with the triple-A Hawaii Islanders (it could be worse), playing for Chuck Tanner.

Fourth in the Order:
Right-Hander Art Mahaffey, 12-9, 4.52

Like many other Phillies stories of this era, that of Art Mahaffey is one of startling promise curtailed by injury. Known for his pickoff move, Mahaffey picked off the first three runners who reached base in his debut game in 1960. Living up to his hype, Mahaffey posted a 7-3 record with a 2.31 ERA in his rookie season, then made the All-Star team in '61 and '62.

In 1963, Mahaffey injured his arm, and lost his fastball and his demeanor on the mound. He could still be effective, but he never again saw his dominance or confidence. He would win 12 games in 1964, but his ERA was a bloated 4.52, and his strikeouts had shrunk to 80 from his 1962 high of 158. By 1965, the once-promising 27-year-old appeared to be washed up. After going 2-5 with a 6.21 ERA, Mahaffey was packaged along with Alex Johnson and sent to the Cubbies. He'd retire in the Mets minor leagues in 1967 at just 29 years of age.

Fifth in the Order:
Right-Hander Ray Culp, 8-7, 4.13

Ray Culp would have a fine career, but mostly in Boston. He'd have two 14-win seasons as a Phillie, but not in 1964. As a 21-year-old rookie in 1963, Culp went 14-11 with a 2.97 ERA, five shutouts (fifth), and 176 strikeouts (fourth), enough to win the *Sporting News* Rookie of the Year Award and to be selected for the All-Star team. People expected a lot from the man in 1964. What they got instead was an 8-7 record, a 4.13 ERA, 80 less strikeouts, four less shutouts, and no All-Star Game. The Phils really could have used the 1963 Culp as they went down that sickening stretch of games in late September. As he was, Mauch bypassed the man entirely.

Culp developed a fine career with the Red Sox after learning the palm ball. He went 16-6 with a 2.91 ERA in '68, and followed it up with a 17-8 All-Star season. He won another 17 in 1970, and another 14 the year after. Culp retired at 31 from the Sox after his 1973 campaign.

The Closer:
Right-Hander Jack Baldschun, 3.12, 21 Saves

Flame-haired Jack Baldschun had an uneventful minor league career until he developed a screwball that caught the Phillies' attention. Joining the Phils in Mauch's inaugural '61 season, Baldschun was the only pitcher with a winning record, going 5-3 with a 3.88 ERA, while appearing in a league-leading 65 games.

Jack became the dependable workhorse over the next four seasons, appearing in a personal-best 71 games in 1964 with a fine 3.12 ERA. For some reason, however, the fiery Mauch lost confidence in his man, declining to put him into pressure situations during that interminable stretch of losses at the season's conclusion. Baldschun went to Cincinnati after 1965, and would call his 1970 season with the Padres the last of his major league career.

And the Rest

At times, Mauch would change things up (like that's a surprise?) and put in starters like right-hander Rick Wise, who went 5-3 with a 4.04 ERA in eight starts, and right-hander John Boozer, who recorded a 5.07 ERA in three.

By 1964, most teams in Major League Baseball had already assigned a specific closer; however, many starters still came in as relief. The '64 Phils were no different as their top five starters made 42 relief appearances. Other than that, Mauch went to his spot starters—right-hander Rick Wise, who went 5-3 with a 4.04 ERA in eight starts, and right-hander John Boozer, who recorded a 5.07 ERA in three, and had 36 relief appearances between them.

Mauch's most prominent alternatives were right-hander Ed Roebuck, a 32-year-old veteran who had his career-best season in 1964, as he posted a 2.21 ERA in 60 appearances. There was also right-hander Dallas Green, who endured the worst season of his eight-year professional career with a 5.79 ERA. He could always turn to left-handed veteran Bobby Shantz. At the end of his career, Shantz would go out with a flourish, posting a fine 2.25 ERA in 14 appearances.

The Season, Part One: On the Rise

For 29 years prior to 1964, the Fightin' Phils had not fought so well. In fact, they'd finished dead last 17 times, and next to last another seven. But this season—thanks to the great play of Dick Allen, the hitting prowess of Johnny Callison, the superb pitching performances of Jim Bunning and Chris Short, and Gene Mauch's cunning use of arrangement and rearrangement that kept opponents totally off balance—the Phils became a uniquely formidable team. They announced their arrival to the party by taking eight of their first 10 games in quite possibly the most talented league that the Nationals had ever supported. Let's take a look at some of their opposition, shall we?

- The San Francisco Giants had the likes of Willie Mays, Willie McCovey, Orlando Cepeda, and Juan Marichal.
- The defending champion Los Angeles Dodgers were buoyed by Sandy Koufax and Don Drysdale.
- Bob Gibson, Curt Simmons, and Lou Brock wore Cardinal red.
- The Milwaukee Braves headlined Joe Torre, Rico Carty, Lee Maye, and of course the great Hank Aaron in his prime.
- The Reds sported stars such as Frank Robinson, Vada Pinson, and Deron Johnson.

Despite the strengths of these opponents, the Phils kept hold of first place at the All-Star Break, where our own Johnny Callison lifted the Nationals to victory with a two-out, three-run walkoff homer.

The Phils would be in a dogfight with the Giants into early August when they finally increased their lead to a season-high three games. And then, remarkably, they began to pull away. When Jim Bunning outdueled the fearsome Bob Gibson 9-3 on

August 23, the Fightin's advanced to their high-water mark: a seven-and-a-half-game lead in the division.

Team	Wins	Losses	Win/Lose %	GB
Philadelphia	76	47	.618	—
Cincinnati	69	55	.556	7.5
San Francisco	69	55	.556	7.5
St. Louis	65	58	.528	11.0
Pittsburgh	64	60	.516	12.5
Milwaukee	62	60	.508	13.5
Los Angeles	60	62	.492	15.5

Of course, you can take nothing for granted, but you have to admit this looked pretty damn good. The Phils were outdistancing the defending champs by 15$^1/_2$ games, had relegated the seemingly inexhaustible Giants to a distant second, and if the Cards were going to challenge, they had better do something and do it quick, because—let's be honest—they were out of it. Sure, in some ridiculously ludicrous universe, they might conceivably make up 11 games on the Fightin's, but they would not be able to surpass the other two clubs at the same time.

Over the next month, the Phillies fought hard for a 14-11 record that kept them at a safe distance from their opposition. On Sunday, September 20, the Phils outlasted Jim Brewer and the Dodgers, as Jim Bunning held off a ninth-inning rally to win his 18th against five defeats. When the Phils woke up the next morning, they could look at the standings with some ease of mind.

Team	Wins	Losses	Win/Lose %	GB
Philadelphia	90	60	.600	—
Cincinnati	83	66	.557	6.5
St. Louis	83	66	.557	6.5
San Francisco	83	67	.553	7.0
Milwaukee	77	72	.517	12.5

It had been a long battle, a hard fight, but no one could blame the Phils for starting to think ahead to the Series. The club began printing and selling World Series tickets, the program went to press, and *TV Guide* featured a photo of Connie Mack Stadium in its World Series preview.

There were only 12 games left in the season. They had a six-and-a-half-game lead. Their magic number was four. With any number of Phils wins and/or Cardinal or Reds losses that added up to four over these 12 games, we'd advance to the World Series. As it ended up, we didn't outlast either one of them.

Phillies Memory

John Cunningham, Philadelphia Author

During the late '50s and early '60s, I'd listen to Phillies games on the radio with my father. I could endure the losses. I was a kid. But I couldn't bear to hear the loud click when he'd snap the radio off. In early June of 1964, my father died of a heart attack. Numb and alone, I watched on the television set that he'd bought only the month before as Jim Bunning pitched his perfect game. It was Father's Day. The next morning, my mother shipped me off to our small farm in New York State for the summer to "get me away from everything."

I managed to keep track of the Phillies in a semiweekly newspaper where the first-place Yankees dominated the sports pages. It felt like a dream but the Phillies were playing just like, well, like the Yankees. By the end of August, I returned home looking forward to the impossible—the Phillies in the World Series. And hopefully, against the Yankees. Incredibly, the Phils started to lose, again and again and again. At September's end the losing stopped, and the hurting began. My heart was splintered but I was used to it by then. I was all of 15 years old.

The Season, Part Two: The Collapse

September 21 Through 23:
Reds at Philadelphia (Three Games)

I looked and there before me was a pale horse! Its rider was named Death, and Hell was following close behind him.

—Revelation 6:7-8

That pale rider was one Chico Ruiz of the Cincinnati Reds, who came to town on September 21, and came home in a scoreless game at the top of the sixth. Oh the day had started off so very bright. The sun high upon the horizon, children laughing in the streets. Phils starter Art Mahaffey looked as poised as ever in his career. He'd allowed but three hits, walking none, and with the way the Phils had been hitting in the clutch all season, he seemed destined for his 13th victory against only eight defeats.

But then something strange happened. With two outs and Ruiz on third, Mahaffey went into the windup and...saw Ruiz dart for home. WHAT? It should have been an easy out, one that even you or I could have recorded. Any little leaguer in the city could have recorded it. But Mahaffey got excited and uncorked a wild one that Clay Dalrymple could not get a hold of. Ruiz scored, and Hell followed close behind him.

Chris Short got knocked around in the second game of the series, the Reds winning, 9-2. It was the club's fourth loss in the last five games, but no one seemed too distressed. Tickets for the series were already selling out. The Reds would tap Dennis Bennett for four runs in the top of the seventh the next night to upend the Phils, 6-4. It was the first time the Phils had been swept since early June against the Giants. Their lead had fallen to just three and a half over the Reds, five over the Giants and Cards. We needed a stopper. Good thing we had Bunning going for us the next day as the Braves headed into town.

September 24 Through 27:
Braves at Philadelphia (Four Games)

Jim Bunning did his job well in the opener, allowing only six hits through six innings, with only one going for extra bases. He'd given up three runs on some timely Milwaukee hitting, but the Phils had overcome deficits much like this all season. And indeed, they gave it their best shot. By the time the club reached the eighth inning, they trailed 5-0. Though they managed a three-run rally, they left the bases loaded, not able to get that timely hit that had seemed to come so easy just a week earlier.

With the defeat, the Phils' lead was now three on Cincinnati, three and a half on the Cards, and four and a half on the Giants. Eight games to go. It was still a healthy-enough lead, but Gene

Mauch knew he needed to staunch the blood flow. So he marched Chris Short back out there on just two day's rest. The move didn't elicit much shock. Mauch had gone through the season thus far employing such unpredictable maneuvers; in addition, Short had gone only a few innings in his last outing. He should have been ready.

Short indeed responded with a fine outing, going seven, while allowing only two earned runs; still, the Phils trailed 2-1 upon his departure. Trailing 3-1 in the bottom of the eighth, the Phils tied the game on a two-out, two-run homer by Johnny Callison. Clutch hitting, late in the game. Could this be a sign that the swoon was over? Could we soon breathe a sigh of relief? Surely, it had been scary, but hey, a great team is a tested team, and when you look at it, they still had a comfortable lead. They could still set their pitching staff by the series. More tickets were sold, more programs printed, and *TV Guide* went to press.

Then Joe Torre hit a two-run blast in the 10th, and the Braves were suddenly in the driver's seat again. But the Phils wouldn't back down. With two outs and Cookie Rojas on first, Dick Allen hit an inside-the-park homer to tie the game once again. This was the team we knew. This was the team we loved. This was the team that was going to give the Phils their first World Series in franchise history.

Right? Right? Um...maybe. Fans sat stunned as the Braves scored two more in the top of the 12th, and even though the Fightin's put two on with two out, John Herrnstein just couldn't get the hit that would have changed this club's history. Instead, he clubbed a meek grounder to first to end the game.

The Phils had now lost five in a row. Meanwhile the Reds had taken a doubleheader from the lowly Mets, the Giants had beaten the Cubs, and the Cards had topped Pittsburgh. With only seven games to go, the Phils' lead had fallen to a game and a half over the Reds, two and a half on the Cards, and three and a half on the Giants. Would this nightmare never end? To answer these questions, Mauch sent Art Mahaffey out for the third game of the series.

Things looked good right from the start in this one, thanks to an RBI triple from Dick Allen and a two-run homer from Alex Johnson in the first inning. When Johnny Callison drove in another in the second, the Phils could look out upon a four-run lead.

Thank God, Mahaffey looked in total control again...or at least until the fifth, when he allowed a leadoff homer to Dennis Menke and an RBI double by Lee Maye. The lead had fallen to 4-2.

Mahaffey stayed strong into the eighth, but when he allowed the first two runners on, Mauch had seen enough, calling in closer Jack Baldschun. He retired the first man to face him, but after allowing a single to load the bases, Mauch marched right back out there to replace Baldschun with Bobby Shantz. Catcher Gus Triandos allowed a ball to squirt past him to make the game 4-3, but Shantz retired the next two batters to keep the lead intact. The fans were certainly not breathing easily, but at least they were breathing...if only for a little while longer.

Shantz came back out to protect the lead in the ninth, and immediately allowed a leadoff single to Hank Aaron, followed by a sharp single to right by Eddie Matthews. Thank the Lord that pinch hitter Frank Bolling followed up with a tailor-made double-play grounder to Bobby Wine, who tossed to Tony Taylor, who couldn't catch the ball.

Instead of two outs and a runner at third, the Braves now loaded the bases with nobody out. But Bobby Shantz had been here before. While many of these players were untried in situations like this, the wily veteran Shantz surely knew how to steady the ship, take one pitch at a time, and serve up a hanging curveball to Rico Carty, who ripped it to right center for a bases-clearing triple to give the Braves the lead, 6-4. Ed Roebuck came to put out the fires, but the Phils couldn't start one of their own. They'd lost their sixth straight. Meanwhile, the Reds had topped the Mets, the Cards had beaten the Cubs, and at least the Giants didn't win...only because they didn't play.

The Phils were still in first, but barely. With six games to play, their lead on the Reds had fallen to only half a game. The Cards were now within a game and a half, while the Giants had crept all the way back to within three games. Somehow even the Braves, who were eight games out and mathematically eliminated, looked like they had a better shot at winning the pennant than the Phils. Our boys would be facing the Cards and the Reds in their last two series. At least their fate was still in their own hands. Only thing was, fate was not being kind to our beloved Fightin's lately.

Now before we get to these last six games, let me remind you that just because I have to write about this, you don't have to read it. You can skip right to 1980, if you like, or move on to 2008. So...go ahead. I won't think less of you. In fact, I'd think more of you.

You still there? Really? Glutton for punishment. Typical Phils fan. It's one thing not to turn away from an accident. It's something else to keep driving around the block so you can revisit the travesty. It's like Art Mahaffey said. Every time he closes his eyes, he sees Chico Ruiz streaking for home once more. Then once more after that. Then once more after that.

On Sunday, September 27, the fans dutifully piled into Connie Mack Stadium, but the mood was sullen. Even the fiery, red-faced Mauch seemed to have folded in on himself. He had become morose, standing with arms folded, his face was blank. It seemed that instead of trying to figure out whether to hit and run or swing away, he was trying to transport himself to a nice beach in the Caribbean with calming breezes and icy blue drinks.

As for me, I wish Mauch would have gotten what he'd been dreaming of. Then we might not have seen the exhausted Jim Bunning trundle himself back out to the mound after only two days' rest. Bunning still had that dead-eyed glare as he looked in on the plate, but as he reared back for his first delivery, you could see there was some pop missing from the pitch.

It certainly wasn't missing from the Braves' bats. Felipe Alou led the game off with a single over second; Lee Maye followed with a double off the left field wall; Aaron crushed a double to left to bring home both. And Gene Mauch...well, Gene Mauch looked out on the field, his arms crossed, his face a mask of nothing: Aaaahhhh, nice warm breezes, icy blue drink.

This time the Phils would bounce back. Tony Gonzalez led off with a double in the bottom of the first, and was promptly singled in by Dick Allen. Clay Dalrymple doubled to lead off the second; Tony Taylor tripled him home to tie the score; and Jim Bunning himself hit a line drive to right that brought home Tony to give the Phils the lead. It didn't last long.

In the top of the fourth, Bunning had nothing left. Joe Torre led off with a single; Rico Carty singled to follow; Dennis Menke singled to tie the game. And Mauch stood with his arms folded: Just a little salt around the rim, thank you very much.

Ty Cline doubled to right to put runners on second and third, and give the Braves the lead. Then pitcher Tony Cloninger singled to short center for the fifth consecutive hit of the inning. Even Mauch saw the signs of depletion now, and he replaced Bunning with future star Dallas Green. The problem was, that stardom wouldn't come for another 16 years. Right now, Green was just another one of the frazzled Phils. By the time Green was removed in the fifth, he'd allowed seven hits and five more runs. The Phils trailed 12-3, and would squander a three-homer day from Johnny Callison in their eventual 14-8 drubbing. The Phils had dropped seven straight.

The Cardinals won their fifth straight that afternoon, shutting out the Pirates 5-0 to pull within a half a game of the Phils. But they didn't have their sights on the Phils any longer. No one did. They stood a game and a half behind the Reds, who had taken sole possession of first with a doubleheader sweep of the New York Mets to increase their winning streak to nine games. At least the Giants had the decency to drop a doubleheader to the Cubbies to fall four and a half games behind the pace. They weren't mathematically eliminated, but with five games to go and three teams ahead of them, it seemed a tall order. Then again, this was 1964. Anything could happen. Among the "anything" was the shocking managerial decision that Mauch was going to go back to Chris Short to open up a three-game series against the St. Louis Cardinals.

September 28 Through 30:
Philadelphia at Cardinals (Three Games)

For a man who clearly had little left in the tank, Style Short pitched incredibly well. Throwing into the sixth inning, he allowed only three runs on seven hits. Not a stellar performance, but he kept the Phils in the game. It's just a shame the Phils could scratch out only one against Cards ace Bob Gibson. The Phils, who had just been on top of the world a week before, had fallen into third place with the loss.

Mauch went to Dennis Bennett for the crucial game two. He hadn't been impressive since injuring himself in mid-September during the second game of two consecutive shutouts. Still, it was a better choice than Bunning or Short. You just had to close your eyes and hope.

Mauch made another rather curious move in sitting the incredibly hot hand of Johnny Callison. It would be just the third time he decided to sit the man all season. Odd, but you can't blame the guy for trying to shake things up at this point. At least he'd stopped sipping blue drinks on the shores of the Caribbean. So, with one eye closed, and perhaps one hand on a Rosary, the Philadelphia fan tuned in the radio, adjusted the rabbit ears, and got ready for the next game.

Like many games before it, this one didn't start off pretty. After the Phils squandered a leadoff double by Cookie Rojas in the top of the first inning, Dick Groat doubled in a run in the bottom. The Cards began the second with three consecutive hits, followed by runs batted in from Tim McCarver and Curt Flood. The score stood at 3-0, and there was only one out in the second. Dennis Bennett's day was over. The Phils managed a brief flourish in the fourth when Gus Triandos hit a two-out, bases-loaded single to make the game 3-2. Sadly, however, the Phils would get no closer than this.

Philadelphia would lose again. Nine in a row now. Newspapers had stopped selling. No one was calling for World Series tickets. The *TV Guide* was embarrassed. Jim Bunning and Chris Short readied themselves to find more life in lifeless arms.

Meanwhile, the Reds had finally succumbed, losing to the Pirates and Bob Friend, 2-0. This would put the Cards and the Reds in a flat-footed tie for first with records of 91-67. With the Giants' 5-4 loss to Houston, they fell to three and a half out, mathematically eliminating them, while the Phils—I can barely bring myself to say it—had dropped to a game and a half out, with only three to play. Mathematically, they still had a shot. Realistically, the season was over.

Just to make certain of this, Mauch trotted Bunning back out to the mound on September 30. Bunning removed the sling from his arm and prepared to take the mound. He didn't stay long. He was removed with one out in the third, having allowed eight hits and six runs. The Phils tried bravely to rally late in the game, putting together five runs over the last three frames. But it was too little, too late. When the dust cleared, the Cards had won, 8-0, having swept the Phils in the three-game series. The Phils had dropped their 10th straight game. Mauch was philosophical. "Losing streaks," he said, "are funny. If you lose at the beginning, you got off to a bad start. If you lose in the middle of the season, you're in a slump. If you lose at the end, you're choking."

Makes sense, Gene. The only problem with that theory is that if you lost at the beginning of the season, it's doubtful whether you would have kept pushing Bunning and Short out there until they could barely lift their arms.

Things had not been going so well for the Reds of late either. Ever since their nine-game winning streak vaulted them from third place, six and a half games out, to alone at the top of the league, they'd been shut out for two consecutive games by the lowly Pirates, the last coming over 16 innings.

Going into the last frame of the season, the Cards stood a half game ahead of the Reds, two and a half ahead of the Fightin's. While the Cards had a three-game series to play against the Mets, the Reds would host the Phils for two. Granted, the Cards would have to drop three straight to the Mets, and the Phillies would have to break their slide with a two-game sweep of the recently red-hot Reds, but this was 1964. The rulebook had been thrown out.

October 2 Through 4:
Philadelphia at Reds (Two Games)

The eyes of the nation turned to the National League. And if you weren't a Philadelphian, you had to admit this was all pretty incredible stuff. Whatever you want to call it (a slump, a choke, or fate), this was a failure of mythic proportions.

The Reds brought their ace, Jim O'Toole, to the mound. O'Toole was having one of his best seasons, coming in at 17-6 with a 2.66 ERA. Mauch countered with (surprise of surprises) Chris Short! Style responded with his usual pluck. He might not have been the same pitcher as when well rested, but he was a gamer. He held the Reds to four hits and three runs (only one earned) over his six-plus innings of work. Meanwhile O'Toole looked to be just breezing right along, throwing a two-hit shutout.

But something odd happened. The Phillies bats came to life. After Tony Taylor singled home the first run, Dick Allen hit a clutch two-out triple to tie the game, followed by an RBI single from Alex Johnson to give the club a 4-3 lead. Gene Mauch then turned the game over to Jack Baldschun, the man he'd basically been shunning for the last 10 games. Baldschun retired all six men he faced, striking out two and never allowing a ball to leave the infield. See what happens when you get your rest?

The Phils' losing streak had come to an end. But there was no jubilation—not on the field, not in Philadelphia. We all knew the hell we'd just gone through. We all knew that we were still in third place with just a game to play. On the other hand, we knew we were still alive. The Cards' incredible eight-game winning streak had come crashing down at the hands of the Mets. We stood just a game and a half behind the Cards, a game behind the Reds.

The Phils and the Reds had a day of rest on Saturday, October 3, while the Cardinals lost again, getting trounced 15-5 by the Mets. The absurd and unlikely suddenly seemed possible again. Going into the last game of the season, the Phillies were back in the hunt indeed. While the Reds and the Cards stood tied for first, the Phils were a game behind. If the Fightin's could beat the Reds, and the Mets could beat the Cards, there would be a three-way tie for the league lead.

On Sunday, October 4, there was an audible groan from the collective fans of Philadelphia when Jim Bunning took the mound. Only this time, he was up to the task. Thanks to the several days off in the schedule, he had some semblance of rest. As such, he pitched a six-hit complete game shutout for his 19th victory of the season.

The Phillies offense knocked out Reds starter John Tsitouris with three runs in the third. Dick Allen added a solo shot in the fifth, then a three-run homer in the sixth. When the dust settled, the Phils had taken the Reds out, 10-0, to finish their season at 92-70, tied with Cincinnati a half game behind the Cards. We all know the final tally, however. As exciting as it was for the other teams, the Phils would sit back and listen as the Cards summoned up the offense to take the final game of the series from the Mets, and thus the division title.

It was over. The Phils had dropped the ball. Indeed, they'd dropped many balls, overthrew some others, underthrew some more, swung and missed at dozens, and, worst of all, kept handing them day-in and day-out to the two most exhausted players ever to have to keep walking out to the pitcher's mound: Jim Bunning and Chris Short.

THE AFTERMATH

While the Cardinals defeated the Yanks in seven to take the World Series, the Phils sat home and wondered what went wrong. It wasn't Billy Penn's hat. It wasn't fate. It wasn't bad luck. It was simply some very bad managerial decisions, together with some critical errors and the loss of timely hitting.

The Phillies would put together a decent season in 1965, behind another fine year from Chris Short (18-11), Jim Bunning (19-9), Cookie Rojas (.303), and Dick Allen (.302), but their tidy 85 wins were only enough to place them in the sixth position, 11? games behind the Koufax-Drysdale Dodgers. (The Cards fell to just a game above .500, in seventh place.)

The next year saw the Phils put together 87 wins that would bring them back to the upper half of the division, but eight games behind the Dodgers, who won the Nationals for the third time in the last four seasons. By 1967, the team was on the wane. Only Bunning managed a winning record, and even that was just 17-15. The Phils did have a winning record once again, but at just 82-80, they didn't provide much of a scare in the pennant champion Cardinals. Still, it was their sixth straight winning season, a franchise record; you had to go back to the 1800s to find a club that had even gone four straight.

By 1968, however, it was over. The club finished just 76-86, good enough for seventh place, 21 games behind the Cardinals once again. Mauch would be fired a third of the way through the season. Bunning was gone, Covington was gone, Callison was hitting at just .244.

The Phils would not be able to claim redemption or any other kind of championship for another 12 years, under a whole new regime, one that would claim the First Philastic Dynasty.

THE FIRST
PHILASTIC
DYNASTY

1977: Yes We Can!

1977 National League Standings

Team	Wins	Losses	WP	GB
Philadelphia Phillies	101	61	.623	0
Pittsburgh Pirates	96	66	.593	5
St. Louis Cardinals	83	79	.512	18
Chicago Cubs	81	81	.500	20
Montreal Expos	75	87	.463	26
New York Mets	64	98	.395	37

NLCS:
LOS ANGELES DODGERS 3; PHILLIES 1

Preseason

By the time 1977 rolled around, the First Philastic Dynasty had clearly taken hold. The new era had begun on April 6, 1974, when second baseman Dave Cash completed an Opening Day double play and loudly announced, "Yes we can!" Shortstop Larry Bowa looked over his shoulder and asked, "Who you talking to?" to which Cash simply said, "Anyone who'll listen, man. Anyone who'll listen."

Mike Schmidt certainly listened. Trailing 3-2 going into the bottom of the ninth, he launched a one-out, two-run homer to give the Phils the game and, if only for a moment, a share of first place. The Phils would complete their seventh straight losing season that year, but would finish in third place, only eight games behind the winning Pirates. More important, however, the Phils began to have swagger. This team was up and coming, and they knew it. They climbed to the top of their division in 1976 with 101 wins. Although the Big Red Machine shut them down 3-0 in the National League Championship, the Phils had gotten their first taste since 1950.

The Manager

Just coming off a 1976 Manager of the Year award, Danny Ozark entered his fifth season with more confidence than ever. A baseball lifer, Danny had played minor league ball for 18 years before becoming a manager in 1956. Finally, in 1963, after 25 years of baseball, Ozark made it to the majors as the coach for Walter Alston's Los Angeles Dodgers. He would earn his first managerial assignment for 1973 when he took over the Phils.

Danny was loved by his players and stayed out of their way, serving as a strategist and leaving the game to the boys. The media loved him as well, but for different reasons. Once, after a Phils loss eliminated them from contention, a reporter asked how he felt now that the Phillies were out of the pennant race. Ozark lost his temper, demanding that his boys could still win this thing. Hmmm. You would think that the manager would keep track of the standings. He once told an audience that "Half the game is 90 percent mental." And after a bitter defeat, he lamented that "Even Napoleon had his Watergate."

You had to love Danny. Really. If you didn't love him, you'd end up weeping. And the Phillies were going through too great a renaissance to weep—that is until the very end of '77, when perhaps the greatest Phils club to ever take the field succumbed to one bad managerial decision.

The Batting Order

Leading Off:
Center Fielder "The Secretary of Defense"
Garry Lee Maddox, .292, 85 R, 22 SB

Most people, including myself, were none too happy the day it was announced that the Phils had acquired Garry Lee Maddox back in 1975. We didn't have anything against Garry per se; it's just that we loved the man that the Giants were taking in return: outfielder and first baseman Willie Montañez. The flamboyant Montañez always knew how to entertain an audience—with a circus catch, a bat flip, or a hearty laugh. Plus, the guy could hit.

It didn't take us long to see the wisdom behind the move. Starting with his first year on the club, "The Secretary of Defense" would rattle off eight straight Gold Gloves. With his long, loping strides, he could spring off that already springy AstroTurf to make highlight reel catches.

Mets broadcaster Ralph Kiner said of his playing, "Two-thirds of the earth is covered by water. The other third is covered by Garry Maddox." Indeed, his partner in left, Greg Luzinski, who had little mobility, would actually line up facing the left field line, allowing Maddox to cover anything from center all the way to left. And it worked...until Game Three of the National League Championship Series, but we'll get to that later.

In 1977, Maddox was just coming off a season where he'd been third in the league in batting with a career-high .330, and first in the league in putouts for a center fielder. He would dominate both offensively and defensively for the club right up to his retirement after the 1986 campaign. After he left baseball, Maddox remained in the Philadelphia area, enrolling at Temple University and being elected a director of the Philadelphia Federal Reserve Bank, serving from 2003 to 2006.

Leading Off:
Right Fielder Shake 'n Bake McBride, .339, 27 SB

Shake 'n Bake McBride came to the Phillies in a midseason trade with the St. Louis Cardinals for pitcher Tom Underwood and third baseman Dane Iorg. It proved to be an incredible move for the Phils as McBride took over the regular right field duties from Jay Johnstone (who was having a splendid year himself), while Iorg and Underwood failed to live up to potential. McBride's speed of bat and foot served well in the leadoff position, freeing up the grace and power of Garry Maddox to take over the sixth spot in the order.

Bake was the real deal, having won Rookie of the Year honors in 1974, when he hit .309 (eighth) on his way to hitting over

.300 in each of his first five years as a pro. Injuries shortened his season in '76, however, which may have been one of the guiding factors in the Cards' decision to let him go. Hitting only .262 when he was traded in mid-June, McBride proceeded to hit .339 the rest of the way. Bake would be a starter with the Phillies through the 1980 season before being traded to Cleveland. He would retire in 1983.

Batting Second:
Shortstop Larry Bowa, .280, 93 RBI, 32 SB

Larry Bowa is Philadelphia. Everything about him screams Philly: tenacity, temper, and talent. The guy just never backed down, and really didn't care what people thought of him. His whole goal, on the field and in life, was to find a way from "point the first" to "point the last," and he'd do whatever it took to get there. Period. You don't have to look any further than his first tryout to see proof of the story. After not making his high school team, Bowa finally earned a spot at his junior college, where he played well enough to bring a scout down for a look. Now you wouldn't blame any kid for getting so nervous that he couldn't focus on the game. Not so with Larry. He didn't give a damn. In fact, he got thrown out of the game for arguing a minor call, and never got the chance to perform for the scout.

Bowa didn't make a whole lot of friends on the field, but that was never his goal. People respected him. Like 1990s All-Star first basemen John Kruk said in his book, *I Ain't No Athlete, Lady:* "A helluva coach. A great field manager. God, what a dickhead. I thought he was the biggest asshole in the United States of America. Of course, there are still days when I think that, but only some days. Not every day like before. Oh yeah, one more thing. The best thing that ever happened to me in my career was him becoming my manager."

No matter the temper, Larry Bowa was like a Swiss watch at short, providing security and consistent stewardship unlike any other in Phillies history. Commanding the field from 1970 through 1981, Bowa won two Gold Gloves, led the Nationals six times in fielding percentage, posted a then-record single-season fielding percentage of .991 in 1979, and still holds the record for highest all-time fielding percentage at .980.

Bowa came up as the typical good-field, no-hit shortstop, much in the footsteps of the Whiz Kids' Bobby Wine. But the tenacious firebrand continued to work on his skill and became more disciplined and focused as each year went by, until he saw his average rise from a 1973 campaign when he hit .211, to a .275 the next season, and a .305 the season after that. Hitting at .280 in 1977, Bowa became the perfect number-two man. Always a contact hitter, he could move the runners along, and, once aboard, he used his speed to keep the pitcher distracted.

Though Bowa remained a productive hitter and field lieutenant through his career, the Phils traded him to the Cubs in 1981, along with some minor league kid named Ryne Sandburg, for the vaunted Ivan de Jesus. Bowa helped lead the Cubs to the division title in 1984; Ryne led the way thereafter, and Ivan helped pave the way to the conclusion of the First Philastic Dynasty.

After Bowa retired in 1985, the Padres chose him to manage their club, but quickly found out that his tenacity led to a great deal of disgruntled ballplayers. It seemed a better fit when he signed on to lead the Phils in 2001. Bowa was fiery. Philadelphia was fiery. Philly would throw snowballs at Santa. Bowa would throw a grenade.

We'd just gotten through with the seemingly enervated Terry Francona. (I don't care what the guy's done in Boston; he's just boring; Philly doesn't need boring.) The Phils had seven consecutive losing seasons and were just coming off a last-place finish. We needed a punch in the arm.

That's exactly what Bowa gave us. And considerably more. On his way to marching the team to the cusp of the division title in his first season, he locked down the 2001 Manager of the Year Award. The fans loved him. The press loved him. The players—well, that's another story. Bowa was known for looking at the cameras and saying the right thing, but he would speak off-the-record quite often, and be as frank as any Philadelphian. The fans might not have heard what he said, but that didn't prevent the players from learning.

Bowa managed Philly to three more fine seasons, but was summarily fired with two games remaining in the 2004 season.

Batting Third:
Michael Jack Schmidt, .274, .574 SLG, 38 HR, 101 RBI, 114 R, 104 BB, 15 SB

There will never be another Michael Jack Schmidt. In his 16 full seasons of major league play, Schmitty made the All-Star team 12 times; won the MVP three times; collected nine Gold Gloves, six Silver Sluggers, eight home run titles, and four RBI titles; led in slugging average five times, on-base percentage three times, and total bases three times. How many times on warm summer nights did the city erupt as Harry Kalas called out the familiar, "There's a drive, deep left, that's ball's OUTTA HERE! Michael Jack JACKS one!"

1977 was a familiar story for the statuesque Schmidt. He racked up a then-career high of 38 round-trippers (fourth), smacked 11 triples (second), crossed the plate 114 times (third), drove in 101 runs (ninth), and drew 104 walks (third). He had a .574 slugging percentage (fourth) and a .393 on-base percentage (seventh). He drove the ball for 76 extra base hits (third) and amassed 312 total bases (fifth). He led all third basemen in assists (396) and finished fourth in putouts (106) and fourth in fielding percentage (.964). And just for the hell of it, Schmidt came in fourth in getting hit by the pitch (nine times) and third in sacrifice flies (nine).

It's pretty uncanny when you consider that such a season constitutes an off-year for the likes of Michael Jack. On any given day, you could find Michael defending his play to the press. Don't worry. He'd get it together. He was only 27. There was a lot of time to learn the craft. In 1977, Schmidt changed his game a bit. A dead-pull hitter, Schmitty always lagged a bit in terms of average. He began to adjust his stance so that he could hit the ball with more consistency and to all fields.

Despite his incredible career, Schmidt never really had a warm relationship with the fans. He played the game right, he played the game well, but he played it cool, like a precision clock. Philadelphia, whatever you want to say about it, is certainly not run like a precision clock, and neither is the heartbeat of its people. We're more likely to cheer wildly for the antics of a Lenny Dykstra, the calisthenics of a Willie Montañez, the affable nature of a John Kruk, than for someone who keeps the game within himself, even if he is the greatest player of all time. Schmidt was just as likely to criticize us as well. Oddly enough, it was one of these criticisms that endeared him most to Philly fans. After lambasting the fan base of Philadelphia during a road trip interview, they came out in droves to boo him upon his return. When Schmitty took to the field, however, he did so in costume, wearing a ridiculous wig and clown glasses. Michael Jack was laughing right along with us. And suddenly we loved him. Hey, any family member can make a mistake. Even during winning efforts, people seemed to turn against him in some way. As Schmitty said, "Philadelphia's the only place where you can experience the thrill of victory and the agony of reading about it the next morning."

Schmidt excelled straight through the 1987 season, winning MVP honors in '80 and again in '86. When his average slid to .203 in early 1989, Schmitty hung up the spikes at age 39. When he addressed the press and the fans to announce his decision, he cried, and we wept along with him. Mr. Cool had stopped playing ball. The precision was out of that clock. He could be emotional. He was one of us, but he would always be more than that. He would always be Michael Jack.

Batting Cleanup:
Left Fielder Greg "The Bull" Luzinski, .309, 39 HR, 130 RBI, 99 R, 3 SB

Always a fan favorite, The Bull patrolled our left field grasses from 1970 until 1980. One of the most formidable power hitters of his era, Greg set personal bests for homers in 1977 (39, third) and batting average (.309, ninth). With 130 RBI (second), 99 runs scored, a .594 slugging percentage (second), 35 doubles (10th), 77 extra base hits (second), and 329 total bases (third), Greg was one of the best players in the league during the '77 season, finishing in second in MVP voting.

The only thing Greg couldn't do was move all that fast. But with The Secretary of Defense roaming center, he didn't have to. And when the Phils took a fair lead, Jerry Martin would trot out to take care of the outfield business—save for one very critical time, but we'll get into that at the painful conclusion to this chapter.

Having first broken into the majors as a Phillie in 1970, Luzinski helped lead the team to their rebirth in 1975, when he finished second in MVP voting with league-leading totals in RBI (120) and total bases (322), to go along with a .300 batting average, 34 homers (third), 35 doubles (second), and a .540 slugging percentage (second).

Greg made the All-Star team for four years running, from 1975 to 1978, and was the National League's top vote-getter in '78 when his first-half stats were nearly inhuman. The Bull was always a streaky hitter who could carry a team on his shoulders for weeks (sometimes months) at a time, and then go dormant. But he was always good-natured about this, both before the crowds and at home. He even named his dog Ofer, hoping that by hanging the moniker of "O for" on a high-spirited dog he might dismiss whatever demons had brought him to the slide. Luzinski went through the worst slump of his career in 1980, hitting just .228, leading the Phils to trade The Bull to the White Sox, where he would flourish until his retirement in 1984 at age 34.

Phillies Memory

Michael A. Ginsberg, Longtime Fan

I idolized Greg Luzinski, who remains my favorite Phillie of all time. It seemed that almost every game I went to came down to a moment when The Bull stepped to the plate, needing to hit a home run to win it for us. I remember the "Bull Pen" above left field, a section of tickets Luzinski donated for charity, and thinking what a great guy he was to do such a thing.

I've never met Luzinski, though there are plenty of opportunities to do so these days. But there's a part of me that wants to keep him larger than life in my mind, a god on Mount Olympus, not a regular human being who has moved on to other things after retiring from baseball.

I swear one day I'm gonna buy an old Luzinski baseball card, take it with me to Cooperstown, and leave it in that sacred space. He belongs there because to me it's the least I can do for a young kid's hero.

Ninth-Inning Replacement for Luzinski:
Right Fielder Jerry Martin, .260, .447 SLG, 6 HR

Good with the bat and the glove, Jerry Martin served primarily as a late-inning fielding backup for Greg Luzinski. For the most part, however, Martin's story is of promise unfulfilled, especially the promise of playing the ninth inning of Game Three of the NLCS (see below). He became a regular when traded to the

Cubs in '79, where he had served with moderate success.

In October 1983, Martin was arrested—along with Royals teammates Willie Wilson, Vida Blue, and Willie Aikens—for trying to purchase cocaine. All were sentenced to six months in a minimum security prison, while Baseball Commissioner Bowie Kuhn gave them a one-year suspension. In the end, the group would serve only three months, while Kuhn reduced their suspension on appeal. Martin returned to baseball and the New York Mets in 1984, but a wrist injury limited his playing time. He retired at the end of the season after hitting just .154.

Batting Fifth:
First Baseman Richie Hebner, .285, 18 HR, 62 RBI

A hard worker who spent the off-season digging graves at his dad's cemetery, Richie Hebner brought a sense of dogged determination to whatever team he played for. Coming up in the Pirates organization in 1970 as a third baseman, he teamed up with Dave Cash at the top of the lineup to help the Bucs to five division titles and one World Series ring over six years. Hebner signed with the Phillies after the 1976 season as a free agent. A man who could hit for average and power, he was a nice fit as the number-five man to follow Schmidt and Luzinski.

The acquisition of Pete Rose for the '79 season made Hebner expendable. Going to the Mets for pitcher Nino Espinosa, Richie broke his personal RBI record the next season, and then when he was traded to Detroit in 1980, he broke it again. He retired as a Cub in 1985 at age 37.

Batting Fifth:
First Baseman Davey Johnson, .321, .408 OBP, .545 SLG

Davey Johnson provided some additional veteran leadership and playoff experience on a team that needed it. The full story of Johnson—from his All-Star career, to his stunning move to Japan, to his American resurgence, to his wildly successful managerial career, to the strange conclusion of that tale—is one for the ages. It's just that it's really not one that can be covered in this book.

Johnson played one year for the Phils after his sojourn in Japan, and he was a more-than-able backup to Richie Hebner. He was traded to the Cubs late in '78 for a man we will speak a good deal about in chapters to come: Larry Anderson. In short, Johnson came up through the Orioles organization and was their starting second baseman during their glory years in the early to mid 1970s, when they won four division championships and two World Series titles.

Johnson joined the Braves in 1973 and continued to excel, hitting 43 homers to break Rogers Hornsby's record for second basemen. When the Braves released him four games into the '75 season, he made the startling decision to move to Japan. Davey set a record with two pinch-hit grand slams in 1978 while playing for the Phils, then was traded to the Cubs where he finished out the year and his playing career at 35. He became a manager of the New York Mets in 1984, and led one of the greatest teams of all time—the '86 club—to the World Championship. In his seven years with the Mets, he never finished below second place.

Johnson joined a fifth-place Reds team in 1993, immediately leading them to two division championships. He took the helm of the '96 Orioles after that, and though the O's had finished below .500 the previous season, he brought them to two division championships as well.

After taking the Orioles to the American League Championship Series two years running, and taking the Manager of the Year Award in 1997, Johnson was summarily fired because of disagreements with the owner, Peter Angelos. The Dodgers would pick him up in 1999, where he would finally finish below .500 for the first time in his career. Davey turned it around quickly, however, moving the Dodgers to second in 2000 before retiring after the season at the age of 57.

Batting Sixth:
Right Fielder Jay Johnstone, .284, 15 HR, 59 RBI

Jay Johnstone was the everyday right fielder until the Phils acquired Shake 'n Bake McBride in midseason. Joining the Phils in 1974, Jay had played a great role in the team's resurgence. He was always a fine hitter for average, batting .295 (1974), .329 (75), .318 (76), and .284 (77). He could also smack some doubles to the wall and could usually be found with over 50 RBI per season.

Best known as a clubhouse prankster and jokester, Jay kept things loose in the clubhouse as well as on the field. He would nail players' cleats to the floor, sneak up behind others to set their shoes on fire (the invariable hot foot), and once locked his Dodgers manager, Tommy Lasorda, in his office during Spring Training. My favorite, however, is when Johnstone leapt on top of his dugout during a game, walked up through the crowd and stood in line to get a hot dog.

The Phils needed this kind of player. The team had the intensity of Mike Schmidt, the guru nature of Steve Carlton, the fiery antics of Larry Bowa, and the keen-eyed leadership of Bob Boone. In Jay, they had someone who could remind them that underneath it all, this was a kid's game and they were all supposed to be having fun. It was a bonus that the man also brought a bat.

Johnstone was traded in early 1978 to the Yankees for Rawly Eastwick. Although he'd retire in 1985, his personality led him to the broadcast booth for the Yankees ('89–'90) and the Phillies ('92–'93).

Batting Seventh:
Catcher Bob Boone, .284, 11 HR, 66 RBI

They say that if you want to know how strong a team is, you need look no further than the catcher. He's the quarterback of the team, the engine that keeps the car running. And Bob Boone was one of the best. Always a consistent if not a commanding bat, Boone provided a prowess behind the plate that was uncanny. The Phils nearly made one disastrous trade with Boone back in 1974 when they agreed on a move at the Winter Meetings, only to have it vetoed by owner Ruly Carpenter. They eventually would sell him outright to the California Angels after the '81 season, when his offensive stats began to decline.

Boone was far from finished, however. He remained with the Angels for seven years, where he anchored a young pitching staff and won five more Gold Gloves. At 40 years old, he hit a career-best .295, but the Angels, in a pro-youth move, granted him free agency. The ageless Boone won another Gold Glove while playing for the Royals in '89, but when a broken finger limited his play in 1990, he retired at the age of 42. Boone didn't leave baseball, however. His leadership ability naturally led to management opportunities. He was the Royals manager from 1995 through '97, then took over the Reds from 2001 to 2003. But none of his teams finished with a record above .500, and Boone stepped aside.

Batting Seventh:
Catcher Tim McCarver, .320, .527 SLG

In his second stint with the Phillies (the first was from 1970 to 1972), Tim McCarver worked as Steve Carlton's personal catcher. The two were so closely tied to each other that people often said they would be buried 60 feet, six inches apart.

McCarver came up through the Cardinals organization, making the major league club for a brief time when he was all of 17 years old in 1959. This, of course, is when he met the young Carlton and became Bob Gibson's personal choice for catcher as well. Always a competent hitter, he made two All-Star teams in the mid-'60s, and finished second in the 1967 MVP voting to teammate Orlando Cepeda.

Tim came to Philadelphia in the historic 1969 trade, when Curt Flood refused to report, thus kicking off the lawsuit against the MLB that would result in free agency. It was in Philadelphia during this time that he caught Rick Wise's 1971 no-hitter. McCarver briefly teamed with Harry Kalas and Richie Ashburn as a color analyst, before reaching national prominence as a sportscaster for all three major networks. He has won three Emmy Awards for his work.

Batting Eighth:
Second Baseman Ted Sizemore, .281, 47 RBI, 64 R

A former Rookie of the Year recipient, when he broke in with the Dodgers in 1969, Ted Sizemore enjoyed a brief but memorable stint with the Phillies organization, as he helmed the middle infield for two division championship teams in 1977 and '78. Sizemore had a decent bat (.262 lifetime in an era when second basemen usually hit .250 or below) and a fine glove; he didn't hit for power, and was made expendable when Davey Lopes appeared on the horizon.

In 1970, Ted was traded to the Cardinals for former Philly great Dick Allen. Sizemore formed a good one-two punch with Lou Brock at the top of their order to keep the Cards in the pennant run during his five years with the club. Lou Brock credits

Sizemore's patience at the plate for some of his incredible achievements as a base stealer.

Sizemore joined the Phils in 1977, and had a fine season both at bat and in the field, where he came in second in putouts (348) and third in assists (427). He would put up similar defensive numbers in 1978, though his batting average slipped dramatically to .219. The Phils traded Ted to the Cubbies, after the season, for Greg Gross and Manny Trillo. He would finish his career with the White Sox in 1979 at age 35.

The Pines

Depending on the platoon, the Phillies could always call on Jay Johnstone, Bob Boone, Tim McCarver, or Davey Johnson for pinch-hitting or fielding relief. All were more than expert at their positions, hit for good average, and had pop in their bats. Danny Ozark could also turn to fan favorite Tommy Hutton, who had served as a pinch hitter and spot starter with the club since 1972. Hutton would hit a career-best .309 in '77, while getting the most limited playing time in his career, thanks to the two starters ahead of him at first and the five in the outfield.

Then there was Downtown Ollie Brown, who at 33 was serving the final year of his storied career. He'd been with the organization since 1974, serving a primarily pinch-hitting role. Terry Harmon, who was in the last year of a decade-long major league career served with the Phillies, could always be counted on for infield relief and light pinch-hitting duty.

The Starting Staff

The Ace:
Left-Hander Steve "Lefty" Carlton, 23-10, 2.64, 198 K

What do you say about Steve Carlton? Everything the man did, including his silence, seemed geared toward controversy. He went through incredible ups and downs with the media, and even though the fans offered him unrivaled love, he never spoke to them, rarely even looking in their direction.

Carlton broke into the majors on an incredibly talented 1967 Cardinals pitching staff, where he went 14-9 with a 2.98 ERA.

After making the All-Star team the next two years, Steve felt he deserved a much better raise than the Cards were willing to offer. After initially refusing to report to Spring Training in 1970, Carlton had one of his most disastrous seasons, leading the league in losses with 19.

Blaming his performance on his temperament, Carlton changed his mental approach to the game. He became a student of Eastern philosophy and changed his training regimen entirely. In a time when most players played ball, then went out drinking, Carlton began practicing martial arts to build up his mental strength both on and off the field. One of his favorite exercises was to twist his fist to the bottom of a five-gallon bucket of rice.

Steve proceeded to go 20-9 in '71, and reclaimed a spot on the All-Star team. It was this kind of attitude that led battery mate Tim McCarver to say, "Carlton does not pitch to the hitter, he pitches through him. The batter hardly exists for Steve. He's playing an elevated game of catch." Once again, however, he got into a contract dispute with the Cardinals, which eventually led owner Gussie Busch to swap aces with the Phils, taking Rick Wise in return. At the time, it didn't seem like a bad trade for either club. Wise was a 25-year-old right-hander who'd just thrown a no-hitter, and was coming off a 17-win season while posting a 2.48 ERA. Carlton was a 25-year-old left-hander, coming off a 20-win season. Tim McCarver, who had caught both players, said that it was a trade "of a real good one for a real good one."

It didn't remain so even-keeled, however. Though Wise had a consistently fine career, winning 16 games for each of his two seasons with the Cardinals, Carlton became a legend. And he did so immediately.

Lefty's '72 season just might be the greatest that any pitcher has ever recorded in baseball history. The Phils had been going through another rough patch before the trade, having finished last or next-to-last the past three seasons. Carlton, however, turned all that around. In his very first season with the club, he led the league in wins (27), strikeouts (310), ERA (1.97), complete games (30), innings pitched (346.2), games started (41), and strikeouts-to-walks ratio (3.563). During one incredible stretch, from July 19 to August 13, he threw six straight complete games, allowed only one run and recorded four shutouts.

All this for a team that finished in last once again, going 59-97, a full $37^1/_2$ games behind the Pirates. Carlton's 27 wins accounted for 46 percent of the club's wins that season—a record in MLB history. He started the All-Star Game for the Nationals, was the unanimous winner of the Cy Young Award, and received the Hickok Belt as the top professional athlete of the year.

Steve Carlton worked with three dominant pitches: the sinker, the rising fastball, and the looping curveball. Famed Pirates slugger Willie Stargell said of Lefty's signature sinker, "It was like trying to drink coffee with a fork." After another 20-win season in 1976, Carlton turned it on in '77, going 23-10 (first in wins), while sporting a 2.64 ERA (fourth) with 198 strikeouts (fourth). This was also the year when he stopped talking to the media entirely. From his early days in St. Louis, Steve felt that the press never game him a break. Feeling that the media was making his newfound spiritual regimen look ridiculous, Carlton simply stopped addressing the press for a decade. In 1981, a reporter remarked about the relationship between Steve Carlton and upcoming Mexican pitcher Fernando Valenzuela: "The two best pitchers in the National League and neither speaks English."

Carlton broke his media silence with the local press when he granted an interview to *Philadelphia* magazine's Pat Jordan in April 1994. One wishes, however, that he would have remained silent. During the interview, Carlton said he believed that the world was ruled by the Russian and U.S. governments, which "fill the air with low-frequency sound waves." He claimed that the "Elders of Zion" were fighting both of these governments for control, along with "British intelligence agencies," "12 Jewish bankers meeting in Switzerland," and "a committee of 300 which meets at a roundtable in Rome." And, just for the hell of it, he made mention of his discovery that President Clinton had a black son and that the AIDS virus was created at a secret American site "to get rid of all gays and blacks." Suffice it to say that Carlton has denied making these statements and has not spoken to the press since. Who could blame him?

Second in the Order:
Right-Hander Larry Christenson, 19-6, 4.05 ERA, 118 K

Larry Christenson was one of those rare (and becoming rarer) baseball figures who spends his entire career with one organization. In his very first game in the major leagues, the 19-year-old Christenson hurled a complete game shutout against the New York Mets. He saved his best seasons, however, for the Phillies division championship years, winning 13 games in both 1976 and 1978, with a career-best 19 victories in '77. Injuries, however, derailed this quickly moving locomotive.

In 1979, Christenson would finish at just 5-10, thanks to two trips to the injured reserve list, one of which occurred when he fell off a bike at a charity event. He was sidelined again in 1980, and had to have surgery in '83, after which the Phillies gave him his unconditional release at just 30 years old.

Third in the Order:
Left-Hander Randy Lerch, 10-6, 5.07 ERA

Here in his rookie season, Randy Lerch struggled with his control but could look surprisingly strong, especially when under pressure. After winning 10 or more games in his first three seasons with the club, he was traded to Milwaukee in 1982. Lerch would eventually complete his career back in Philadelphia where it began, posting a 7.88 ERA in 1986.

Fourth in the Order:
Left-Hander Jim Kaat, 6-11, 5.39 ERA

Jim Kaat pitched for 25 seasons, won 283 games, and claimed 16 Gold Glove awards. However, by the time he joined the 1976 Phillies at age 37, his best seasons were behind him...just behind him. He was coming off two consecutive 20-win seasons for the White Sox, where he perfected his quick pitch delivery.

In 1977, Kaat didn't have much to add but veteran leadership, as he went 6-11 with a bloated 5.39 ERA. He'd bounce back in 1978 with an 8-5, 4.10, but the Phils would sell him to the Yankees in early '79. Kaat would throw with consistent success until he retired from the Cardinal organization after the 1983 season at age 44.

Fifth in the Order:
Right-Hander Jim Lonborg, 11-4, 4.11 ERA

A former Cy Young Award winner when he went 22-9 with a 3.16 ERA for the 1967 Red Sox, Jim Lonborg had pitched for the Phils since 1973. In '77, he was just coming off his best season for the club, where he'd gone 18-10 with a 3.08 ERA. At 35 years of age, however, Lonborg appeared to tire. Though he had a fine record of 11-4, his ERA would rise by more than a full run per game, and would continue to rise over the next two seasons, until he was released by the Phils midway through the 1979 expedition.

The Bullpen

When you look at the earned run averages of the starting staff of the Phillies, you have to wonder how they were ever able to put together 101 victories. Two of their starters posted ERAs over five, while two others couldn't fight their way below four. These kinds of numbers wouldn't even look good in a league where they allowed the designated hitter. On average, Jim Kaat and Randy Lerch didn't make it through the fifth inning, while Jim Lonborg and Larry Christenson barely made it through the sixth. That left a lot of work for the bullpen. And they were up to the task. Hell, this was the bullpen that could use Tug McGraw as a setup man most of the time.

The Closer:
Right-Hander Gene Garber, 2.35, 19 Saves

After pitching with modest success for Pittsburgh and Kansas City, Gene Garber was purchased by the Phils during the 1974 season and immediately set up shop in the bullpen. The 26-year-old, who was on his way to 19 major league seasons, turned in a 2.06 ERA, and was the official closer of the team into the '78 season.

Garber had something to prove in 1977. Although he'd had a fine '76 season, posting a 2.82 ERA together with 11 saves, he'd taken the loss in the heartbreaking third and final game of the Championship Series against the Reds, allowing a three-run rally to end the game and the Phils' dreams. He would get his chance at redemption in 1977.

With their wealth of relievers, Garber was traded in early '78 to the Braves, as the Phils reacquired Dick Ruthven in hopes of shoring up the starting staff. He pitched with great success for the Braves through 1984, serving mostly as the closer, notching up double figures in saves most every year with typical ERAs hovering at 3 or below. Garber would finish his career in 1988, still going strong for the Royals, where he earned a 3.58 ERA in 26 appearances.

Another Closer:
Left-Hander Tug McGraw, 7-2, 2.62, 9 Saves

One of the most beloved Phillies of all time, Tug McGraw did it all in 1977. He could close a game, be called on in mid-inning situations to put out a fire, set up Gene Garber for the ninth, and actually start a game or two. He did it with charm, energy, enthusiasm, and a wink to the fans. He could ignite a team from the mound, and indeed almost saved the fourth game of the '77 Championship Series, as he tried to rally the club in the pouring rain.

Always a screwball just like his best-out pitch, Tug got his start in professional baseball in a typical oddball way. His brother, a minor league player himself, asked scout Roy Partee if he would have a look at his younger brother. Partee agreed but only as a favor. Tug took the mound as a starter that day and threw a perfect game. He wasn't typically a starting pitcher, had never thrown a perfect game in his life, and never would again.

McGraw finally made a landing with the Mets in 1974 at age 24 and began building a legacy, serving as the closer with identical 1.70 ERAs in both '71 and '72. After struggling in '74 (4.16 ERA), the Mets traded him to Philly for Mac Scarce and Del Unser. Tug quickly became one of the cogs that brought the team to their '76, '77, and '78 division titles. And, of course, to their first World Championship. But more on that later.

Yet Another Closer:
Right-Hander Ron Reed, 7-5, 2.75, 15 Saves

Ron Reed was a two-sport superstar, playing professional basketball for the Pistons from 1965 to 1967 and professional baseball for the Braves during the summer. The Braves finally contracted him out of basketball for 1968, and by '69, he went 18-10 to lead them to their first division title.

A starter for most of his career, Reed was converted to a reliever when he came to the Phillies in 1976 and quickly teamed up with McGraw and Garber to give the Phils one of the most formidable bullpens in history. He would finish in the top 10 in saves from 1976 through '78, and earn 13 wins as a long reliever in '79. Always a consistent arm, Reed would continue to prosper in the pen, going 9-1 with a 3.48 ERA in 1983, his last season with the club. The Phils traded him to the White Sox for Jerry Koosman at the end of the season, where Reed would complete his career with another typically strong season, retiring at 40.

Yet Another Closer:
Left-Hander Warren Brusstar, 7-2, 2.65, 3 Saves

We all know the story of the much-beleaguered J.D. Drew, who was drafted by the Phillies in 1997 and yet refused to sign. Less known is the tale of Warren Brusstar, who at 18 was drafted by the Giants in 1970, but refused to sign; he was again drafted by the Giants in 1971, and refused to sign. He was drafted by the Mets in '73, and once more didn't sign. But when the Phils drafted him in '74, he upped in and signed on. In 1977, his rookie season, the 25-year-old Brusstar began what would be a nine-year career.

Although he battled shoulder problems throughout his career, Brusstar was a successful pitcher everywhere he went, serving mostly in long relief. He'd pitch for the Phils until the White Sox purchased him during the 1982 season. He would spend four good seasons with the Cubs before retiring at 33 in 1985.

Phillies Memory

Christine Qualtieri, Longtime Fan

My dad loved the Phillies. His wine cellar showed it. Other than the pictures of Sinatra, the only thing on its wall was an old "Yes We Can" bumper sticker.

In the'70s, the wine cellar is where Dad would sit on his beach chair working on his fishing darts, with a beer at his side and Whitey and Harry on the 5&10 radio talking about baseball. It seemed like it was really just a conversation rather than an intricate game description. And I sat nearby playing with my dolls and just enjoying the company of my "family."

Jim Kaat was my favorite because my mom liked him and he had the same pleasant mannerisms as my dad. Of course, my criteria for a favorite player would change over the years, because within a year I would have a huge crush on Randy Lerch.

In the summer of '77, I spent almost every night in their company: Dad, Richie Hebner, Michael Jack Schmidt, The Bull (did he have his glasses then?), and Garry LEE Maddox. These were the days when I knew the players' middle names. Of course I knew them; they were family. I loved to see the yearbook pictures of the players with their kids. (Little did I know that I should have saved that picture of the Boone family!) They were just like my dad, with their arms around their kids, smiles on their faces and Phillies red in their blood. The Phillies were and are part of the family, and they will always be the only bumper sticker on my car!

The Season

The Phillies started slow out of the box this year, and by mid-May, they were still trying to shake off the lethargy, standing at 12-13. This was good enough for fifth place in the National East, a full seven games behind the streaking Pirates. At 18-10, however, they righted the ship, pulling into fourth among a tight group that left them only three games behind a constantly shifting first-place tandem of the Pirates, Cubs, and Cards. A mediocre June, however, left the Phils limping again, falling eight and a half games behind the Cubs. On Thursday, June 30, Steve Carlton threw a complete-game six-hitter over the Pirates for his 10th win of the year. From that point on, the Phillies became a force of nature, going 62-29 and winning the division by five games over the Pirates, and 20 over the Cubs.

THE 1977 NATIONAL LEAGUE CHAMPIONSHIP SERIES

The Dodgers won 98 games during the season to coast to a division title, topping the Reds by a full 10 games. Their offense sported a mixture of grace, speed, and strength. The power came from four 30-homer men, led by Steve Garvey (.297, 33 HR, 115 RBI, 91 R), Reggie Smith (.307, 32 HR, 87 RBI, 104 R), Dusty

Baker (.291, 30 HR, 86 RBI, 86 R), and Ron Cey (.241, 30 HR, 110 RBI, 77 R). Their speed came from Davey Lopes (.283, 47 SB, 85 R) and Bill Russell (.278, 16 SB, 84 R). Their pitching staff was helmed by Tommy John (20-7, 2.48), Don Sutton (14-8, 3.18), Burt Hooton (12-7, 2.62), Rick Rhoden (16-10, 3.74), and Doug Rau (14-8, 3.43). Charlie Hough was their designated closer with a 3.32 ERA and 12 saves. The Phils had split the season series with the Dodgers, scoring 52 runs against their 50. It was going to be a helluva series.

Game One

Tuesday, October 4 (Dodger Stadium)

The opening game featured two 20-game winners in Steve Carlton and Tommy John. It didn't take us long to launch an assault as Greg Luzinski hit a two-run homer in the top of the first inning. We made it 4-0 in the fifth when Davey Johnson plated Schmidt and Luzinski. The Phils were coasting 5-1 going into the bottom of the seventh when Carlton lost his command. He offered up a one-out walk to Jerry Grote, a single to Davey Lopes, and another walk to Reggie Smith to load the bases with two outs. Ron Cey followed with a gargantuan grand slam that brought all of Dodger Land to its feet. After Carlton allowed a single to Steve Garvey to follow, Gene Garber came in to shut the door.

The Phils got something going in the ninth inning when Bake McBride hit a one-out single off Dodger reliever Elias Sosa. Larry Bowa followed with a single of his own to put runners at the corners, before Schmidt got the lead once again with a sharp single. Sosa then balked in another run to give the Phils a 7-5 lead. Gene Garber came into the bottom of the ninth, and just like he'd done in the eighth, put the Dodgers down in order. The Phils had won their first playoff game in 62 years, dating back to when the 1915 Phillies won their opening game of the World Series against the Boston Red Sox behind Grover Cleveland Alexander.

Game Two

Wednesday, October 5 (Dodger Stadium)

Bake McBride hit a fourth-inning leadoff homer against the Dodger's Don Sutton to break a scoreless second game. Suddenly, you couldn't blame the loyal Philly fans for dreaming of a sweep. Jim Lonborg couldn't hold onto that lead very long, however. Rick Monday hit a ground-rule double to lead off the bottom of the frame, and two outs later, he was brought home by a line-drive single from Davey Lopes.

The Phillies fell behind for the first time in the series in the bottom of the fifth inning, when Steve Garvey hit a grand slam, putting the Dodgers ahead, 5-1. Los Angeles added single runs in the sixth and seventh, not that Sutton needed it. Although he allowed nine hits, he walked none, and worked himself out of trouble each time it arrived. Still, the Phils had managed a split in Los Angeles and would now be coming back to Philly where we had put together a remarkable 60-21 record through the season.

Black Friday

October 7 (Veterans Stadium)

Veterans Stadium was packed to capacity and then some. Thanks to some exceptional ticket scalpers, many duplicate tickets were sold. But no one cared. The ushers let the duplicates stay. Everyone wanted to see history made. They got their wish. But it wasn't exactly the history they were looking for.

Phils starter Larry Christenson got himself into trouble in the second inning, as the Dodgers touched him up for three runs, thanks to a double by Dusty Baker and a two-run single from Steve Yeager. This didn't silence the Philly faithful, however. In fact, what happened next is one of Philadelphia's proudest baseball moments. It started tamely enough with a Greg Luzinski leadoff single, and when Richie Hebner grounded into a force and Garry Maddox struck out, things didn't look like they were going anyplace fast. But Bobby Boone hit a two-out single to set some fire to the crowd, and then Burt Hooton walked Ted Sizemore to load the bases.

With the fans going absolutely insane, Hooton fell behind pitcher Larry Christenson, and then as he threw ball three, people began taunting him...en masse. Seventy thousand voices turned against one Burt Hooton, and he felt it. He threw ball four to walk in a run, then he walked Bake McBride to tie the game. And then, throwing his hands out at the crowd, he let them know that he didn't appreciate what they were doing.

Bad move, Burt. What this did, of course, was let the fans know that they were really getting into his psyche. That's when they screamed with the strength of 10 grinches...plus two. Result: Hooton walked Larry Bowa to give the Phils a 3-2 lead, and Burt was taken out of the game. He showed his displeasure with the fans as he left, which was the equivalent of giving them a bouquet of flowers.

Rick Rhoden managed to retire Schmidt to end the inning, but the tide had turned. Everyone in that stadium, including every single Phillie, knew we had just won the game, and were well on our way to our first World Series appearance in 27 years. Christenson didn't hold the lead for long, however. Ron Cey doubled to lead off the fourth, and came around to tie the game on a Dusty Baker single to right. When Rick Monday singled to follow, Christenson left the game for Warren Brusstar, who got himself out of the inning with no further damage. With the game still knotted going into the bottom of the eighth, the Phils put an attack together against reliever Elias Sosa. Richie Hebner led off with a double, and scored when Garry Maddox laced a followup single to right. Maddox advanced to third on a throwing error by Reggie Smith, and then scored on a throwing error from Davey Lopes.

The Phils carried a 5-3 lead into the ninth inning with ace closer Gene Garber on the mound. Garber had already taken the Dodgers down in order through the seventh and eighth, and he looked at the very top of his game. Including his performance in the opening game, where he'd been credited with the victory, Garber had retired all 10 men he'd faced—eight by groundout, two by strikeout. No one had yet to get a ball out of the infield on Gene. The game was in the bag.

Too bad that's what Danny Ozark thought as well. In defiance of the strategy he'd employed for the last two years, Danny did not replace Luzinski for the speed and glove of Jerry Martin. Still, when Garber retired the first two men he faced on grounders, it didn't look like it would much matter. But then pinch hitter Vic Davalillo stepped into the box and saw Ted Sizemore playing unusually deep at second. He set a drag bunt down that Sizemore was unable to get to, bringing the tying run to the plate. No fear, though. Garber had now faced 13 batters in this postseason, and not one had hit the ball out of the infield.

Manny Mota pinch-hit for the Dodgers and quickly fell behind 0-2, but then hit a long, lofting ball to left. Jerry Martin could have easily ranged under it for the catch, the win, and a chance for the Phils to take it to the World Series itself. However, Luzinski loped to his left, then his right, then tried to dart back as fast as he could; all this time, Garry Maddox was rushing over from left center. The ball, Luzinski, and Maddox converged; Luzinski lunged, it tipped off the glove, and caromed off the wall. Luzinski recovered, made an excellent throw to second that beat Mota to the bag, but Sizemore could not hold onto the ball.

With the score now 7-6, Davey Lopes hit a sharp grounder to third that Mike Schmidt set up for what looked like a clean and easy out. However, the ball hit a seam and then bounded off Schmidt's knee. Larry Bowa made an incredible play off the carom and gunned the ball to first. Replays show that ball beat Lopes to the bag, but he was called safe; Mota meanwhile scampered around third and the game was tied.

Now it was Garber's turn to come unglued. He rushed a pick-off throw to first that went wildly past Hebner, putting Lopes in scoring position. Bill Russell followed with a seeing-eye grounder that scored Lopes and gave the Dodgers the lead. The crowd of 70,000 plus sat in stunned silence. Mike Garman came in to close the bottom of the ninth, and give the Dodgers a 2-1 lead in the series.

Game Four

Saturday, October 8 (Veterans Stadium)

The gods wept for Philadelphia on this day. You can't blame them, but one wishes they could have kept their composure. The game was delayed two hours due to incessant rains, and when it resumed, the Dodgers jumped on top of Carlton in the second inning, thanks to a two-run homer by Dusty Baker. Carlton, citing the wetness of the ball, threw a wild pitch that brought in a run in the fifth, followed by an RBI single from the bat of Bill Russell. The Dodgers led 4-1, and the skies really opened up. Certainly, the game looked like it should have been called or at least delayed. However, forecasters noted that the showers were not supposed to stop until the next day. Surely, if the game had been delayed, it would not have resumed.

No one made a move, however, allowing the Phillies to play the bottom of the fifth. The game was now official. There was no life left in the crowd, no hope. We all watched, besotted and besoaked, as the Phils grimly consecrated what we already felt was an inevitability. Tug McGraw tried to will the team and the fans to a rally after he recorded his second consecutive scoreless inning in the eighth, but though the club managed to bring the tying run to the plate, pinch hitter Jerry Martin grounded out to end the last gasp of the Phils' 1977 fire.

It was over. Again. Just like it had been in 1915, just like it had been in 1950, and in '64, and in '76, and now in '77. The Phils had played their 16th postseason game, and were the proud winners of only two. No one even had the audacity to say, Wait until next year. The rains, by the way, stopped shortly after play concluded.

Phillies Memory

Matt Cowell, Philadelphia Author

Time condenses my memories, squeezing away a thousand events, but sharpening the remainder to a jewel brilliance, like the sun that streamed down on my brothers and me as we sat in the 700 level, the second row from the top, in center field, on October 7, 1977.

Even from there, I could see that Steve Garvey missed the plate in the second inning, but was called safe. Even from there, I could see Burt Hooten losing his composure as all 65,000 of us clapped and stamped and screamed, coming to a crescendo with each pitch until he walked in three runs. Even from there, I could see the disaster unfold in the top of the eighth: that refugee from the Mexican League beating out a drag bunt on a 0-2 count with two outs, Mota's line drive down the left field line, the ball bouncing off Schmidt's leg and Bowa snagging the carom throwing Lopes out, only to be called safe.

The only part of the park I couldn't see was the left field corner, where Luzinski had no business being, when he trapped the ball. It wasn't the best game I ever saw, by any stretch of the imagination, but it was by far the most amazing. Like jewels those memories became treasures to me, as with almost everything to do with the Phillies, they are touched by pain, but treasured all the more because of it.

THE AFTERMATH

The depression at the stadium didn't remain at the stadium. Many connect the collapse of the 1977 Phillies with the collapse of the Philadelphia economy shortly thereafter. The town just didn't have the heart to buy anything. Even the bars lost business. Philadelphia sunk into a mass depression. It would be three years before we'd climb out of it.

1980: The Team That Forgot to Lose

1980 National League Eastern Division Standings

Team	Wins	Losses	WP	GB
Philadelphia Phillies	91	71	.562	0
Montreal Expos	90	72	.556	1
Pittsburgh Pirates	83	79	.512	8
St. Louis Cardinals	74	88	.457	17
New York Mets	67	95	.414	24
Chicago Cubs	64	98	.395	27

NLCS: PHILLIES 3; HOUSTON ASTROS 2

WORLD SERIES: PHILLIES 4; KANSAS CITY ROYALS 2

Preseason

Although the Phillies had met some success in the previous two years, there was no question about it: the ravenous buzzards from Black Friday were still tearing at the fabric of our very being. We'd tried to cheer them on as they won their division again in 1978, and even mustered up a boo or two when the Dodgers returned for another NLCS. The results were the same: a 3-1 ousting that included the return of Burt Hooton, this time earning a victory against us. What a jerk.

We'd finished in fourth in 1979, 14 games behind the eventual World Series champion Pittsburgh Pirates. Mike Schmidt had had another fine year in '79, smacking 45 homers (second in the league), collecting 114 RBI (third), and crossing the plate 109 times (third). Pete Rose added his usual fire and gusto to go along with a .331 average (second), 95 walks (fifth), and .418 on base percentage (first), but the rest of the offense slumped to varying degrees. Greg Luzinski, always prone to periods of quiet, hit only .252 with 18 homers; Larry Bowa fell to a .241; and although both Bake McBride and Garry Maddox stole over 25 bases apiece, neither managed to climb into the .300 sphere.

Steve Carlton was still mowing them down to the tune of 213 strikeouts (second), while winning 18 games (third); still, his 3.62 ERA was elevated. Nino Espinosa made a nice addition, winning 14 and producing a 3.65 ERA; Randy Lerch managed 10 wins and a 3.74. But Dick Ruthven failed to impress, going 7-5 with a 4.27, a far cry from the 13-5 he'd posted for us the year before, while Larry Christenson simply tanked, going 5-10 with a 4.50.

The biggest problem, however, had been the Phillies' greatest strength in '77: the bullpen. Tugger played the part of closer and posted a 5.16 ERA. Read that again. A 5.16? Come on, Tug! Ron Reed was only modestly better, sporting a 4.15, while rookie Kevin Saucier notched a 4.19, and newcomer Rawly Eastwick chimed in at 4.90.

Phillies Memory

Mike Aronovitz, Philadelphia Writer,
Author of Seven Deadly Pleasures

I was in my first year of college when Pete Rose caught Bob Boone's bobble by the dugout in the big show against Kansas City. I watched it with my fraternity brothers at Temple University's Pi Lambda Phi on Broad and Norris Streets. Our house was a wreck. A female guest once said that it looked like something out of *The Munsters*. When you walked through the middle room downstairs, your feet stuck to the floor. That was where our beer-pong table was. We had a *Playboy* pinball machine and a soda machine set up to dispense five-ounce Rolling Rocks for seventy-five cents apiece. The place smelled like beer, puke, and Pine Sol. The whole place was a train wreck, and I saw the Phillies win a World Series, right there in the front chapter room with the bay windows that had bars on the outside of them, the mismatched furniture, and the rug that looked like the fur of an elk that just came through a mudslide. We drank, we yelled, we gave big chesty hugs and high fives. We drank a lot and played "Positive Pete Rose," which had clear rules and clear consequences. Every time Pete Rose did something positive, you had to chug. When he caught the bobble by the dugout, we chugged twice in a row. With reverence.

When Philly won that series in '80, it was a signpost in all our lives. It showed us that brotherhood mattered, whether you were wearing the holy red pinstripes or the purple and gold of Pi Lambda Phi. It showed us that playing to the last strike still meant something, that stigmas and curses could be broken, and finally, that these were the very best of times.

The Manager

Dallas Green provided a much different atmosphere than the laid-back Danny Ozark. You think Gene Mauch had a bad temper? That was nothing compared to Green. He could scream at a cup of coffee for getting cold. He took the reins in 1979 with typical bravado and candor: "I'm a screamer, a yeller, and a cusser. I never hold back."

And neither did the Phils. Green clashed with them all. They clashed with him. They clashed with each other. While Ozark would sit back in his comfy office chair and let the players' personalities sort things out, Green was the kind of person who threw kerosene on a fire, and enjoyed the ensuing blaze.

Green led the club to their first World Series championship in 1980, a year in which he claimed Manager of the Year. After earning part of the split-division crown in 1981, he left the Phils to accept a front-office job with the Chicago Cubs the very next year. He made an immediate impact on both the Cubs and the Phils in '81 by trading for Larry Bowa and an otherwise unknown shortstop by the name of Ryne Sanberg. Bowa provided veteran leadership at short for three years, while Sandberg went on to a Hall of Fame career.

Green's uncanny moves brought the 1984 Cubs to their first postseason since 1945. They earned him Executive of the Year honors and a bump to the title of team president. After the team finished in last in 1987, Green fired the manager, blasted the team for quitting in all the papers, and then resigned, citing "philosophical differences" with the team ownership.

Green stepped in to manage the Yankees in 1989, but his personality and that of George Steinbrenner were a ridiculous match. One wonders how the two ever made it past the interview process. He moved across town to manage the Mets from 1993 to '96, but could never get them over .500. He now serves as senior advisor to Rubén Amaro.

The Lineup

Leading Off:
First Baseman Pete Rose, .282, 185 Hits, 95 R

What is there to be said for Pete Rose? Many books have been written about the guy, his career, his legacy, and his run-ins with the law, with Major League Baseball, and with life. I can't add much here other than to say he is a storied personality that brought his energy to Philly for a brief moment, allowing us to make the most out of that spark.

Going into his first game in 1979, Rose learned that the Pirates had lost that afternoon, whereupon he rallied the team, earnestly telling them they had the opportunity to pick up a full game on the Bucs. This was opening night, and Rose was already in a pennant race. Pete had spent most of his career with the Reds, breaking in with them in 1963 at the tender age of 22, and earning Rookie of the Year honors. He would make the All-Star team 12 times in his 16 seasons there, and do it for four of the five years he spent in Philly. He'd lead the league in hits seven times, runs four times, and in batting average three. Rose's 4,256 hits are more than anyone who has ever played.

And as every baseball fan knows, he is not in the Hall of Fame because of a gambling problem.

Pete signed with the Phils as a free agent after the 1978 season, at 38 years of age. He had a fine 1980 season, leading the league in doubles with 41; his 185 hits ranked him fifth, while his 95 runs scored brought him at fifth as well. He would spend the early part of the season leading off, but as Greg Luzinski's slump began to reach mythic status, Lonnie Smith took over the left field and leadoff duties, which would place Rose at second in the order.

Pete's offensive numbers began to slide in 1983, after which, at the age of 42, he moved on to Montreal. He signed on as player-manager of the Reds in midseason, helping to lead the club out of fifth place and into respectability, finishing in second for all four full years he managed the club. And then everything imploded.

Phillies Memory

Maria Ceferatti, Philadelphia Music Teacher

Maybe it was because I lived just blocks away from Veterans Stadium, or maybe it was because I was a tomboy and my father treated me like the son he never had, teaching me how to hold a bat, field a grounder and catch a pop fly, but whatever the reason, I was a dedicated Phillies fan. When I was nine years old, on the night of August 10, 1981, my father took me to a game. It was just after the two-month strike and the Phils were playing the Cardinals.

There was a sense of excitement in the air, and I thought it was just the drinking going on in the 700 level, but my father told me that everyone was waiting for Pete Rose to break a record and tonight could be the night. I didn't know who Stan Musial was, but I learned quickly when Charlie Hustle got a hit at his fourth at-bat and broke Musial's National League record with his 3,631st hit. I thought an earthquake had hit Pattison Avenue. The stadium shook. I mean, I could feel the concrete floor shifting and moving. People were going crazy and my father held onto me like he was afraid I was going to get swept away in the chaos. Thirty years later, I still have the complimentary poster of Pete Rose that was distributed that night, and I'll never forget that ground-breaking moment.

Leading Off:
Right-Handed Left Fielder Lonnie Smith, .339, 33 SB, 69 R

As it became more and more clear that Greg Luzinski was not going through one of his normal cold spells, Lonnie Smith took over left field and the leadoff spot in the order. His fine offensive statistics earned him a third-place finish for Rookie of the Year. He followed up with a .324 season in 1981 before going to the Cards in a three-team deal that brought Bo Diaz to the Phillies. He quickly became one of the Cardinals' offensive leaders, helping to take them to a World Series championship in 1982.

Smith's crash began in '83, when despite good offensive numbers, he was sidelined for a month for illicit drug use. His average dropped over the next two years, causing the Cards to trade him to the Royals early 1985. He would get his revenge in that season's World Series as he hit .333 for the Royals' victory over St. Louis in the October classic.

Lonnie was released by the Royals after the 1987 season and found it very difficult to find another position. He blamed Royals owner John Schuerholz for blackballing him. As he later revealed, Smith decided in a cocaine-induced state that he should kill Schuerholz, going so far as to purchase a gun for the crime.

Smith would hook up with the Braves in '87, and earn Comeback Player of the Year in '88 when he had one of his most incredible seasons, hitting a career-high 21 homers, batting .315, and leading the league with a .415 on-base percentage. He would finish his career as a pinch hitter for the Orioles in 1994.

Batting Second:
Right Fielder Bake McBride, .309, .453 SLG, 87 RBI, 13 SB

After hitting over .300 in his first six seasons as a professional, Bake McBride had faltered in 1979, batting at only a .280 clip. He rebounded in 1980 and then some, having arguably the greatest season of his career. Certainly he never received a higher MVP voting, as he finished in 10th overall in the National League. His .309 average was fourth in the league, his 171 hits 10th, and his 33 doubles eighth. McBride led the league in putouts for a right fielder (282), while coming in third in fielding percentage (.990). But more than anything else, Shake 'n Bake could make things happen. Rarely striking out, you could always count on Shake to get the bat on the ball, moving Lonnie and Pete on the bases. He would take deep pitch counts, allowing the meat of the order to get a good look at the opposing pitcher. And once on the base paths, his speed was a constant distraction.

McBride would move to third in the lineup behind Pete Rose after Lonnie Smith began to take over the leadoff role more consistently. This would be his last great year in the majors, however. Injuries curtailed him in 1981, and after a trade to the Indians in '82, Bake would finish out his career as a high average reserve player in '83.

Batting Third:
Third Baseman Michael Jack Schmidt, .286, 48 HR,
121 RBI, 104 R

In one of his most extraordinary years, Mike Schmidt set personal bests in homers with 48 (first in the league) and runs batted in with 121 (also first). He led the league in slugging percentage with a .644, in extra base hits with 81, and in total bases with 342. To this he added 104 runs scored (second), a .380 on-base percentage (fourth), 89 walks (fourth), and eight triples (ninth). Mike also led in assists-at-third (379) and in sacrifice flies (13). Oh, and what the hell, he also upped his average 30 points to .286 and stole a dozen bases. Schmitty would earn MVP honors for his achievements, and would follow it up with an 1981 campaign that would earn him the same. He would move to cleanup when Lonnie Smith replaced Greg Luzinski.

Batting Cleanup:
Left Fielder Greg Luzinski, .228, 19 HR, 56 RBI

1980 saw Greg Luzinski continue to fall from the lofty peaks of '77. His average had dipped 44 points to .265 in '78, then another 13 to hit .252 in '79, and another 24 to his career worst, .228. He would be sold to the Chicago White Sox after the season concluded. There he reclaimed some respect over the next four years, collecting 102 RBI and a .292 batting average in 1982, and clubbing 32 homers in '83. He would retire after the 1984 season at age 33.

Batting Fifth:
Center Fielder Garry Lee Maddox, .259, 73 RBI, 25 SB

While The Secretary of Defense was still a formidable outfield force, Garry Maddox's bad back began taking a toll on his offensive numbers, his average falling from the .330 heights of 1976 to .259. Maddox still had a keen eye, however, and could be counted on to move runners along with some strength, thus accounting for his 73 runs batted in this season, only three short of his career high. Garry's batting average would rebound, hovering around .280 through 1985, but his chronic back pain progressively impaired his power, speed, and glove until he retired in 1986.

Batting Sixth:
Second Baseman Manny Trillo, .292, 68 R

Not many second basemen draw attention to themselves when it comes to their arm. Not so with Manny Trillo. He would effortlessly take his time ranging to a ball, then after calmly studying the ball, he'd wing it to first so rapidly that it seemed a blur. A career .263 hitter with little power, Trillo nonetheless had his greatest offensive years while in Philadelphia, hitting .292 in '80, .287 in '81, and .271 in '82. He would be traded along with four other players, after the 1982 season, in the infamous five-for-one deal that brought Von Hayes to the club.

Batting Seventh:
Shortstop Larry Bowa, .267, 21 SB, 57 R

The fact that Larry Bowa was able to steal 21 bases from the seventh position says a great deal about how he was used. Bowa, in effect, acted as a second leadoff hitter. Once on, he would dart and scramble, throwing the pitcher off center, and hope to move up, either by his own effort or that of Bobby Boone. This is one of the reasons why the leadoff tandem of Pete Rose and Lonnie Smith collected total of 84 RBI. Always impeccable in the field, Bowa came in third in fielding percentage with a .975, while coming in fifth in both assists (449) and putouts (225). It would be Larry's last hurrah with the club, however, as he moved on to the Chicago Cubs after the '81 season to join Dallas Green.

Batting Eighth:
Right-Handed Catcher Bob Boone, .229, 55 RBI

The 1980 season would see Bob Boone begin a precipitous offensive fall. Despite the low average, Boone had a fine eye, allowing runners the time to maneuver, and he could be counted on to get the bat on the ball, moving Bowa and Maddox along the base paths for the likes of Rose or Smith.

Bob Boone followed up his .229 1980 season with a .211 in '81, giving the Phils the mistaken impression that the 33-year-old was on the wane. Boone, however, would rebound with a fury and continue to play through 1990 with an alarming bat, great leadership, and incredible defensive skills.

The Pines

The Phillies had an extremely diverse and talented bench in 1980, giving Dallas Green a great number of weapons in his arsenal at all times. Behind the plate, they could turn to Keith Moreland (.314, .440 SLG) to spell the offensively struggling Boone. In his first year with the Phils, Greg Gross offered pop off the bench, and a strong outfield arm. A former *Sporting News* Rookie of the Year in 1974, Gross had been a starting outfielder with the Astros, but with four strong outfielders in front of him, he would serve mostly as a pinch-hitting specialist and late-inning defensive replacement.

At 35, Del Unser was nearing the end of a fine career. Providing an unrattled demeanor at the plate and field, he would fill in for Maddox in center or Rose at first until he retired at the end of 1981. Ramón Avilés gave the Phils a nice infield glove to relieve Trillo and Bowa, together with a consistent bat at .277. Aviles would get more use this season than in any other, and would see his last major league at-bats the next season, though he tarried in the minors for several more years.

The Starting Staff

The Ace:
Left-Hander Steve "Lefty" Carlton, 24-9, 2.34, 286 K

Steve Carlton had done well since the 1977 season, posting 16 and 18 wins, respectively, but his 1980 season was one for the record books. On his way to winning his third Cy Young Award, Lefty led the league in wins (24) and strikeouts (286), while coming in second in earned run average (2.34) and complete games (13), and recording three shutouts (fourth). Steve would continue to dominate, winning his fourth Cy Young only two years later, before age caught up with the once mighty salvation for the Phils in 1985, and began the tailspin of a storied career.

Second in the Order:
Right-Hander Dick Ruthven, 17-10, 3.55

In his second stint with the Phils, Dick Ruthven posted some of his best numbers in 1980, providing Steve Carlton with one of those rare dependable backups that the club had not been able to offer since Larry Christenson's 1977 season. Ruthven had come up through the Phils organization in the early '70s, making his debut with the last-place '73 club; however, his injury-riddled '75 season led the Phils to send him off to the White Sox, who quickly shipped him to Atlanta.

Ruthven earned his first All-Star Game appearance in 1976, but he would suffer from injuries again in '77. When he stumbled off the block in '78, Atlanta unloaded him back to the Phils for reliever Gene Garber. It would be a fine trade for both clubs. Ruthven went 13-5 with a 2.99 to help the Phils to the division title in 1978, while Garber anchored the Braves bullpen for years to come. After a promising 6-0 start to his 1979 season, Ruthven succumbed to injuries again before finally landing in 1980 with personal bests in wins, winning percentage, and starts.

Dick once more sprinted from the starting gate in 1981, collecting an 8-3 record before the baseball strike closed him down. When play resumed a month later, Ruthven could not find his stride again. The Phils would trade him to the Cubs in '83 for reliever Willie Hernandez, who would factor in the Phillies' World Series run that season. Ruthven would retire from the Cubs after his 1986 season.

Third in the Order:
Right-Hander Bob Walk, 11-7, 4.55 ERA

Bob Walk broke into the majors with 11 wins this season and recorded the opening game victory in the World Series. He had an unhurried demeanor that made him seem even calmer, and thus more formidable, in times of trouble. Many expected great things from him in the future of Philadelphia sports. The Philly brass, however, could not walk away from the opportunity to pick up star outfielder Gary Matthews when Atlanta offered him up in trade just before the '81 season opened. While Matthews helped the Phils to their 1983 World Series appearance, Walk would struggle with the Braves, constantly bouncing from triple-A to the majors before finally being released after the '83 season.

Walk would make the All-Star team with the Pirates in 1988, but would save his greatest moment for the 1992 National League Championship Series. With the Pirates trailing the favored Braves 3-1 in the best of seven, Pirates manager Jim Leyland surprised everyone by taking Bob from the bullpen and naming him the starter in this pivotal game. Walk proceeded to throw a complete game three-hitter. He would retire after the next season at age 36, when his ERA ballooned to a 5.68. Walk now serves as a broadcaster for the Pirates.

Fourth in the Order:
Left-Hander Randy Lerch, 4-14, 5.16 ERA

You have to ask yourself: How can a World Series champion team have a man with a record of 4-14 and an incredibly high 5.16 ERA as their number-four guy? It really is a mystery. Randy Lerch had once been an extremely promising pitcher who posted double figures in wins in '77, '78, and '79, while whittling his ERA down to a 3.74 the previous season. However, after he broke a bone in his wrist nearing the end of 1979, Lerch was never the same pitcher again. The Phils traded him to the Brewers before the kickoff to the '81 campaign. He would go to the Expos in '82, the Giants in '83, and then to the minors for a couple of seasons before finishing his career with the Phillies in '86. Lerch was only 31 when he hung up his uniform for the last time.

Fifth in the Order:
Right-Hander Nino Espinosa, 3-5, 3.77 ERA

A fly-ball pitcher, Nino Espinosa starred for the Mets in 1977 and '78, when he posted double-figure win totals. The Phils traded Richie Hebner for him in 1979, and Nino continued to impress.

After going 14-12 with a 3.65 ERA in '79, he began putting up good numbers in 1980 before arm trouble sent him to the disabled list and then to the minors. Espinosa missed out on the postseason madness, but he returned for the '81 season, only to be released late in the year after going 2-5 with a 6.11. The Blue Jays picked him up, but only gave Nino an inning's work before releasing him as well. He tried unsuccessfully to make the Pirates in 1983, then retired, having thrown his last game at age 27. To mark an even sadder end to an unfulfilled career, Nino Espinosa died of a heart attack on Christmas Eve 1987. He was only 34 years old.

Sixth in the Order:
Right-Hander Larry Christenson, 5-1, 4.03 ERA

Hampered by injuries that had curtailed his 1979 season, including a broken collarbone incurred during a fall at a charity bike race, Larry Christenson kicked off 1980 with a 3-0 start, only to succumb once more to injuries. After elbow surgery, he returned late in the season to finish at 5-1.

September Starter:
Right-Hander Marty Bystrom, 5-0, 1.50 ERA

Marty Bystrom was an unheralded early-September callup for a club looking for help wherever they could find it. His 6-5 record in triple-A ball didn't exactly send the marketing media to proclaim him the next coming of Bob Gibson. But after one shutout inning against the Dodgers on September 7, Bystrom became a starter. He went on to shut out the Mets on a complete game five-hitter, and then proceeded to win each of the next four games he started. Hey, Bob Gibson didn't do that. Who was this kid?

Without Marty Bystrom, the Phils would have never won the division championship in 1980. Unfortunately, Bystrom was hampered by arm problems for the rest of his short career. He would be traded in midseason 1984 to the New York Yankees for Shane Rawley and, after going only 24-26 for the rest of his major league career, he would retire as a Yankee in 1985 at age 26. But for one shining moment, Bystrom was greater than Bob Gibson, and all of Philadelphia will forever thank him.

The Relief Corps

The Closer:
Left-Hander Tug McGraw, 5-4, 1.46 ERA, 20 Saves

Tug McGraw looked like a broken man after the 1978 season, sitting dejectedly after the Phils had dropped another NLCS to the Dodgers. After pitching so phenomenally well for so long, Tugger had undergone a rough two seasons in '78 and '79, ratcheting his ERA up to 5.16 in '79, a career worst. At 35 years old, however, he attacked the 1980 season with an intensity that went beyond his normal exuberant self. There was something in his Tug's this season. He knew what he had to do, and he did it. Dallas Green would have to go to the well many times this season, thanks to an erratic staff, but Tugger would constantly be called upon, always ready and able to get the Phils out of trouble. It was as if he single-handedly willed this team to a championship

McGraw would finish fifth in the Cy Young Award voting—the first and only time he received votes. He would pitch only four more years for the Phils, and would still be effective in 1984 (3.79 ERA in 25 appearances), when he would retire at 39. Tugger would take his popularity to broadcast news over the next few years. Sadly, Tug McGraw contracted brain cancer and passed from this world at age 59 in 2004. But he will always live in Philadelphia, ever flying from the mound after the last strike that brought the Phils their first World Championship.

Phillies Memory

Joseph P. Gehling, Longtime Fan

Of the many events that shape our lives, few occur the day we are born. My younger brother was one of the lucky few who came into this world and was molded by the evening's events. In October 1980, the Phillies won their first championship, with Tug McGraw on the mound. The classic photograph of Tug jumping from the mound, a fist and a glove over his head, was timed nicely for my brother's birth—so nicely that Tug could have been celebrating the delivery.

To this day I have never called my brother by his real name; no one does. He is Tugger, and always will be, as his link to the late great Tug McGraw does not fade. Number-45 jerseys littered our home growing up; as many of Tug McGraw's as my brother's. Having inherited the moniker, he had adopted the number in all sports. Both the name and number have a special significance to him, as it does to our whole family, and we'll never forget that October night in 1980 when our team and our family became forever linked.

Long Relievers:
Right-Hander Ron Reed, 7-5, 4.04,
and Right-Hander Dickie Noles, 1-4, 3.89

This was a club that really needed their long relievers. Christenson, Lerch, and Walk didn't average more than five innings per start, while Espinosa could make it through six, but only just. In his fifth year with the Phillies, the 37-year-old Ron Reed made 55 appearances, getting Phils starters out of trouble, keeping them in games, and trying to bridge to McGraw. At age 23, Dickie Noles served the same purpose, completing one of his best seasons in a career that would see him bounce over six teams in 11 years before retiring in Philly in 1990 at 33.

Spot Relievers:
Left-Hander Kevin Saucier, 7-3, 3.42,
and Right-Hander Warren Brusstar, 2-2, 3.72

Kevin Saucier might not have been the most talented pitcher, but he sure was fun to watch; the 23-year-old sophomore was never hesitant to show his emotions. Though it may have led him never to live up to his potential, his strong reactions to each and every play—sometimes each and every pitch—fit in well with the Philadelphia fan. He'd leave for Detroit after this season, put in a couple good years (including a 1.65 ERA in 38 games in 1981), but retire at 25 in 1982.

Warren Brusstar had been with the Phils since coming up in 1977. He'd just come off an injury-riddled year in 1979, when he posted a 6.91 career-worst ERA, but he would rebound well in 1980. The White Sox purchased his contract in late '82, and Brusstar, battling shoulder problems, would retire in 1985 at age 33.

The Season

The fact that the Phillies had gone 19-11 under Dallas Green at the end of 1979 gave people some hope for the 1980 season. However, by August 11, with the Phils languishing in third place at just four games over .500, the club didn't seem to have the spark that could take the team over the top. In fact, with the Phils barely managing a .500 record since May 24, people predictably began to call for Green to be fired. Dallas would have none of it, though. He simply fired back, and fired at the team.

Keith Moreland responded, getting incredibly hot in August and September. Michael Jack continued to jack the ball all over the place. Lonnie Smith took over the left field and leadoff duties with flame and desire, and a little guy named Marty Bystrom came up from the minors to win all five games that he started. When Steve Carlton defeated the San Francisco Giants on September 1, we moved into a tie for first with the Expos and the Pirates. September would be an endurance test. We would get involved in nine extra inning games and win seven of them.

While the Pirates tanked, winning only 19 of their final 50 games, the Expos kept pace with us, and as fate would have it, both teams entered their last series of the season, facing off against each other in a flat-footed tie. For all intents and purposes, though, it was only October 3, the playoffs had already begun.

In the opening game, Dick Ruthven went up against the Expos' Scott Sanderson, both with records of 16-10. Mike Schmidt hit a sacrifice fly to bring home Rose in the first inning, then a solo homer in the sixth to give the Phils a 2-0 lead. Ruthven had shut the Expos down through five, and though he hadn't allowed many hits, he was all over the place, constantly walking himself into trouble. When he walked two and allowed an RBI double in the bottom of the sixth, Green removed the man for late-season acquisition Sparky Lyle. Lyle managed his way through seven before Tugger came on in the eighth to close out the game. The Phils moved a game into first with two games to play. Just one more win against the Expos was needed to advance to the postseason for the fourth time in five seasons. This was unchartered territory.

Larry Christenson, back from injury, was deemed healthy enough to be given the starting assignment in game two, going up against Expos ace Steve Rogers (16-10, 2.88). Expos right fielder Jerry White hit a two-run homer in the bottom of the third to open the scoring, but the Phils battled back in the fifth, thanks to a bottom-of-the-lineup rally. Larry Bowa, batting eighth, opened with a single, then proceeded to dance and feint off first, throwing off Rogers' rhythm. This allowed a particularly fat pitch to be served to Christenson, who belted it for a single, sending Bowa to third. Pete Rose promptly singled Bowa home to put the Phils on the board.

In the seventh inning, still trailing by one, the Phils got three consecutive singles to load up the bases with one out. Greg Luzinski followed, roped one to center to bring two runs home, and give the Phils their first lead of the game. In relief of Ron Reed in the bottom of the seventh, Sparky Lyle allowed a sacrifice fly to tie the game and then a double from Rodney Scott that gave the Expos back the lead at 4-3.

The Phils tied the game in the ninth, when Bob Boone hit a two-out single to center that scored Bake McBride from second. Hoping to send the game into extras, Dallas Green once again turned to Tug McGraw, who, as usual, proved more than up to the task. He retired the Expos in the ninth, then the 10th, setting the Phils up to regain the lead in the 11th, when Mike Schmidt hit a two-run homer that scored Rose ahead of him.

McGraw shut down the Expos again in the bottom of the inning to give the Phils a hard-earned division championship. No one could blame them for relaxing for a bit, popping the corks and celebrating the intense victory. They'd just been through a war, and they'd won. The thing is, they had no idea about the war that was just around the corner, when they would face the Houston Astros in what just might be the greatest championship series ever played in Major League Baseball.

THE 1980 NATIONAL LEAGUE CHAMPIONSHIP SERIES

The Houston Astros had to wait until the very last game of the season to clinch the division title, tipping the second-place Dodgers behind Joe Niekro, 7-1. The Phils had owned the Astros in the season series, beating them in nine of their 12 games, but the Astros had finished with a better record, 93-70 to 91-71.

The Astros' pitching staff was formidable. Joe Niekro had won 20 games while posting a 3.55 ERA. Nolan Ryan had only won 11, but he had a better ERA than Niekro (3.35); he struck out 200 men during the season, second only to Carlton. Their number-three man, Ken Forsch, had a 3.20 ERA. After that, oddly enough, the Astros got better. Vern Ruhle, their number-four guy, was 12-4 with a 2.60 ERA, while J.R. Richard backed up the startling group with a 10-4, 1.90 season. What the hell? And they didn't get weaker once you got to the pen. Closer Joe Sambito notched 17 saves with a 2.19 ERA. Joaquin Andujar served as the long man, posting a 3.91 ERA. The setups were Dave Smith (1.92) and Frank LaCorte (2.82).

If the Phils struggled to find a consistent staff, the Astros struggled to find playing time for all their great arms. You couldn't dismiss their offense either. The club prided itself on speed, led by César Cedeño with 48 steals, José Cruz with 36, Terry Puhl with 27, and Joe Morgan with 24. Cedeño led the team with a .309, Cruz with a .302. No one hit a hundred RBI and no one scored a hundred runs, but they were consistency personified as five of their starters collected double figures in round-trippers.

The Stros were going into their first postseason in their 19-year history, while the Phils were going into their fourth in the last five years. Nonetheless, all Philadelphians knew it wouldn't be a cakewalk. As a matter of fact, all Philadelphians knew were going to get killed.

Game One
Tuesday, October 7 (Veterans Stadium)

The Phils entered the opening game with a franchise postseason record of 3-17. Cole Hamels won more games in the 2008 postseason than the franchise had won collectively in 97 years! No wonder the fans weren't confident. So you really can't blame the hometown Philadelphia crowd when we released a "Yeah-we-figured-as-much" sigh after right fielder Gary Woods singled home José Cruz in the third to break the ice. The fact that we kept squandering runners on base in the early innings didn't help. Ken Forsch had control of the game and cruised easily into the bottom of the sixth without having allowed a run. However, of all the heroes, it would be Greg Luzinski who punished a Forsch fastball over the left-center wall for a two-run shot that gave us the lead.

When Steve Carlton allowed Ken Forsch himself to lead off the seventh with a single, we knew what was coming: the typical implosion. However, oddly enough, Carlton picked him off on the very next play. That's not what's supposed to happen in Philly. Carlton is supposed to have overthrown Rose, sent Forsch to third, and then allowed him to score on fan interference. Instead, Carlton proceeded to get out of the inning, and the Phils scored again in the bottom when Greg Gross, pinch-hitting for Carlton, singled home Garry Maddox.

Going into the ninth inning, the Phils were protecting a 3-1 lead. Dallas Green sent in his closer and, surprise of surprises, he removed Greg Luzinski for a defensive replacement. The fans were perplexed. What was up with this? Hadn't Green read the *Phillies Playoff Handbook*?

Despite the fact that McGraw brought the tying run to the plate when he walked the leadoff batter, he retired the rest in order, and the Phils had won the game. The fans cheered, some wildly, some furiously, more than a few drunkenly. But, really, most of us just seemed kind of confused.

Game Two

Wednesday, October 8 (Veterans Stadium)

The Phils made a hash of things in the second game as they managed to get to Astros starter Nolan Ryan for eight hits, but stranded 14 base runners in his six innings of work. Meanwhile, the Astros would capitalize with three hits they garnered off Phillies starter Dick Ruthven. It was a tight game that would feature the Phils coming from behind, not once but twice. And who's the man who came through for us in this blizzard of frustration? None other than Greg Luzinski, the man who couldn't buy a hit, timely or otherwise, during the season. Trailing 1-0 in the fourth, The Bull doubled in Mike Schmidt, then came around himself on a Garry Lee Maddox single. Trailing 3-2 in the eighth, he smacked a single off Stros' reliever Dave Smith, then came around to score the tying run on another Maddox single. They proceeded to load the bases with one out in the eighth, but Bob

Boone struck out swinging, and pinch hitter Del Unser flew out to end the inning.

The Phils would again get their chances in the bottom of the ninth when McBride and Schmidt hit back-to-back one-out singles. When Lonnie Smith followed with a single to right, everyone felt the Phils had just won the game. McBride could have easily scored from second, but lost sight of the ball, lost sight of the third base coach waving him home, and then held up at third. Still, the Phillies had the bases loaded again. Only one out. All that was needed was to lift the ball out of the infield and...Manny Trillo followed with a strikeout, then Maddox hit a foul pop to end the inning. The Phils had stranded six in the last two innings alone.

The Astros rallied for four runs in the top of the 10th, the big hit coming on a two-run triple from Dave Bergman to put the game away. We were upset, we were annoyed, we were irritated and angry, but we'd been taught well how to deal with these emotions. This was much easier to handle than the victory in game one. Somehow, we felt like we were home again.

Game Three

Friday, October 10 (Astrodome)

The best-of-five went to Houston for the pivotal third game of the series, the Astros going with their 20-game winner Joe Niekro, while the Phils countered with their five-game winner Larry Christenson. Today, however, they were evenly matched. The game went into the 11th inning with nothing but goose eggs on the board. Christenson had given way to Dickie Noles, who had given way to Tugger. Niekro scattered six hits in his 10 innings of work, now giving way to reliever Dave Smith.

In the 11th inning, Smith got through the first two easily enough, but then Garry Maddox launched a double off the center field wall that for one brief instant looked like it was going to head out. After Larry Bowa was intentionally walked, Del Unser came in to pinch-hit for Bob Boone, and he struck out swinging. Another groan. More crossed fingers. We headed into the bottom of the 11th.

Joe Morgan led off the inning with a sinking drive down the right field line that sunk the Phils' emotions. McBride chased the ball into the corner and hurled it toward Trillo, who relayed it to third, way too late. When the dust cleared, the winning run stood just 60 feet away from home. McGraw intentionally walked the next two batters to set up a force, but Astros first baseman Danny Walling drove a ball to left to bring home the game winner.

The Astros grabbed hold of a 2-1 series lead. Sadly, all of Philadelphia could play out the rest of the scenario. We go home, we drink a few beers that have no effect on us, we go to bed, we go through the next day robotically, and then we watch our club fold up their bats in the next game as they prepare to head home to lick their wounds and wait for 1981. Freaking Texans. They had their champions. They had their Cowboys. Couldn't we just have this one freaking series? One beer. Two. Maybe a third. Damn.

Game Four

Saturday, October 11 (Astrodome)

Dallas Green began the fourth game with a controversial move that would have made Danny Ozark squirm. He benched the hot hand of Greg Luzinski for the fleet Lonnie Smith. The Bull sat quietly on the bench, but the cameras showed how perturbed he really was. He knew he could contribute to this game, possibly the last game of the season, possibly the last of his Philadelphia career. Steve Carlton was brought to the mound to help stave such a dire conclusion to the series, but while the Phils predictably couldn't bring any run around against Vern Ruhle, the Stros managed single runs in the fourth and fifth innings.

There were some fireworks in our top of the fourth that resulted in a triple play that got revoked. It turned into a double play, then back to a triple play, finally returning to a double play that ended up having both teams protesting the game. What happened was this: with runners on first and second, Garry Lee hit a soft liner to Vern Ruhle, who caught the ball and threw quickly to Art Howe at first for the double play. Home plate umpire Doug Harvey called Ruhle's catch a trapped ball, but was overturned by the umpires on first and second. During the confusion, Howe ran toward second and tagged Bake McBride for the third out. Triple play!

Dallas Green erupted onto the field. There followed a 20-minute conversation between the umpires that went back and forth with one official ruling after another. Finally, after a conference with National League president Chub Feeney, it was ruled that the double play stood, but a time-out should have been called when the umps disagreed with each other. McBride could then return to second. It didn't matter in the end. McBride didn't score.

We sat in our homes and in our pubs, watching stone-faced as our boys left two runners on in the second inning, two more in the third, another two in the fourth, and one in scoring position in the sixth. So when Greg Gross and Lonnie Smith led off the eighth inning with singles, many of us simply clenched our teeth. A few of us cheered, certainly, because we were supposed to. But no one had his heart in it. Everyone was already ordering another beer, trying to fend off the impending disappointment that would surely come in only six outs. We'd been here before. Many times.

But then something strange happened. Pete Rose singled home Gross. Dave Smith came in to relieve Ruhle, immediately allowing a game-tying single from Mike Schmidt. Smith was quickly replaced by Joe Sambito, who managed to strike out Bake, but Manny Trillo followed with a fly to right that brought Rose home and the lead into the hands of the Phillies at 3-2. It was our first lead since game two.

These boys were off script. No one understood what was going on. No one even touched a beer. Hardly anyone spoke. When Warren Brusstar allowed a one-out run in the bottom of the ninth to knot the game back at three, we felt sanity had returned. The traditional letdown. But then Bake McBride made an unbelievable grab in right, stealing extra bases from Enos Cabell that would have won the game and the series for the Astros. Everyone was surprised, especially Terry Puhl, who had already begun marching around the bases. McBride fired the ball to Rose at first and the inning was over. We were going extras for the third time in as many days.

Things got even stranger in the 10th inning. With two outs and Rose on first, Dallas Green called Bake McBride back from the on-deck circle to bring in Luzinski. This didn't make sense. McBride was 2-4 on the day, had just saved the team with an incredible catch in the last of the ninth, and had earned a hit in every game of the series thus far. But Green knew his players. He knew when to make a move and when not to make a move. It was as if he knew that The Bull had a hit in him from the moment the game began, as if he knew to keep that hit on the bench until it was needed most. Luzinski responded with a blast off the wall in left that scored Rose to give the Phils the lead, and set up Manny Trillo for a double of his own to send our boys ahead 5-3.

When Tug McGraw put down the Astros in order in the bottom of the 10th, Philadelphians didn't know what to do with themselves. We cheered, we wailed, we drank, we sang, and we wondered what the hell was going to happen tomorrow. Surely we wouldn't make it to the World Series. That just didn't happen in Philadelphia. Did it?

Game Five

Sunday, October 12 (Astrodome)

For the biggest game that the Phillies were to play in their last 30 years, they went with rookie right-hander Marty Bystrom. No one questioned Dallas Green at this point. He seemed to have his hand on the pulse of his team and just knew what he was doing. The fact that Bystrom was going up against veteran ace Nolan Ryan looked peculiar, but so was the fact that we were still playing baseball.

The Stros got off to a quick start when José Cruz stroked a two-out double that scored Terry Puhl in the bottom of the first. But the Phils would come right back, manufacturing two runs off Ryan in the second, when Bob Boone singled home Trillo and Maddox.

Even though his command was not with him, Bystrom held the Astros down till the bottom of the sixth inning, when Denny Walling reached first base on an error by Luzinski, then scored on a single by Andy Ashby to tie the game at 2. In the seventh, Green turned to Larry Christenson, who had done exceedingly well in game three. It wasn't the best decision. Larry got rocked for three runs, allowed two hits, walked one, and wild-pitched a run home.

Trailing now by a score of 5-2, and with Nolan Ryan moving easily through the Phillies order, all seemed at a loss. That's okay. We'd already had our rationalizations prepared before this game even began. We had to consider ourselves lucky to even have gotten this far. But then Larry Bowa singled to start off the eighth. Bob Boone singled to follow. And Greg Gross bunted for a hit down the third base line that loaded 'em up with no one out. That was weird. We should already have been heading back to the locker room at this point. Instead, Pete Rose patiently waited out a tiring Nolan Ryan to earn a walk and bring Bowa home to make the score 5-3. Joe Sambito came in to face Keith Moreland, who brought Boone home with a grounder. And suddenly the score stood at 5-4 with runners on first and third and only one out.

It was the Astros who started to press the panic button now. They brought in their third pitcher for as many batters. Ken Forsch looked to take command of the game when he struck out Mike Schmidt for the second out of the inning, but Del Unser singled home Gross to tie the game. Manny Trillo, who would win the series MVP, followed with a rip down the left field line for a bases-clearing triple that gave the Phillies a sudden 7-5 lead.

With their backs to the wall, the Phils had come up with a five-run, eighth-inning rally. Were we on the doorstep of a World Series? And we were going to send in our master, Tug McGraw, who had been stingy with runs all year, for the eighth and ninth innings. Could this really be in the bag? No, of course it couldn't. The Astros came up with a two-out rally that tied the game when they strung four singles together off the hapless Tug.

Neither team could tally a run in the ninth, though the Phils did manage to get two runners on, which sent the deciding game into extra innings, just where the last three games had gone. With Frank LaCorte on the mound for the Astros in the 10th, Del Unser hit a one-out double to right. One out later, Garry Lee Maddox drilled a double to center to score Unser and put the Phillies ahead by a score of 8-7.

When Dick Ruthven sent down the Astros in order in the 10th, Philadelphia simply erupted. People poured out of their houses, streamed from the bars, flew from their parties. Behind the unlikely heroes of Manny Trillo, who hit .381, and Greg Luzinski, who hit .291 and led the team in slugging percentage, doubles, homers, RBI, and runs scored, the Phils were advancing to their first World Series in 30 years.

In so many ways, the rest seemed like an anticlimax. The city had finally emerged from the depths of Black Friday, and had, in one incredible five-game series, gotten its swagger back. This team wasn't just the Phillies. These were the 1980 Philadelphia Phillies, and everyone suddenly knew that they were destined to win.

Phillies Memory

Patti Petrash, Phillies Fanatic

Writing this while I'm sitting in the parking lot of Bright House Field, waiting for the gates to open to watch a split-squad Spring Training Phillies game. All because we are Phillies fans from way back. While sitting here in my car, I happened to focus on the Phillies flags flapping in the breeze, heralding the teams' accomplishments. The 1980 flag got me to reminiscing about that crazy, nail-biting time of my life.

We played the Houston Astros in the National League playoffs that year. The team who won the best out of five was going to the World Series. THE WORLD SERIES!! Even though we had some world-class players like Mike Schmidt, Pete Rose, and Steve Carlton, it seemed like a pipe dream that we'd even get there.

As you can recall, the Phils did make it to the Series that year and won! But to me the Astros series was a moment in my life that will remain the highlight of that tumultuous time. Each game was a back-and-forth tug-of-war between each team. The Astros were leading the series 2 games to 1.

And that brings us to game four. A win-or-die situation for my team. My husband and I were up visiting my in-laws and watching the afternoon game. It didn't look good for our guys. We were scoreless through the first eight innings and the Astros were up 2-0! I would go upstairs and put my hands over my ears to keep from hearing the Astro fans cheer. I was beside myself.

Unfortunately, we had to leave to go to church before the game was over. I really didn't mind because this way I wouldn't be around to watch the Astros win.

The walk back from church was so depressing for me. I walked with leaden feet. My beloved Phillies were done. Oh yeah, there was a slight chance that they came back to win it; but come on, in Philadelphia we all know better than that.

As soon as we came home, we turned on the TV and—what?—the game was still on. How could that be? Extra innings, baby! We made it just in time to see the last out and the Phils win. I couldn't believe they pulled it out. I started crying and jumping up and down with joy.

Oh and I also was thankful I had gone to church.

THE 1980 WORLD SERIES

Led by manager Jim Frey, the Kansas City Royals had walked away with the American West by 14 games. Like the Phils, these Royals had made the playoffs in 1976, '77, and '78, but had been set back in the American League Championship Series until finally emerging in 1980 year after blanking the Yankees 3-0. Their pitching was led by righty Dennis Leonard (20-11, 3.79, 155 K) and lefty Larry Gura (18-10, 2.95); Dan Quisenberry closed for the club, collecting 33 saves to lead the league with a 3.09 ERA.

The catalyst for the Royals' offense was none other than Mr. Pine Tar himself, the inimitable George Brett, who hit .390 this season (first in the league), the highest batting average since Ted Williams' .406 in 1941. Brett added another 118 RBI (second), 24 homers (ninth), and 87 runs scored. His on-base percentage was .454 (first) and slugging average a healthy .664 (also first). He was the MVP for the American League. Willie Wilson provided the speed, leading the league with 133 runs scored, 230 hits, and 15 triples, while coming in second with 79 stolen bases. Willie Aikens added pop with 20 homers and 98 RBI, while designated hitter Hal McCrae hit .297 with 14 homers and another 83 RBI.

Game One

Tuesday, October 14 (Veterans Stadium)

One good thing that the Phillies had going for them in this World Series was the fact that the Royals' star player, George Brett, was suffering from an intense bout with hemorrhoids. And everyone knew about it. The poor guy had millions of people wondering what was up his butt during the entire Series. What's worse, he actually had to speak intelligently on the subject to a national audience. One wonders who let the cat out of that bag. Probably someone George owed money to.

As for the Phillies' starting pitcher, manager Dallas Green had a bit of a problem. He had just thrown four of his six starters only two days before at the Astrodome. He didn't have much choice but to go to with inconsistent rookie Bob Walk to face Royals ace Dennis Leonard. The Royals jumped on Walk early, when Amos Otis cracked a ball to deep left for a two-runner in the second inning. They struck again when Willie Aikens sent a ball to deep center for two in the third. And just that quickly, Kansas City had grabbed a 4-0 lead.

The Phils didn't seem daunted, however. They bounced right back in the bottom of the third, when a Bob Boone double-plated Larry Bowa with one out; after Leonard hit Pete Rose, Shake 'n Bake would hit a gargantuan three-run homer to give the Phils a surprising five-run rally. We'd add another when Bobby Boone hit his second RBI double of the evening in the fourth inning, and then sit back as Walk found his stride, retiring the Royals in order in the fourth, fifth, and sixth. The Phils made it 7-4 on a Garry Lee Maddox sacrifice fly in the bottom of the sixth.

Willie Aikens would bring the Royals within one in the eighth inning, when he produced a two-runner again, this time chasing Walk from the mound. No worries, though. Tugger walked out calmly and coolly, closing out the game and allowing only one hit and one ball out of the infield in his two innings of relief.

The Phils had won their first World Series game since 1915. And when they left the field, although they were excited, there was also something else in their eyes. This was a big win, yes, but just one step toward their ultimate goal.

Game Two

Wednesday, October 15 (Veterans Stadium)

The Phillies were able to turn to their ace, Steve Carlton, for Game Two, but Carlton was far from ace-like. In his eight innings of work, he allowed 10 hits and six walks, resulting in a

Royals on-base percentage of .415. The fact that Lefty allowed only four runs is really quite remarkable. The Phils opened the scoring, plating two in the bottom of the fifth against Royals starter Larry Gura. NLCS hero Manny Trillo sacrificed home Keith Moreland, just before Bowa singled home Garry Lee. And just that quickly, the Phils seemed in control of the entire Series.

The Royals struck back in the sixth inning, when a Manny Trillo error resulted in an unearned run. Carlton then walked the bases loaded with one out in the seventh, before Amos Otis doubled in two more runs to give the Royals their first lead, 3-2. Royal catcher John Wathan followed with a sacrifice fly to extend the lead to two.

Sensing the opportunity to steal a win in Philly, the Royals brought their closer, Dan Quisenberry, to the mound in the bottom of the eighth. It seemed an odd choice. Gura had looked devastating thus far on this evening. He'd allowed only four hits through the seventh, three of them coming in the fifth. Still, you couldn't argue with a fresh arm, especially one so talented as the Quiz.

The Quiz got himself into immediate trouble by walking Bob Boone to lead off the inning; then he sealed his problem by allowing an RBI double to Del Unser to bring the Phils back within one. Quisenberry shook it off as any veteran would do, especially one with the steely nerves of a closer, and promptly coerced Pete Rose to groundout for the first out of the inning. It was a start. Unser now stood at third, but Quiz knew how to work the plate. If only he could manage to strike out McBride, or coax him into a popout. Bake turned that whole scenario upside down and turned the whole stadium inside out with a single to right that tied the game.

With one deep breath and one more fastball, Michael Jack himself roped a double. McBride was off with contact and scored the leading run for the Phils on a close play at home. A lead. Another comeback. To make things even more uncanny, Keith Moreland followed with a line single to right to score Schmidt, and put the Phils ahead 6-4. The fact that Greg Gross hit into an inning-ending double play to follow mattered very little. Ron Reed came out to retire the Royals in the ninth and the Phils, for the first time in their history, had won two World Series games.

Game Three

Friday, October 17 (Royals Stadium)

It was the Phils' turn to squander offensive opportunities in Game Three, as they managed to score only three runs on 14 hits, leaving 15 runners on base. They wasted a fine effort from Dick Ruthven, who went the full nine, retiring from the game with the score tied at three. George Brett had gotten to Ruthven first, blasting a solo homer in the opening inning. Lonnie Smith knocked in a run in the second to tie the game off of Royals starter Rich Gale. But Willie Aikens tripled down the left field line in the fourth, then scored on a Hal McCrae single to give Kansas City a 2-1 advantage.

The Phillies would again answer right back with a solo shot by Schmitty to lead off the fifth and to put an end to Gale's evening. It was a victory of sorts. The Phils had knocked him out of the box in only four innings, but despite having gained seven hits, they plated only two runs, one on a solo homer. The clubs continued to trade runs when Amos Otis homered in the seventh, only to see the Phils tie it with a two-out Pete Rose RBI single in the eighth. When Dick Ruthven persuaded Darrell Porter to fly out and end the bottom of the ninth, he set the game into extra innings, all tied at three apiece.

The Phils would threaten in the 10th against Dan Quisenberry, when they put two runners on with one out. Schmitty hit a beeline right up the middle. For a moment, it looked like the ball was going to drop, but Frank White was playing him that way. He nabbed the ball on the line, touched second for the force, and ended the inning. Tugger came on in the bottom of the 10th, but despite the fact that he'd had a couple days' rest, he looked a little rusty. U.L. Washington singled to lead off the inning, Willie Wilson walked, and McGraw looked to be in great trouble. But then Boonie nailed Washington on an ill-advised steal attempt, and Tugger struck out White for the second out of the inning. There was light at the end of the tunnel.

But between that light and Tugger stood George Brett, the fiercest hitter in the game. Tug played him well, or at least he played Wilson well. He paid little attention to Willie on first, basically allowing him a free pass to second, and then gave Brett the intentional pass as well. First and second, two out. Willie

Aikens at the plate. Tugger took the sign, toed the rubber, and let hurl. But Aikens turned on the pitch and delivered a game-winning RBI single to left center to give the Royals their first game of the Series.

Game Four

Saturday, October 18 (Royals Stadium)

Larry Christenson would get the ball for the Phillies to start Game Four, but he found his start only a third of an inning long. The Royals actually hit for the cycle against him with a single from Willie Wilson, a triple from George Brett, a homer from Willie Aikens, and back-to-back doubles from Hal McCrae and Amos Otis. Before the smoke cleared, he'd allowed four runs. It was a disaster.

Dickie Noles got some of our frustrations out by knocking down Brett his next time up at the plate, and we felt satisfied. But the Phils weren't. They actually mounted a comeback. What audacity! Every other Phillies team over the last 97 years had been taught that this was the time to simply lay down and die. These Phils, however, scored solo runs in the second, seventh, and eighth innings to make the score 5-3. They brought the tying run to the plate in the eighth, but this time the team of Dennis Leonard and Dan Quisenberry was too much for them, and the Phils fell, 5-3. It was a brand-new series, tied 2-2, but the Phils proved something this night. They were never going to quit.

Game Five

Sunday, October 19 (Royals Stadium)

The Royals hoped to keep the momentum alive by sending left-hander Larry Gura out against Marty Bystrom, who had still never lost a major league game. But he did his best to do just that today, as he allowed 10 hits and a walk in just five innings of play. Somehow, however, the Royals found it difficult to score off the man, and a two-run homer by Mike Schmidt in the fourth opened the scoring.

Kansas City would finally get to Bystrom in the fifth inning with an RBI grounder from Brett. Then they chased him from the mound in the sixth when Amos Otis tied the game with a lead-off homer, followed by back-to-back singles from Clint Hurdle and Darrell Porter. Ron Reed came on immediately to allow a sacrifice fly to give Kansas City the lead, but got out of the inning with no further damage. Despite the heavy offense that the Royals had been throwing, the Phillies trailed only by a score of 4-3. The Phils got two runners on in the seventh inning with one out before Kansas City turned to the Quiz, who went and turned us away. We countered by sending out Tugger in the bottom of the seventh. Both aces were facing each other in a tight game that would determine the momentum and thus the Series.

The score remained the same until the ninth inning, when Schmitty opened with a single over third. Del Unser then ripped a Dan Quisenberry special down the right-field line for a double that scored Schmidt from first and tied the game. That would again set up Manny Trillo, who had more than accepted his hero status for the 1980 playoffs. He calmly delivered a two-out hit over the outstretched glove of the Quiz, and the Phils were back in the lead, 5-4. Tugger didn't have an easy time of it in the ninth, walking the bases loaded before finally striking out José Cardinal to end the game. It was an incredible victory, one that any other Phils team would have found a way to give up, give away, give back, or give in to. But not this club. This club seemed to have left the blueprints in another locker room. This club was heading back to Philadelphia with a chance to hand Philly their first World Series of all time.

Phillies Memory

Julie Conover, Philadelphia Attorney

In the summer of 1980, I had my first real job and lived in Center City. Although I wasn't a Philly native, I was a life-time baseball fan, and in 1980, I was falling in love with the Phillies.

When the Phillies made the playoffs, my boyfriend (now my husband) and I were ecstatic. Folks at his work got play-off tickets, and we bravely volunteered for Game 6 of the World Series, knowing that we would miss out completely if the Phillies floundered before then. But our luck held, and we were privileged to be at Veterans Stadium to see the Phillies win their first World Series ever.

What an experience! I can still recall holding my breath when Bob Boone bobbled a high pop-foul with the bases loaded in the ninth inning, only to have Pete Rose miraculously appear and grab the ball out of the air. Although I've seen film of that play dozens of times, in my mind's eye I always picture it from where we sat, high in right field. And then the final pitch from Tug and we won!

Almost as exciting was riding the Broad Street Subway back to Center City with hundreds of celebrating fans. We partied in the streets and bars of Center City until the wee hours of the night. I felt like a true, lifelong Phillies fan and I have been ever since.

Game Six

Tuesday, October 21 (Veterans Stadium)

With all of Philadelphia in riotous expectation, our boys marched back into Veterans Stadium. The stadium itself seemed a living and breathing beast that day, ready to ingest the Royals. Steve Carlton rode that energy, mowing Kansas City down as only Lefty could. He allowed only three hits and no runs through the seventh, while the Phils got all the runs they would need on a Michael Jack two-run single in the third off Royals starter Rich Gale. They'd add another when Shake 'n Bake grounded home Lonnie Smith in the fifth, and one more when Boone singled in Bowa in the sixth, but that was just window dressing. A 4-0 lead when destiny was already in our hip pocket? Too beautiful to believe.

Carlton finally began to wear down in the eighth, when he walked catcher John Wathan to lead off the inning. After he allowed a single to José Cardenal, Tugger came in to try to nail down the Series. After recording a flyout, Tug walked Willie Wilson to load the bases, gave up an RBI sacrifice fly to U.L. Washington, then gave up an infield single to George Brett to reload the bases, and suddenly we could feel that familiar tightness in our throats. A 4-1 lead, the tying runs on, the leading run at the plate. Black Friday was only three years gone. But this time McGraw was up to the challenge, inducing the hard-hitting Hal McCrae to ground modestly to second.

We took that same 4-1 lead into the ninth. And, as usual, it didn't come easy. McGraw walked Willie Aikens with one out.

No big deal—or at least that's what we thought until he allowed back-to-back singles to John Wathan and José Cardenal to load up the bases. Still only one out. The tying runs were again on the paths. The leading run at the plate was by Frank White, who popped up down the first base line. Boone pushed back his mask and drifted easily under, Rose sauntered down the first base line and drifted easily under, and while no one called it, the ball began to drift easily to the ground. Boone struck out his glove at the last moment, but it ticked off his mitt—and right into the mitt of Rose. Two outs. Easy peasy.

Tug McGraw then put it all to rest with the legendary strikeout of Willie Wilson to end the game, end the World Series, and end the seemingly endless misery that Philadelphia had had to endure for the entire history of the franchise. The picture of Tugger leaping off that mound as the ump called that final strike will always be stitched in the collective memory of a city that never gave up on its team, not through the constant losing seasons of the '20s, the '30s, and the '40s, not through the harrowing demise of the '64 club or the series of circumstances that led to Black Friday. We'd finally been rewarded, and the champagne flowed for us all.

These 1915 Phillies captured the first pennant in team history.

Erskine Mayer won 20 games for both the 1914 and 1915 Phillies.

Grover Cleveland Alexander (*right*) won the pitcher's Triple Crown in 1915 (wins, strikeouts, and ERA); beside him is rookie manager Pat Moran.

Slugger Gavvy Cravath led the league in homers six times from 1913 through 1920.

The 1950 Whiz Kids breathed life back into Phillies baseball for one miraculous season. National Baseball Hall of Fame Library, Cooperstown, New York

Robin Roberts won 20 games each season from 1950 to 1955.

National Baseball Hall of Fame Library, Cooperstown, New York

Controversial slugger Dick Allen, seen here is his 1960 Elmira Pioneers uniform.

National Baseball Hall of Fame Library, Cooperstown, New York

Lefty Steve Carlton won four Cy Young Awards for the Phillies between 1972 and 1982. National Baseball Hall of Fame Library, Cooperstown, New York

The addition of Pete Rose gave the Phillies the boost they needed to finally achieve the World Series title in 1980.

National Baseball Hall of Fame Library, Cooperstown, New York

One of the greatest players in baseball history, Mike Schmidt is honored in the Hall of Fame. Ken Bingham

Steve Carlton's 1980 uniform sits comfortably beside those of Mike Schmidt and Pete Rose in the Hall of Fame.

Ken Bingham

Lenny Dykstra led the league in runs, hits, walks, and at–bats in 1993.

The 2007 Phillies turned 1964 upside down with an astonishing come-back to take the division title on the final day of the season. John Burns

Together with shortstop Jimmy Rollins, second baseman Chase Utley has given the Phillies the best middle infield in their history.
Stephanie Bingham

Speedsters Jimmy Rollins and Shane Victorino have provided the spark at the top of the lineup for the Second Philastic Dynasty. Stephanie Bingham

Cole Hamels won the 2008 World Series Most Valuable Player after posting a 4–0 record in the playoffs. Patti Petrash

1983: Wheez Kids Get Wizzed

1983 National League Eastern Division Standings

Team	Wins	Losses	WP	GB
Philadelphia Phillies	90	72	.556	0
Pittsburgh Pirates	84	78	.519	6
Montreal Expos	82	80	.506	8
St. Louis Cardinals	79	83	.488	11
Chicago Cubs	71	91	.438	19
New York Mets	68	94	.420	22

NLCS:
PHILLIES 3; LOS ANGELES DODGERS 1
WORLD SERIES:
BALTIMORE ORIOLES 4; PHILLIES 1

Preseason

The Phillies came out strong in 1981, breaking off to a 34-21 record, but then Major League Baseball went on strike. When the clubs returned, ownership decided to kick-start the season again, play a second half, and then have the respective winners meet each other in the championship. The Phils nose-dived in the second half, finishing in third, while the Expos took the division. If the records from the halves had been put together, our Phils would have generated only a third-place finish, the Cardinals taking it all. As it happened, though, the Cards didn't even make the playoffs. Go figure. The Phils lost the division series to the Expos, 3-2. The Cardinals got some revenge in 1982, taking the division over the second-place Phils and going on to beat the Brewers in the World Series.

The Phils had brought a new look to 1982, with Bo Diaz replacing Bob Boone behind the plate, Ivan de Jesus at shortstop for Bowa, Gary Matthews in left for Luzinski, and George Vukovich in right for McBride. At 41, Pete Rose was still going, just not as strong, hitting just .271, his worst batting average since 1964. After winning MVPs in 1980 and '81, Mike Schmidt put together another terrific season, but finished in third. Steve Carlton won another Cy Young Award in '82, going 23-11, while Larry Christenson, still fighting injury, went below .500. Newcomer Mike Krukow (13-11) hung out with us for a year, coming from the Cubs for Dickie Noles and Keith Moreland. Dick Ruthven came in at .500, and Marty Bystrom, completing his fourth year, was having a very difficult time living up to those lofty expectations he had set for himself in 1980.

The Phils knew that they had to retool. We had already picked up John Denny from the Indians late in '82. He hadn't been impressive in his four starts down the stretch, but the guy had a pedigree. We traded away Krukow to the Giants for aging second baseman Joe Morgan and reliever Al Holland. We signed our third Big Red Machine alumnus, Tony Perez, as a free agent. And, of course, we made our whirlwind deal, sending five players—including Manny Trillo, George Vukovich, and Julio Franco—over to the Indians for Von Hayes, who would take over the right-field duties.

This was not a youth movement. Rose was already 41, Morgan was 39, and Perez was 41. They joined Carlton at 38, Bill Robinson at 40, Ron Reed at 40, and Tugger at 38. Clearly, we were not retooling for the future. We were just retooling to make a run at 1983. In that, the Phils were successful. However, it set us up for some gloomy years in the seasons to follow.

Manager Number One:
Pat Corrales

Pat Corrales had taken over for Dallas Green in 1981, helping to take the Phillies into the playoffs. Having made their off-season moves for veteran talent, the future was now, and so ownership had little patience with Corrales after he got off to a slow start in '83. They fired him even though the club was in first place with a 43-42 record.

Manager Number Two:
Paul Owens

Paul Owens had spent his entire baseball career with the Phillies, becoming general manager in 1972. He was the principal architect of the 1980 Champions. After firing Pat Corrales, he personally took over the team. Always a kind and generous man, Owens led with an open heart and spirit that rallied everyone behind him. He would only stay at the helm for two seasons, firing himself at the end of a disappointing 1984.

The Lineup

Leading Off:
Second Baseman Joe Morgan, .230, 72 R, 18 SB

At 39, Joe Morgan's awesome career was nearing its end. Long gone were the days when he'd won back-to-back MVPs for the 1975 and '76 Big Red Machine. Long gone were the days when he would be a perennial 60-stolen-base, 100-runs-scored, 20-home-run man. Still, his spirit helped anchor the Phillies infield in this, his only season in Philadelphia. The Phils would release him after the season, leaving him to sign with the A's where he would complete his career in 1984.

Batting Second:
First Baseman Pete Rose, .245, 45 RBI, 52 R

At 41, Pete Rose's offensive numbers had finally begun to fade. In fact, if it weren't for late-season callup Len Matuszek, who replaced Rose at first base, this team might not have made the playoffs. It was Matuszek's presence that gave ownership the confidence to release Rose at the end of the season.

Batting Second:
First Baseman Len Matuszek, .275, .525 SLG

Len Matuszek quickly proved himself an apt replacement for Rose when he was called up in September. It was an incredible beginning. It's one thing to replace an all-time great in your first month of play, but he did it with ease. Len smacked six doubles and four homers, together with 16 RBI in only 17 starts. Matuszek took over first base full time in 1984, but he would turn in a disappointing .248 batting average, while hitting only 12 homers and knocking in 43. He'd be traded to the Blue Jays at the start of the '85 season. He would complete his career in a limited role with the Dodgers in 1987 at age 32.

Batting Third:
Third Baseman Mike Schmidt, .255, 40 HR, 109 RBI, 104 R

Despite Mike Schmidt's relatively low batting average, the man led the league in walks with 128, which in turn brought him to the lead in on-base percentage as well at .399. He topped all in homers with 40, came in third in runs scored with 104, and was third in runs batted in with 109. He didn't slack off defensively either, coming in first in assists for a third baseman (332) and third in putouts (107). Schmitty made the All-Star team for his fifth straight year, won his fifth straight Gold Glove and his fourth straight Silver Slugger.

Batting Cleanup:
Right Fielder Joe Lefebvre, .310, .543 SLG

Joe Lefebvre was a big midseason pickup from the Padres for Sid Monge. Joe had a fine minor league career with the Yankees, outdistancing peer Ricky Henderson in many areas. Still, he never quite lived up to his potential in the majors. But this year, his bat came alive more than any other season. Platooning in right with Von Hayes and Sixto Lezcano, he gave the Phils some muscle in the middle of the lineup that the 24-year-old Hayes was unable to offer in the early part of his career. Lefebvre continued to platoon with mixed results in 1984, then suffered a knee injury that would take him out of the game completely in 1985. He would retire as a Phillie after the '86 season.

Batting Cleanup:
Right Fielder Sixto Lezcano, .239, .351 SLG

The Phillies acquired 29-year-old Sixto Lezcano from the San Diego Padres in late August. He had come up through the Brewers organization where he played his first 12 seasons of ball. Lezcano had his best season in 1979 for the Brew-club when he batted .321 with 28 homers and 101 RBI. He immediately fell to .229 the next season and never reclaimed those lofty heights. But Sixto would see his power revived once in Philadelphia, where, platooning with Lefebvre in 1984, he had a .480 slugging percentage with a .371 on-base percentage. He would be granted free agency at the end of '84, and sign on with the Pirates where he retired at the end of '85.

Batting Somewhere in the Middle of the Lineup:
Right Fielder Von Hayes, .265, 6 HR, 20 SB

The moniker of Five-for-One that Pete Rose hung upon Von Hayes set expectations pretty high for the young man. Hayes would be moved throughout the lineup from second, thanks to his speed; to third, thanks to his quick bat; to cleanup, thanks to his power; and to fifth, thanks to his timely hitting. But he could never really find a home. Before the end of 1983, he would give way to Lezcano and Lefebvre in right.

Hayes had an impressive career with the Phils, proving himself to be a fine all-around player. He played every outfield position, as well as third and first base, quite well. Von could steal bases, swiping 48 in 1984; he could pop the ball, consistently hitting in the high teens and twenties, slapping 26 in 1989; he led the league in runs scored and doubles in 1986; and he was always among the on-base-percentage leaders through the late '80s. Batting leadoff in 1985, Hayes once collected five runs batted in within a single inning. He led off the inning with a homer, then after the Phils batted around, he hit a grand slam in his second at-bat—a record still.

When Hayes broke his wrist in 1991, it spelled the downturn of his bright career. His average dipped to .225, and he hit a grand total of zero homers. Von was traded at the end of the season to the California Angels for Rubén Amaro Jr. and Kyle Abbot. He retired as an Angel at the end of '92. Hayes has returned to baseball as a minor league manager in recent years, mostly with independent clubs.

Batting Fifth or Sixth:
Left Fielder Gary "Sarge" Matthews, .258, 10 HR, 13 SB

Gary Matthews moved around the lineup from second to third in the early part of the season, then fifth and sixth, even batting cleanup occasionally in the latter part of the season. The Phillies traded for Matthews, just before the 1981 season, with the Atlanta Braves for Bob Walk. Sarge, who had won Rookie of the Year honors in 1973, was a welcome addition to the outfield, where he quickly became a leader, thanks to his powerful bat, affable nature, and confident attitude.

The Phillies would trade Matthews to the Cubs, after the '83 season, for Mike Diaz and Bill Campbell. While Matthews went on to lead the league in on-base percentage and scoring 101 times, Mike Diaz never made the majors, and Campbell would last only one ill-starred season. We were astute enough to bring Sarge back to the club as part of our broadcast team, where he has captured the heart of the fans once again.

Batting Sixth:
Center Fielder Garry Lee Maddox, .275, .367 SLG

No longer the same man who had won seven consecutive Gold Gloves, Garry Lee Maddox had already begun suffering from the back problems that would soon end his career. His best offensive attribute was an excellent eye. He could be counted on to get the bat on the ball and move along the runners ahead of him.

Batting Sixth:
First Baseman Tony Perez, .241, .372 SLG

Tony Perez made his mark on baseball when playing for Cincinnati's Big Red Machine in the 1970s, making the All-Star team seven times, consistently collecting over 100 runs batted in and 20 homers, and hitting for high average. Perez would spell Pete Rose at first until Len Matuszek took over the position in September. The Reds would pick him up as a free agent after the '83 season and use him in a limited role until the end of '86, when he would retire at age 44.

Batting Seventh:
Catcher Bo Diaz, .236, 64 RBI

The Phils acquired Bo Diaz in a three-player deal, at the end of the '81 season, that sent Lonnie Smith to the Cards. He had his best season with the Indians in that strike-shortened year when he hit .313. His greatest triumph for the Phillies came on April 13, 1983, when he hit a two-out, bottom-of-the-ninth, walkoff grand slam to beat the Mets 10-9. Diaz would be traded to the Reds in 1985, where he concluded his career four years later at age 36. Sadly, Diaz would pass away in 1990 when a satellite dish he was installing outside of his Mexican home toppled over on him.

Batting Eighth:
Shortstop Ivan de Jesus, .257

The name of Ivan de Jesus doesn't bring good memories to the average Philly fan, and it's not because of anything that de Jesus did. It's because of what we did to get him. After the 1981 season, we grabbed the young, promising middle infielder from the Chicago Cubs for the aging Larry Bowa, and a throw-in, perennial all-star, future Hall-of-Famer Ryne Sandberg.

The Phils had reason to think highly of the young shortstop at the time, however. He had 595 assists in 1977, the fifth highest total ever for a shortstop, then followed it up with a '78 season where he scored the most runs in the national league. God knows why we decided to ignore the fact that he earned a "reverse Triple Crown" in 1981, finishing last in batting average (.194), with no homers and only 13 RBI. Still, Ivan de Jesus was a fine shortstop, serving us well from 1982 to '84, before he was traded to the Cards at the beginning of the 1985 season. He would spend his last four seasons bouncing back and forth from the majors to the minors, before retiring in 1988 at age 35. Meanwhile, Ryne continued going strong.

The Pines

At any one time, three platooning right fielders were available on the bench in Von Hayes, Joe Lefebvre, and Sixto Lezcano. Similarly, three platooning first basemen could also be counted on in Pete Rose, Len Matuszek, and Tony Perez. Greg Gross continued his stellar Phillies career, serving as a spot starter and a pinch hitter. He could play every outfield position as well as first base.

We could also turn to the speedy Bob Dernier, who was in his second full season in the majors. Dernier spotted outfielders from time to time, and had a fine bat, but he found his real art this season as a specialist runner who would come in to steal a base or to provide extra speed in late innings either as an out-fielder or a baserunner. In very limited playing time, Dernier would steal 35 bases to lead the team.

Catcher Ozzie Virgil would spell Bo Diaz behind the plate, and serve as a powerful pinch hitter. Virgil had served in the Phillies organization since the season before and would become the team's starting catcher at the end of this season, a job he would hold until traded to Atlanta, after the '85 season, for Milt Thompson and Steve Bedrosian.

The Starting Staff

The Ace:
Steve "Lefty" Carlton, 15-16, 3.11, 275 K

Even Steve Carlton's ERA was basically identical to 1982 (3.11 as opposed to 3.10), when he won the Cy Young Award for the fourth time. Although Lefty continued to lead the league in strikeouts and innings pitched, he lost more games than he won, resulting in the end of his four-year All-Star Game streak. What is remarkable is that the Phillies went to the World Series on a relatively down year for Carlton. Lefty would never win as many as 15 games again in his career, and he would finally retire from the Twins in 1988 at age 43.

Second in the Order:
Right-Hander John Denny, 19-6, 2.37

The 1983 Phillies didn't have the great offense that many of the '70s clubs put together. They didn't have the stacked relievers that many of those teams were known for either. What this team had that no other team had in the history of all Philadelphia teams, barring the current era, was a number-two pitcher who could match or even (gasp) outmatch Steve Carlton.

Coming up through the Cardinals organization, John Denny had broken into the league with a thunderclap, leading the Nationals with a 2.52 ERA in 1976. A couple years later, he nailed down 14 wins with a 2.96. However, when his ERA rose to 4.85 and his wins dipped to eight, the Cards lost patience and traded

Denny to Cleveland for Bobby Bonds. The Phils traded for him in September 1982, but Denny wasn't able to improve the club's chances in so short a time. The next year, however, presented a different story. Denny led the league in wins with 19, came in second in ERA with a 2.37 mark, and won the Cy Young Award. A terrific year, certainly, but one he'd never have again. Suffering from arm trouble, Denny went 7-7 in 1984, then 11-14 in '85, before being traded to the Reds where he would retire after the '86 campaign.

Third in the Order:
Right-Hander Charles Hudson, 8-8, 3.35

Charles Hudson enjoyed a fine rookie season in 1983 with a 3.35 ERA in his 26 starts. On July 20, against Houston, he would actually take a no-hitter into the ninth inning. Hudson would pitch for the Phils with sporadic success through 1986, when he was traded to the Yankees for Mark Easler. After a 1-5, 6.35 season in 1989, Hudson began to drink quite heavily. It all came crashing down on him when he rammed his car into a telephone pole, breaking his left leg and shattering his right knee. He would never start another game in his career.

Fourth in the Order:
Right-Hander Marty Bystrom, 6-9, 4.60

In his last full season as a Phillie, Marty Bystrom posted a career high in both wins and losses. When he found himself at 4-4 midway through the 1984 season, the Phils traded him to the Yanks for Shane Rawley, who would have a nice impact on the late-'80s clubs. Bystrom, meanwhile, would win only two for the Yanks in '85, then retire after an '86 season that saw him win only three, while posting a 5.71 ERA.

Fifth in the Order:
Right-Hander Kevin Gross, 4-4, 3.69 ERA

The first-round pick of the 1981 amateur draft, the 22-year-old Kevin Gross joined teammate Charles Hudson as rookies on the '83 Championship team. Called up in midseason, Gross proved he was a confident and poised young pitcher with a great deal of promise. The Phils expected big things from the six-foot-five right-hander, and for a while it looked like those things might indeed be on their way. Gross doubled his win total in 1984, then won 15 in '85. But then he started to suffer from control problems that consistently brought him into the leaders of walks and hit batsmen.

In 1987, Gross was caught sandpapering the ball on the mound, and was suspended for a month. He came back in '88 to make the All-Star team, but floundered at the end of the season, finishing only 12-14. He was traded to Montreal the season after for Floyd Youmans and Jeff Parrett.

Gross threw with mixed results for the Expos for a couple seasons, then for the Dodgers for a couple more. After going nearly a year without a victory, he threw a no-hitter against the Giants in 1991. He signed a lucrative free-agent deal with the Rangers in 1995, but would lead the league in losses. After signing with the Angels in 1997, Gross managed only two victories and a 6.75 ERA before retiring at 36.

Sixth on the Depth Chart:
Right-Hander Larry Christenson, 2-4. 3.91 ERA

Plagued by injuries, the 29-year-old Larry Christenson was at the nadir of his career. No longer the strapping youth who could nail down 19 wins a season alongside Steve Carlton, Larry pitched in near constant pain. And, although he managed a decent ERA for the 1983 season, he saw limited play and would retire at the end of the year.

The Relief Core

The Closer:
Left-Hander Al Holland, 8-4, 2.26, 25 Saves

Al "Mr. T" Holland came into the Bigs with a lightning fastball, posting a 1.75 ERA for the Giants in his rookie season of 1981. He put up another impressive season in a bullpen-by-committee arrangement before being traded to the Phillies along with Joe Morgan for Mike Krukow and Mark Davis prior to the '83 season. A fierce competitor, Holland would stare down the batters before delivery, using intimidation as much as his pitching arsenal. He posted a 2.26 ERA in his first year as closer for the club, while recording 25 saves, second best in the league. For his work, Al earned the Rolaids Relief Award in 1983.

Holland broke the Phillies' saves record the next year with 29, making the All-Star team. But by the end of the season, he had recorded 10 losses and his ERA climbed up to 3.39. His fast-ball appeared to be leaving him at age 31. The Phils traded Mr. T to the Pirates for Kent Tekulve early the next season, and after only a few months with the club, the Pirates sent him to the Angels. Holland signed with the Yankees as a free agent in 1986, retiring after the '87 campaign at age 34.

And the Rest

Left-Hander Willie Hernandez, 9-4, 3.28 ERA, 7 Saves

Knowing they needed some bullpen help, the Phils traded the fading Dick Ruthven to the Cubs for Willie Hernandez in late May. Hernandez had run hot and cold as both a starter and reliever since breaking into the majors with the Cubs in 1977. At 28 years old, he served well as Al Holland's setup man. For Phillies fans, however, Willie Hernandez will always be attached to Ryne Sandberg as one of the ones who got away. After a fine 1983 season, the Phils would trade Hernandez to the Tigers for Glenn Wilson and John Wockenfuss, then sit back and watch as Sandberg won the MVP in the Nationals and Hernandez won the MVP and Cy Young in the Americans. Meanwhile the Phils languished in fourth place.

Many call Willie's 1984 Tigers campaign "The Perfect Season." He went 9-3 with a 1.92 ERA, saving 32 games in 33 opportunities (the only blown save coming in a meaningless, late-season game). He went on to pitch five games in the postseason, allowing only two runs. Hernandez gained another 31 saves the next season, but when he accompanied this with 10 losses, he began to lose favor with the fans. He served as a setup man for the Tigers over the next three seasons, retiring in 1989 at 34 years old.

Left-Hander Tug McGraw, 2-1 3.56

It's really difficult to put the inimitable Tug McGraw in the "And the Rest" category. Just a couple years past the glory of the 1980 season, Tugger, at 38, was nearing the end of his career. He could still look remarkably good on the mound, as can be seen in his 3.56 ERA in 1983, together with the 3.79 he posted in his final year of '84. However, the sparkle was fading, and he was no longer the man to be called on to put out a fire.

Right-Hander Ron Reed, 9-1, 3.48

At 40 years old, Reed was still a fine pitcher, and he knew how to work the plate. Only two other pitchers, one named Denny and the other named Carlton, earned more victories for the 1983 club. Still, the writing was on the wall for the tall right-hander, who would go to the White Sox for Jerry Koosman at the end of the season, and retire after the '84 campaign.

Right-Hander Porfi Altamirano, 2-3, 3.70

A famous amateur pitcher in his home country of Nicaragua, Porfi Altamirano once shut out both the Cuban national team and team USA in a 1977 tourney. His star would shine bright but quickly in the majors, as he lasted only three years, with 1983 being his best. The Phils would send Porfi along with Gary Matthews and Bob Dernier to the Cubs for Bill Campbell and Mike Diaz at the end of the '84 season.

The Season

The brass had high expectations for their 1983 club as it entered its centennial year in baseball. Yes, there were many more good years than bad for the team during that time, but we were supposed to be in one of the greatest periods of franchise history, and as such, the team was expected to climb to remarkable heights. Sadly, it didn't start off that way. They didn't play with a great deal of spirit, made some mistakes and quite a few mental errors, and sluggishly hung around the .500 mark. Still, Pat Corrales had them at the top of their division when he was fired after a 5-2 loss to the Reds on July 17.

Okay, we were only a game above .500 at the time, and in a tight grouping that saw us only a game from being in fourth, but still Corrales had us in a tie with the Cardinals for first place. To date, he is the only manager who has ever been fired when his club was at the top of its division. And really, I don't think you could have had such lofty expectations for this club. I know they had a good pedigree with names like Mike Schmidt, Steve Carlton, Tug McGraw, Garry Maddox, Pete Rose, Joe Morgan, and Tony Perez, but for most of these aging superstars, their glory days were well behind them. Some guy named Len Matuszek replaced both Rose and Perez. Maddox was fighting a bad back with every inside pitch and every sinking line drive. Carlton couldn't keep his record above .500, while Morgan couldn't manage .240. Only one of the six starters had more wins than losses.

Corrales was supposed to at least have Five-for-One Von Hayes to support Mike Schmidt in the lineup, but the guy was still going through growing pains that would have him sitting the bench after Paul Owens took over in midseason. This was a club of patchwork that won and disbanded after they were finished. And Pat was blamed for "only" having them in first place?

Still, when the Paul "the Pope" Owens replaced Corrales, the mood of the club did change. After playing at .500 for a few weeks while the Pope fiddled with the lineup, the team began to put some wins together. On Saturday, August 6, they moved five games above .500 and reclaimed first place over the rival Pirates. They would play cat and mouse with the Bucs for over a month, neither moving more than a game from each other until the Phils beat the Cardinals 5-3 on September 18 and moved into first for good with a 79-70 record. They coasted home after that, winning 11 of their last 13 games, and taking the division by six.

THE 1983 NATIONAL LEAGUE CHAMPIONSHIP SERIES

Helmed by Philly's own Tommy Lasorda, the Los Angeles Dodgers had taken the National League West by three games over Atlanta, but it wasn't as close as it looked. They'd toyed with the Braves for most of the season, but come late August they moved into first for good and comfortably led by three to five and a half games from early September on.

The Dodgers were a club powered by pitching, as they led the league with a team 3.10 ERA, the Phillies just behind them at 3.34. Fernando Valenzuela, then just 22 years old, had an off-year with a 3.75, but he managed a 15-10 record with 182 strikeouts (fourth in the league). Jerry Reuss won 12 while earning a

2.94 ERA (sixth); Bob Welsch won another 15 with a 2.65 (third); while Alejandro Peña won 12 with a 2.75 (fifth). The cherry on top was the closing partnership of Steve Howe (1.44, 8 saves) and Tom Niedenfuer (1.90, 11 saves). Dave Stewart (2.96) and Pat Zachary (2.49) served as setup men. They provided no break on the mound.

Although the Dodgers' team batting average was only a modest .255 (the Phils were at .249), they led the league in homers with 146 (the Phils at 127). Their power man was Pedro Guerrero (.298, 32 homers, 103 RBI), but five other players, including Greg Brock (20 homers), Mike Marshall (17), Ken Landreaux (17), Dusty Baker (15), and Steve Yeager (15), provided punch as well. They also had great speed, what with Steve Sax pilfering 56, Guerrero 30, and Landreaux another 23. What's more, the Dodgers owned the Phillies during the season. On Friday, August 26 at Veterans Stadium, behind Kevin Gross, the Phils topped them, 4-1. It was our only victory against them in 12 meetings.

Philadelphia wasn't brimming with confidence going into the NLCS, but there was also something strange in the air. We had no idea what to expect from this Dodger team. We didn't really know them. We had grown up with the '70s club. There might be one addition or two each season as they pushed forward, but for the most part, they were members of the family.

More than half of the Phil's roster had come to the club over the past two years. And they included three members of the former Big Red Machine that had been part and parcel of the very defeats we had to suffer in the mid-'70s. They weren't a Philadelphia ballclub tried and true. And that was a good thing. We'd been taught over the past 100 years exactly what to expect from our boys. This team didn't share that same history— not with us and not with each other. Anything was possible.

Game One

Tuesday, October 4 (Dodger Stadium)

The Phillies traveled for the opener to Dodgertown, where they hadn't won since July 25, 1982. Mike Schmidt sent an alert to Los Angeles that past history was of no importance when he smacked a two-out homer off Jerry Reuss in the top of the first to open up...and close the scoring in the game.

Steve Carlton pitched near effortless baseball, scattering seven hits in seven-plus innings of shutout ball. The Dodgers put some pressure on Carlton in the eighth when they loaded the bases with one out. But Al Holland induced Mike Marshall to fly to right, ending the inning and the rally.

Holland got into a bit of trouble himself in the ninth inning when eight-hole hitter Derrel Thomas reached first on a two-out error by none other than Michael Jack Schmidt. Thomas proceeded to steal second to put the tying run in scoring position, but Holland retired pinch hitter Greg Brock on a groundout to end the inning and the ballgame.

Game Two

Wednesday, October 5 (Dodger Stadium)

The Dodgers came back in the second game with Fernando "El Toro" Valenzuela. This time it was the Dodgers who drew first blood when Ken Landreaux singled in Dusty Baker in the bottom of the first. Gary Matthews brought the Phils even with a solo shot in the second, but the Dodgers would pull away for good in the fifth when Pedro Guerrero tripled in two to give LA a 3-1 lead. They added an insurance run in the eighth on a Jack Fimple two-out single off Ron Reed.

The Phillies managed to bring the tying run to the plate in the ninth inning after Sarge Matthews led off with a single and Greg Gross followed with a pinch-hit walk, but Tom Niedenfuer struck out Joe Lefebvre, coerced Von Hayes into a popout, and struck out Ozzie Virgil to end the game. The series would go back to Philadelphia tied at one game apiece. We'd been here before, six years ago to be exact.

Game Three

Friday, October 7 (Veterans Stadium)—Black Friday Revisited?

On Friday, October 7, 1977, at exactly 3 p.m., the Phillies faced off against the Dodgers in Veterans Stadium for a pivotal third game three of the NLCS. You could feel the energy buzzing all around the city. And it wasn't a good buzz. Besides, we'd already gone to our two aces down in Dodgertown. Now we had to turn to our rookies. Who knew what would turn out?

Charles Hudson put all questions to rest with the best game of his young career, throwing a complete game four-hitter. For the Phils offense, all we really needed was Gary Matthews. After drawing a walk in the second, he came around to score on a passed ball from Dodger starter Alejandro Peña. He followed this up with a solo shot in the fourth, a two-run single in the fifth, and for good measure, a two-out RBI in the seventh. Hudson would only make one mistake. Ahead 3-0 in the fourth inning, he served up one up to Mike Marshall, who lashed a two-run homer. He'd allow no more hits the rest of the way as the Phils won, 7-2.

Six years earlier, it was the Dodgers' Bill Russell who stroked the hit that scored the winning runs on Black Friday. Remarkably enough, it was Russell who recorded the last out here in game three. It did not go unnoticed by the crowd. They were even bellowing for Burt Hooton, still wearing Dodger Blue and in the dugout, to come to the field and doff his cap. Naturally enough, he refrained. One wonders, if he had done so, whether Hooton would be one of the most beloved personalities in Phillies lore.

Game Four

Saturday, October 8 (Veterans Stadium)

There was an unbelievable amount of tension and expectation from the crowd. This team had already beaten the Black Friday curse. How far could they go? Well, at least one step farther.

Series MVP Gary Matthews again opened the scoring in the first with a two-out, three-run homer that scored Mike Schmidt and Sixto Lezcano ahead of him. And, as in game three, that would be all we would need. The chief architect of the Phillies future when he first arrived in 1972, Steve Carlton allowed only one run, a leadoff homer from Dusty Baker in the fourth, as he pitched through six. The Phils added four more runs, two coming from a double by Schmidt in the fifth and another two on a Lezcano homer in the sixth, but this was just window dressing.

Ron Reed got himself into a little trouble in the eighth inning, when he allowed a leadoff single to Pedro Guerrero, who came around to score on a single by Dusty Baker, but Al Holland quickly doused the flames, and although he allowed a double in the ninth, it was of no account as the Phils won this one walking away, fittingly enough, notching up that last out with a strikeout of Bill Russell. This time they didn't even call for Hooton. Suddenly, he didn't matter anymore. Neither did the Dodgers. The only thing that mattered right now was the Baltimore Orioles, who we'd be meeting for the World Series in our centennial year.

THE 1983 WORLD SERIES

The Orioles were in their first season under manager Joe Altobelli, who took over for the legendary Earl Weaver after 14 years at the helm. Altobelli brought the O's to an Eastern Division title by a full six games, then stopped the White Sox 3-1 in the American League Championship Series. They led the Americans in home runs with 168, coming in second in total runs with 799. They didn't shortchange on the pitching either; their team ERA was at 3.63 (second in the league).

Baltimore led with lefty Scott McGregor (18-7, 3.18), followed with righty Storm Davis (13-7, 3.59), and rounded with Mike Boddicker (16-8, 2.77). They could choose between Mike Flanagan (12-4, 3.30) or veteran Jim Palmer (4.23) as their number-four guy. They closed with Tippy Martinez, who had 31 saves and a 2.35 record. Their offensive power was led by Eddie Murray, who stroked 33 homers (fourth) and 111 RBI (fifth), while hitting .306 and scoring 115 times (second). It was good enough for him to earn second place in MVP honors.

Murray's teammate Cal Ripkin, meanwhile, finished first in MVP voting, thanks to a stellar season only a year after he'd won Rookie of the Year honors. Ripkin batted .318 (fifth) while smacking 27 homers (ninth) and collecting 102 RBI (ninth). He led the league in doubles (47), hits (211), and runs (121). Kenny Singleton added another 28 homers, while John Lowenstein smoked 15. The Orioles had last appeared in the World Series in 1979, when they'd lost to the Pirates. They'd finished in second place every year since then, and they were hungry.

Game One

Tuesday, October 11 (Memorial Stadium)

The Phillies made the short trip down I-95 for Game One, putting their hopes behind their Cy Young winner, John Denny. Denny didn't start off well, giving up a solo homer to the second batter he faced, right fielder Jim Dwyer, but he turned the screws on the rest of the way, allowing only three more hits and no more runs in his 7.2 innings. No batter reached second against him until Al Bumbry hit a two-out double in the bottom of the eighth, after which Al Holland came in to close out the game, retiring all four batters he faced.

O's starter Scott McGregor didn't make things easy on our boys. He only allowed four hits in his eight innings of work. Lucky for us, two of those hits were home runs. Joe Morgan rocketed one in the sixth, and Garry Maddox, with an assist from President Ronald Reagan, hit one in the eighth. How did the leader of our country get involved, you ask? Well, with McGregor breezing right along through seven innings, the game was suspended while Howard Cosell interviewed Reagan, who had come out to see the game. Many believe that this caused McGregor to get cold and serve up an unusual home run ball to Maddox. Whatever the reason might be, the Orioles could mount next to nothing against the trusty team of John Denny and Al Holland, and the Phils had taken the first game of the Series by a score of 2-1.

Game Two

Wednesday, October 12 (Memorial Stadium)

For Game Two, the Phils faced off against Mike Boddicker and his famed "foshball," a cross between a forkball and a changeup. They found they could do little to nothing against it as he went the distance, allowing only one run and three hits while striking out six. The O's got all the runs they needed off Phils starter Charles Hudson when they chased him with three in the bottom of the fifth, thanks to a solo shot by John Lowenstein and runs batted in from Rick Dempsey and Boddicker himself.

With the 4-1 victory, the Orioles would tie the Series and travel up to Philly for a three-game set. Insultingly, they packed up all their champagne. I mean, you have to appreciate the confidence, and any team could always steal a game on the road, but they would have to face Steve Carlton and John Denny in those three games. No way they would just plow through. Right?

Game Three

Friday, October 14 (Veterans Stadium)

O's starter Mike Flanagan got himself into trouble quickly, allowing a second-inning leadoff homer to Gary Matthews; followed by a leadoff homer from Joe Morgan in the third. The Phils would hit Flanagan well, knocking him out in four with six hits; but they were unable to take full advantage, their only two runs scoring on those two solo shots.

In the bottom of the sixth, fate finally began to turn against the Wheez kids. With runners on first and second and two outs, Steve Carlton strode to the plate. Lefty had been throwing a gem thus far, allowing only three hits and a run, that coming from a homer off the bat of Dan Ford in the top of the sixth. Paul Owens came out of the dugout to see if Lefty felt tired. Though Carlton was known as a fine-hitting pitcher, Owens would have gone to a pinch hitter if he had reason. Carlton told him he felt just fine, then proceeded to strike out swinging to end the inning. Still, it looked like Owens had made the right decision, as Carlton retired the first two batters to face him in the seventh. Rick Dempsey followed with his second double of the game, a deep, deep shot to left center. Carlton threw a wild pitch to send Dempsey to third before Bobby Ayala hit a line drive single to left to tie the game.

Al Holland came in for Carlton, and looked to get out of the inning when he induced Dan Ford to hit a grounder to short. Then de Jesus muffed the play, allowing Ayala to score, and the Orioles suddenly had their first lead in the game. The Phils only got one ball out of the infield over the last three innings against the duo of Sam Stewart and Tippy Martinez, allowing the Orioles to prevail, 3-2. With a 2-1 lead in the series, the O's took their champagne out of the trucks and put it on ice.

Game Four

Saturday, October 15 (Veterans Stadium)

Say what you want about Philadelphia fans, but they come out to support their clubs. The crowd of 66,947 was the largest World Series attendance since Game Three in 1964. John Denny went up against Storm Davis in a game that every fan knew could decide the outcome of the Series. If the Phils should lose, they'd trail 3-1 and face heavy odds, but a win would turn it into a best-of-three. Anybody's game.

The Orioles broke a scoreless fourth-inning tie when Al Bumbry hit a bases-loaded single to score two. The Phils, however, bounced right back in the bottom, when Joe Lefebvre hit an RBI double to bring us within one, and then went ahead in the fifth on runs batted in from John Denny and Pete Rose. Perhaps we'd reversed the Game Three fortunes. This time when we let our starter hit, he'd put us in the lead and now had to come out to hold it down. I guess it works for storybooks.

In reality, Denny came unglued in the sixth, allowing a single, a double, and two walks while recording only one out before Paul Owens removed him from the game. Willie Hernandez came in with the bases loaded and the game once again tied. John Shelby lofted a sacrifice fly to left that immediately gave the lead to the O's, and this time they would not relinquish it.

Trailing 5-3, the Phils brought the winning run to the plate in the bottom of the ninth after Ozzie Virgil hit a two-out single that scored pinch runner Bob Dernier. But Joe Morgan lined out to second to end the game. Having mowed through our hometown advantage and our two aces, the Orioles now had a commanding 3-1 lead in the Series. And their champagne was already cold.

Game Five

Sunday, October 16 (Veterans Stadium)

The fans came out for Game Five and cheered for the Phils, but the writing was on the wall. The bars were filled, the TVs were on, but people made conversation while the game was played. For the most part, we'd already moved on from the season. We were used to doing that. The Phils seemed to have moved on as well. O's starter Scott McGregor threw a complete game, five-hit shutout against them. Phillies starter Charles Hudson didn't throw a bad game, but he wasn't at peak performance either. He allowed a leadoff homer to Eddie Murray in the second, another to Series MVP Rick Dempsey in the third, and finally a two-run homer by Murray in the fourth. The O's took us, 5-0. Philadelphians shuffled out of the stadium. The Phils shuffled back into their clubhouse. And the Orioles got to open those cases and cases of champagne they'd hefted along with them.

Phillies Memory

Bruce Graham, Playwright, Author of The Philly Fan

I watched the 1980 World Series in Knoxville, Tennessee, while visiting my girlfriend. The series itself was almost anticlimactic after the Astros' NLCS but still...it was the Phillies. The town had been waiting over a hundred years for a World Series Champ. Unfortunately, I had to watch what would be the final game of the series in a bar at the Atlanta airport on my way home. (Talk about bad planning.) I ran up the concourse every hour saying, "Put me on the next plane." Finally, game over, I scrambled like a maniac and caught the last plane back to Philly that night.

Philly fans have a rough—generally based on truth—reputation. But that night I had a pleasant flight picturing that crazy parade down Broad Street. There was a celebratory feeling among the passengers. Then I landed. My best friend picked me up in the brand new car he had driven off the lot that afternoon. Before I could say, "How 'bout them Phils?" he brandished a loaded .357. "I'm just waitin' for some drunk Phillies fan to jump on my car," he announced.

It was great to be home.

THE AFTERMATH

The Phils needed to get younger and they knew it. Hell, everyone knew it. They released Pete Rose outright, sold Tony Perez, and traded Ron Reed. Paul Owens took the 1984 team to an 81-81 finish, their worst record since Dave Cash announced a decade earlier, "Yes we can."

John Felske took over the reins in 1985. It didn't make things better, as the club sunk to 75-87, finishing fifth, a full 26 games behind the leading Cardinals. By 1989, the last of the '70s heroes had departed with Mike Schmidt and Steve Carlton, the Phillies had gone through four more managers, and had turned into a last-place club. Yeah, we'd been there before, too.

1993: The Monster Show

1993 National League Eastern Division Standings

Team	Wins	Losses	Win/Lose %	GB
Philadelphia Phillies	97	65	.599	—
Montreal Expos	94	68	.580	3.0
St. Louis Cardinals	87	75	.537	10.0
Chicago Cubs	84	78	.519	13.0
Pittsburgh Pirates	75	87	.463	22.0
Florida Marlins	64	98	.395	33.0
New York Mets	59	103	.364	38.0

NLCS:
PHILLIES 4; ATLANTA BRAVES 2

WORLD SERIES:
TORONTO BLUE JAYS 4; PHILLIES 2

Preseason

The team that took the field in Spring Training of 1993 didn't seem all that more promising than the team that did so in 1992, or in 1991, '90, '89, '88, or '87. The Phillies had finished in last in 1992 with only 70 wins, enough to finish 26 games behind the pace; indeed, they hadn't had a winning season since 1986, and even then they finished 21.5 games behind the Mets. In the years since that "winning season," they'd finished in last three times and out of first by 20 games or more five times.

The 1992 squad featured six starters who couldn't hit over .270. While John Kruk and Lenny Dykstra manufactured averages of over .300, they also had starting shortstop Juan Bell at .204 and right fielder Rubén Amaro at .214. Their staff might have spotlighted Curt Schilling, who could dominate any team, pulling in 14 wins and a 2.35 ERA, but it also sported the likes of Kyle Abbot, who went 1-14. I'm serious. The man won one game out of 15. Not only did the Phils keep him on the major league roster, but he continued as part of the starting rotation. And it's a good thing he did keep going out there. Otherwise we would have had to turn to the likes of Pat Combs (4-4, 7.71), Don Robinson (1-4, 6.18), or Andy Ashby (1-3, 7.54). Kyle Abbot, at 1-14, was our number-three guy!

While the Phillies didn't seem to match up on the field, oddly enough, they matched up pretty well with Philadelphia. John Kruk put it best. Looking at the clean-cut Dale Murphy, who left the team early in 1992, Krukker said the Phils consisted of "24 morons and one Mormon." The '92 team was a fun-loving fraternity of friends. You wanted to drink with these guys, eat with these guys, cheer for these guys. It's difficult to conceive of an exultant bash of Mormons.

The next year gave some good reason to hope for better on-field results as well. Catcher Darren Daulton, who led the team in RBI (109) and home runs (27), was a no-nonsense leader of the club. He walked strong and he spoke like he expected the team to win. It was kind of cute. And Daulton wasn't the only one. Lenny Dykstra (.301, 30 SB) already knew the taste of victory; he'd been a part of the World Series Champion New York Mets in 1986, and carried himself as if he could will this group of afterthoughts to a championship of their own. And when Curt Schilling took the mound, suddenly we looked like a professional team.

In addition, the Phils had the spark of John Kruk, who'd led the club with a .323 average the year before, and had such a good time on the field that the sheer joy of the game he brought with him put a club at ease with itself and with its energy. Then, of course, you had Mitch Williams, who could hump that ball up there. He often had no idea where it was going, but that was part of his charm; the batters didn't know where it was going either. They just knew that it was going toward them, quite possibly at them, it was going fast, and the game was on the line. Mitch laughed at himself, laughed at the world, laughed at us when we booed him, and, more than anything else, he believed that the team could do it.

The Phils had made a few key acquisitions in the off-season as well. There was David West, who had at one time been a top prospect of the New York Mets, but due to injuries and a myriad of other problems, had not lived up to his potential. He was one of the very few who had actually participated in a World Series. Unfortunately, he'd managed a wildly high ERA for the luckless 1991 Minnesota Twins. In a five-year career, he'd managed an ERA of less than five only once and was just coming off a 6.99 with the Twins. But he had at one time been a phenom. We didn't have many of those.

We also signed outfielder Jim Eisenreich, another onetime phenom who had gone into voluntary retirement for three years because of Tourette's syndrome. He was coming from the Royals, where'd he'd only managed a .269 batting average with 28 RBI the year before. Still, like David West, he was a guy who "could do it." Or at least at one time, the best minds in baseball thought he "could do it."

Then there was Pete Incaviglia (you guessed it: another former phenom). He's best known for the fact that he never spent one pitch of one game in minor league ball, and for being the greatest power hitter in the history of college baseball, where he'd crushed 100 homers in 213 games, with a career slugging average of .913. In his junior year, Pete had a 1.14 slugging average. He hadn't faired so well in the majors, however, hitting only 11 homers in each of his last two seasons as he bounced from Texas to Detroit to Houston. But again the guy at one time seemed to have limitless potential—at one time.

You can add to this the likes of Milt Thompson, a sure-handed center fielder who had played with the Phillies in the mid-'80s and had done well in a part-time role for the Cardinals in the past two years; Danny Jackson, who had managed more than six wins only once in his past six seasons, but in 1988 had won 23 games for the Reds; and Larry Andersen, a spirited left-hander, who was returning to the team from the Padres.

In short, the team had gone through some wholesale changes. They might not have looked statistically superior to the team that had come the year before (and indeed were again predicted in last by most baseball forecast publications), but the attitude had changed. These were players who had known what it was like to win and had known adversity since. Many had been relegated to the bench, given up on by their former clubs, forgotten by their fans and foes alike. Nonetheless, they all held a small silver light deep within them, something that still gave them hope, a small flame that was waiting to be stoked into a fire. All that had to happen was for a team to believe in them once again, even if that team were the lowly Phillies.

This was a true Philadelphia ballclub. They were hardnosed, they knew what it was like to be disrespected, and they fought like hell to earn respect every single day on that playing field. Indeed, they have known what it was like to lose, especially on a major league level. However, despite the fact that they'd been bumped around from major league team to major league team, despite the fact that some had known ERAs in the high digits, despite the fact that they'd battled psychological problems that forced them into early retirement, relegated to the bench, and demoted to minor league ball, this was a team that had a drive unlike any other.

And they knew had to play as a unit. Say what you will about those clubs from the '70s, including our first World Series Champions, but they didn't get along. This club had a ball together. When the games were over, they might leave the field, but they didn't leave the locker room. They hung out, they worked out, and when it was all said and done, they went out drinking. Many of us wanted to be right there with them.

The Manager

Jim Fregosi was as hard-nosed as the team he led. Coming off a stellar playing career where he'd set records for the Los Angeles and California Angels in hits, triples, doubles, runs, RBI, and double plays turned, he took the managerial reins and led the Angels to their very first postseason appearance in 1979. Replacing Nick Leyva in 1991, Fregosi led the Phils to a 74-75 finish before retooling in '92. The '93 club perfectly fit his to-the-grindstone house, unblinking personality, and managerial style.

The Starting Lineup

This team looked like a picture postcard of exactly what John Kruk had called them a year before: a motley crew. Baseball historian Robert Gordon aptly claimed that they were more like a collection of "beards, bellies, and biceps" than a baseball team. But, as he also noted, they were much more than that.

Leading Off:

Center Fielder Lenny "The Dude" Dykstra, .305, 19 HR, 143 R

If I close my eyes, I can still picture The Dude with a cheek full of chaw, spitting on himself and all of center field. From the very start of the season, it seemed that Lenny wouldn't be happy unless he threw himself onto the ground at least 10 times a game, virtually destroying his uniform in dirt, mud, and dust. By midseason, it seemed that he simply had stopped washing his uniform.

Once you got past the grooming habits, Lenny's play was nothing short of exemplary. He led the league in runs (143), hits (194), and walks (129), finishing second in MVP voting. He led the charge right from the opening bell with grit and determination. Coming from the New York Mets, where he'd experienced a World Championship in 1986, Lenny was reluctant to report to what was at the time a secondary franchise. However, he made a huge impact on the 1990 Phils, leading the league in hits with 192 and in on-base percentage with a .418. He actually batted over .400 into June. In 1991, he also made a big impact; the only problem was that it was with a tree. While driving drunk, he and teammate Darren Daulton ran off the road, injuring both players. Dykstra, suffering from a broken collarbone among other ailments, returned in two months and ran directly into the center field wall. Result: another injury, another broken collarbone, and the end of his season.

The next year didn't provide any better results. On Opening Day of 1992, he was hit by a pitch, broke his wrist, and ended up sidelined again. These two seasons rested him up for his spectacular 1993, when he played in 161 games, leading the league in at-bats and plate appearances.

Thanks to injury, Dykstra was never able to repeat these endurance markers. He would never accrue 400 at-bats again, or even a .280 batting average. He would retire as a Phillie after the '96 season. Lenny went into business and investments in his post-baseball career, making millions for himself and his investors with his uncanny knowledge of the stock market. In 2009, however, he went belly up and had to declare bankruptcy.

Batting Second:
Second Baseman Mickey Morandini, .247, .355 SLG

Not one of the bulky, beer-swilling bruisers on this Phillies club, Mickey Morandini nonetheless fit in perfectly. Wearing his hair to his shoulders, he played free, easy, and confident, whether in the field or at the plate. Despite a low average, Mickey was a perfect fit for the number-two hole. He led the team in triples (nine) and was second in stolen bases (13), always utilizing both bat speed and foot speed to make things happen so as to set up the big men in Macho Row. Mickey improved at the plate during his career, raising his average as high as .295 in 1997. It was enough for the Cubs to offer up their top-notch prospect, Doug Glanville, for Mickey.

Mickey had his greatest season in 1998 for Chicago, posting career highs in batting average (.296), hits (172), runs (93), and RBI (53). After a weak 1999, he was granted free agency, returned to Philly for a brief period in 2000, and then completed his career that same year, batting ninth for the Toronto Blue Jays.

Batting Second:
Second Baseman and Shortstop Mariano Duncan, .282,
11 HR, 73 RBI

Mariano Duncan might not have had the same dexterity of glove as Mickey Morandini, but he had a more consistent bat and some power. He would spell Juan Bell at shortstop in the first half of the season, before Kevin Stocker took his regular spot in the middle infield, and would trade off with Morandini at second base thereafter.

Duncan made his bones with the Cincinnati Reds when they won the World Championship in 1990; he batted .306 while leading the league with 11 triples. He came to the Phils as a free agent in '92, earning his at-bats as a utility player, moving from left field to second base. He took over third base in 1994 for the injured Dave Hollins and made his first All-Star team.

Duncan saved his greatest season for the 1996 World Champion New York Yankees, where he played five positions and hit .340. When his playing time was cut down the next season, he did something foolish: he mouthed off to George Steinbrenner, who traded him immediately to the last-place Blue Jays. When Duncan couldn't find an everyday job there either, he went to Japan to finish out his career.

Batting Third:
First Baseman John Kruk, .316, 100 R, 85 RBI, 14 HR, 111 Walks

You just had to love John Kruk. The lovable and slovenly Krukker was in many respects the leader of this team. Curt Schilling and Lenny Dykstra had the monomaniacal drive toward victory, and Darren Daulton had the field generalship, but Kruk rallied everyone around him with good humor and a fine sense of what really mattered. When a woman once chastised him that athletes who smoked and drank made for bad role models, he responded, "I ain't an athlete, lady. I'm a baseball player."

Krukker came up with the San Diego Padres in 1986, where he hit over .300 in his first two seasons. After slumping in '88, the Padres were quick to send him to Philly for Randy Ready and Chris James. Thank you, San Diego.

John managed to inspire people even when off the field. During the winter of 1993, he had surgery for testicular cancer, and returned on Opening Day of '94 to the delight of all. Neither the operation nor a knee injury later that season would curtail him from batting over .300 once again.

Kruk was granted free agency after this season, and he finished his career with the Chicago White Sox in 1995. He has gone on to become a popular ESPN analyst, and has served as a coach for the Phils' minor league organization.

Batting Cleanup:
Third Baseman Dave Hollins, .273, 104 R, 93 RBI, 85 BB

Dave Hollins came up with the Phillies in 1990, making the starting team in '91. He had his greatest year for the Phils here in 1993 at just 27. Big things were expected of Hollins, a no-nonsense player who moved through the game like a locomotive intent on crushing anything in its way. Unfortunately, the locomotive proved a little more fragile than it looked.

Beset by injuries that shut him down early in '94, Hollins returned in '95 to face mechanical problems that caused his defensive game to falter. As he tried to regain his composure, his average dropped to a career low of .229. He was traded to Boston for Mark Whiten in midseason, and spent the rest of his career as a journeyman.

Dave Hollins played for seven teams over his last six years, enjoying his best post-Phillies season with the Anaheim Angels in 1997, when he hit .288, while scoring 101 runs and collecting 85 RBI. Dave retired as a Phillie in 2002, having been brought on by Larry Bowa. Sadly, he only got 17 at-bats, having succumbed to—of all things—spider bites, which aggravated his diabetes. He retired at age 36.

Batting Fifth:
Catcher Darren "Dutch" Daulton, .257, 24 HR, 90 R,
105 RBI, 117 BB

Looking at the team photos of this club, it seems as if Darren Daulton just doesn't belong. While the rest stand around wearing bandannas, chewing tobacco, shirt tails out, bellies proudly forward, Darren Daulton stands poised, perfectly coiffed and trim, with a dimpled chin, an eye of intensity, and an aura of strength. Indeed, he may have learned this fortitude through the hard knocks he took coming up in the organization. Considering Daulton the catcher for their immediate future in 1984, the club traded away Ozzie Virgil and Bo Diaz, but multiple injuries limited Dutch's playing time. At full strength in '86, he endured a home plate collision that tore up his knee and ended his season in June. With the Phils signing Lance Parish in '87, Daulton returned as a backup. Then, after finally becoming a regular starter in '90, it looked like his future had finally arrived. However, a car accident in 1991, with Lenny Dykstra behind the wheel, would limit his play again.

Daulton became a force in the '92 and '93 seasons, winning the RBI crown in '92 with 109, and finishing sixth in '93 with 105. He finished in the top seven in MVP voting and made All-Star both years. His knee problems began to take a toll on him after 1993, as his power numbers, average, and playing time consistently decreased until the Phils traded him to the Marlins at the deadline in '97. Daulton's leadership and experience helped the young Marlins to their first World Series title. He would retire on top after that season at 35 years of age.

Things did not go so well for Darren after baseball, however. Krukker put on a suit and tie and went into broadcasting; Lenny went off to make millions in the stock market; and Mitch Williams became a baseball and broadcasting sage. But the poised former Phil was arrested for domestic violence, and he did an ESPN interview in which he claimed that he had the ability to do astral projection. Daulton added that he wasn't even in his body during some of the most important plays of his baseball career. Having begun to shrug off these views, Darren is now doing color work on Comcast Sports, and he can be heard on FM 97.5, "The Fanatic." He still looks cool, poised, and collected with that dimple proud and strong.

Batting Fifth:
Right Fielder Jim Eisenreich, .318, .445 SLG

Jim Eisenreich proved to be one the greatest heroes the team had, both on and off the field. Touted as one of the finest bats of his generation, Eisenreich came up with the Twins in 1982. The 23-year-old was batting .303 when he suddenly collapsed in convulsions in the outfield of the Metrodome. He tried to battle his way through it, but ended up sitting out most of the season as doctors tried to figure out what the problem could be. Eventually, Jim was diagnosed with Tourette's syndrome, which played hell with his nervous system, causing both physical and psychological setbacks. This is a rare disease for an adult, made even more difficult given his job's very public nature.

Eisenreich made two abortive attempts at a comeback in 1983 and '84, then he officially retired. After working intensely on his problems and finding the right medication, Eisey returned to professional baseball in 1987, hitting .382 for the Royals' double-A affiliate. He entered the majors again and served well under the radar as a pinch hitter for the Royals until 1989, when he began to platoon in the outfield. Jim truly blossomed when he came to the Phils as a free agent for the '93 season, platooning with Wes Chamberlain in right field. Not much of a power hitter (he broke double figures in homers only once), Eisey was always a good hitter for average.

You could always find Jim Eisenreich getting the big hit during his Phillies tenure. When Eisey took the plate, you could rest at ease. I suppose, after all he'd gone through, he didn't feel much pressure when a pitcher came at him with a game on the line. That was nothing compared to what it took just to march out onto the field.

In 1995, at 36 years of age, Eisenreich became an everyday player for the first time, and he made it count, hitting .316. Jim was clipping along at .361 the next season when he fell to injury in early September. He signed as a free agent with the Florida Marlins in 1997, left there along with the rest of the Florida fire sale in '98, and retired from the Dodger organization at the end of the season.

Batting Sixth:
Right Fielder Wes Chamberlain, .282, .493 SLG

Wes Chamberlain platooned with Jim Eisenreich in right field, adding more power in shifts when he was teamed up with speedy left fielder Milt Thompson. Among starters, Wes' .493 slugging percentage was second only to Pete Incaviglia's .530.

Wes came up with the Phils in 1991, finishing fifth in the voting for Rookie of the Year. After his fine all-around 1993 performance, the Boston Red Sox traded both Billy Hatcher and Paul Quantrill in order to acquire his services in '94. Following two disappointing seasons with the Bosox, Wes went on to play for Japan's Chiba Lotte Mariners in 1996. He continued to play ball in the Canadian Northern League after his professional career came to a close.

Batting Seventh:
Left Fielder Pete Incaviglia, .274, 24 HR, 89 RBI, .530 SLG

Pete Incaviglia was one of those huge mythic figures that typified the 1993 Phillies. Named the College Player of the Century in 2000, Inky was touted as one of the most promising players ever to play the game when he was drafted by the Expos in 1985. Inky refused to go to the minors, and demanded an immediate trade to a team that would back his refusal. He landed in Texas, where he thrilled crowds with gargantuan home runs as well as gargantuan swings and misses. Incaviglia was an old-time slugger who would swing with all he had in him. If he connected, you had better watch out. If he didn't, it would usually end up in the catcher's mitt.

Inky was a big, lumbering hulk of a guy who was never known as much of an outfielder, but he would give it all he had in the outfield, just like he did at the plate. In 1994, he injured himself by running into the wall while trying to catch a ball he had virtually no chance of reaching. His high strikeout totals and poor fielding sent him from team to team until he wound up signing with the Phils as a free agent for the '93 club. Needing someone to believe in him again, Inky gladly accepted the platoon work with Milt Thompson. Together they posted 131 RBI. No platoon duo has ever fared better.

Inky's 1994 injury curtailed his great resurgence, taking a toll on his offensive game when he returned. In 1996, he landed a job with Japan's Chiba Lotte Mariners. He hit just five round-trippers, to go along with his .181 average, before returning to the U.S. There he'd travel around to five teams in his last three years with little success. Oddly enough, Incaviglia finally accepted a minor league contract at the end of his career as he tried to latch on with the Arizona Diamondbacks in 1999, but he could not make the squad.

Batting Seventh:
Left Fielder Milt Thompson, .262

Every team has to have that one great circus outfielder, the one who can scale a wall and rob a ball that is destined to zip away from the park. Milt Thompson could accomplish this with the best of them. A gazelle in left, Milt was always off with the crack of the bat. You could count on him to make the difficult catches look effortless and the impossible ones look, well, effortless.

Thompson came up with the Braves in 1984 and hit .300 in a supporting role for his two seasons there, before being traded along with Steve "Bedrock" Bedrosian in 1986 for Ozzie Virgil. Milt was a great find for the club, starting in center field and batting leadoff. He hit .302 in 1987, when he swiped a career-best 42 bases. After three years of service, the Phils sent him along to the Cardinals in '89, where he hit his career-best .307. He returned to the Phillies as a free agent in 1993, and became part of the glue that made the team work.

Milt Thompson went into coaching in 1997, eventually becoming the Phils' first base coach in 2003 under Larry Bowa. He earned many accolades as the hitting coach for the 2008 World Champions, but during a team-wide offensive slump in 2010, he was relieved of his duties. Thompson now works in the Astros minor league operation as an outfield coach.

Batting Eighth:
Shortstop Kevin Stocker, .324

The Phils had a tough time finding just the right shortstop in 1993. They began with Juan Bell, who at one time had been considered the successor in the Orioles organization to Cal Ripkin Jr. However, with Bell hitting at the Mendoza line after the first month, and considering his whopping .204 average the year before, they began to look in other places. Eventually, they dipped into the minors to find the little-known Kevin Stocker, who became the anchor for the organization. Though not a steady hitter at any level in the minors, Stocker came through with a .324 average for the big league club, as well as a deft hand in the field. While the Phillies moved through the season with swagger and arrogance, gut and gristle, Stocker had a wide-eyed enthusiasm, like a kid who couldn't believe that not only had Christmas morning finally arrived, but he'd gotten that 10-speed bike he'd been asking for.

Kevin played steady and strong for the Phils until selected by Tampa Bay in the 1998 expansion draft. He had a .299 batting average for them in '99, but finished his career batting .197 for the Angels in 2000. Stocker now owns an Emerald City Smoothie franchise in his home state of Washington.

The Pines

Jim Fregosi could turn to the platoon mates of either left or right field during any one game, which would always give him a mix of power (Incaviglia, Chamberlain), speed (Thompson), or average (Eisenreich).

Ricky Jordan (.289, .421 SLG), who had been a platoon player until 1993, could come in to play first base to spell John Kruk and be counted on in key at-bats. Kim Batiste (.282, .436) served as a pinch hitter and a late-inning defensive replacement in the infield, mostly for Dave Hollins at third. Reserve catcher Todd Pratt (.287) actually had the highest slugging percentage on the team with a .529, and was a warrior on the field.

The Starting Staff

First in the Order:
Left-Hander Terry Mulholland, 12-9, 3.25

At 30 years old, Terry Mulholland was one of the staff's elder statesmen. He might not have been our best, but he was certainly our leader on the mound. While Tommy Greene seemed edgy, and Curt Schilling appeared steely-eyed in determination, Mulholland looked at ease. He might as well have been strolling to the mound at the family Fourth of July picnic.

Terry had some fine success with the Phillies after coming from the Giants in the 1990 trade for Steve Bedrosian. He threw a no-hitter in '90, led the league in complete games with 12 in '91, made the All-Star team in '92, and led the team to the World Series in '93. He was traded to the Yankees for Kevin Jordan in 1994, and continued to pitch effectively through the 2006 season. A man who kept his poise on the mound and could start as well as relieve without bothering to consult his ego, Mulholland was an attractive bonus to many teams who were preparing for a playoff run. For this reason, Terry moved 13 times over his last 12 seasons of ball, concluding his career with the Diamondbacks at age 43.

The Ace:
Right-Hander Curt Schilling, 16-7, 4.02, 186 K

Curt Schilling didn't approach the mound, he attacked it. While Carlton might have been playing a game of Zen meditation out there, it was clear that Curt really didn't like his opposition. He reacted to them as if they had just broken into his house and demanded dinner. Schilling dominated the game for 20 years, first making a name for himself at 25 when he came from the Astros to the Phillies in 1992 to go 14-11. From then on, his combination of fastballs, splitters, and sliders served him well. He earned at least 20 victories three times in his career, struck out 619 over 1997 and '98, and made the All-Star Game six times.

Schilling's undying dedication came out every time he took the mound. You need look no further than the "Bloody Sock Game," when Curt took the mound despite a painful ankle injury in order to face the New York Yankees in the ALCS that would eventually lead the Red Sox to their 2004 World Championship. Unfortunately, it could also lead him to ignore everything else off the field. In 1999, while his wife was rushed to the hospital with a life-threatening blood clot, Curt arrived at the clubhouse prepared to take the mound. Manager Terry Francona turned him away.

Curt could always be counted on to stand up for what's right. The attitude resonated well with the fans, but could backfire within the clubhouse. During the Phillies' slide into mediocrity after 1993, Curt complained that the club didn't show the necessary commitment to victory. General manager Ed Wade told the *Philadelphia Inquirer*, "Every fifth day, Curt has the opportunity to go out and be a horse on the mound. Unfortunately, on the other four days, he tends to say things which are detrimental to the club and clearly self-serving."

However you want to look at it, Curt was an icon wherever he went, and—love him or hate him—he set a winning standard that others followed, bringing championships to Boston, Arizona, and nearly to Philadelphia.

Third in the Order:
Right-Hander Tommy Greene, 16-4, 3.42

Tommy Greene was a meteor. In the 15th game he ever started, in place of the injured Danny Cox, he threw a no-hitter, then proceeded to go 13-7 with a nifty 3.38 ERA. Greene looked destined for a very bright future. He had the best year of his career in 1993, winning 16 with a 3.42 ERA. He was the pitcher of record when the Phils finally pulled in the division crown with a 5-0 win over the Pirates on September 30. But Greene began to fight shoulder ailments thereafter. He would pitch only 20 more games over the next three years, record only two more wins, and retire before the age of 30. He is currently the general manager of the Monroe Chattel Cats of the Southern Collegiate League.

Fourth in the Order:
Right-Hander Danny Jackson, 12-11, 3.77

After winning 23 games (tops in the National League) for the Reds in 1988, Danny Jackson went through a spate of years that were lost either to injury or control problems. Through 1992, he never won more than he lost, and had a 1991 season for the Cubs in which he walked more players than he struck out. Over the course of two years, Jackson was traded by the Cubs, unprotected by the Pirates (The Pirates didn't want him?), and swapped by the incoming Florida Marlins (The Marlins didn't want him either?). By the time Danny arrived in Philadelphia, the MLB had basically told him he was unloved and unwanted.

It was the perfect recipe for success. Danny Jackson had a career resurgence in 1993, taking 12 games and pulling in a 3.77 ERA. The dominant picture of Danny had him standing shirtless on the mound, flexing his pecs in celebration of the National League championship after the Phils downed the Braves. It wasn't just the offense that put the macho in Macho Row.

Jackson was having the year of his life in 1994, going 14-6 with a 3.26 ERA, when the baseball strike cut short the season. He signed as a free agent with the Cardinals for 1995, but saw his career go back into hiding afterward. Over the next three years, he won only five games against 31 defeats, and retired at the end of the '97 season from the San Diego Padres.

Fifth in the Order:
Right-Hander Ben Rivera, 13-9, 5.02

Despite his poor ERA, Ben Rivera won more games than either Terry Mulholland or Danny Jackson, and without those victories, the Phils would have finished well off the pace in the National League East. Ben was only in his second year of major league baseball, having completed a rookie season split between Atlanta and Philly, where he collectively went 7-4 with a 3.07 ERA, good enough to earn him seventh place in the voting for Rookie of the Year.

Although he set a personal high for victories in 1993, Rivera's ERA ballooned to a dangerous number. It continued to rise in '94 to a 6.87, while his win total plummeted to three. The Phillies granted him free agency at the end of the season, but

Rivera had no takers. He eventually went to Japan to play for the Hanshin Tigers in 1998 and '99.

The Pen

The Closer:
Left-Hander Mitch "The Wild Thing" Williams, 3.34, 43 Saves

Mitch Williams lit the crowd on fire every time he walked in from the bullpen, and then lit everything else on fire when he got there. Known as The Wild Thing for a reason, Mitch managed to strike out 60, but on the way, he walked 44 and threw six wild pitches, one every 10 innings. While wildness has gotten into some pitcher's heads, thus destroying their mound careers (Steve Blass and Rick Ankiel, for instance), Mitch actually had fun with it. During pregame warmups, he would sometimes hurl a ball way over the batter's box, arching up and into the stands.

A typical Mitch game can be exampled by an April 28 outing against the Padres. Leading 5-2 in the ninth, Jim Fregosi called for Mitch to close out the game. After allowing a leadoff single, he walked the next two batters to load the bases, then enticed the next batter to ground out into a double play. After falling behind the next hitter 3-0, he served one up across the plate, which was stung on a bead, but right to Mickey Morandini. Result: one inning pitched, one hit, no runs, and one save. Take a breath. Clap your hands. Record the victory. And move on. This was the reason why Curt Schilling sat in the dugout with a towel over his head when Mitch came in to "save" his game. He couldn't bear to watch. Fregosi, though he still refused to blink, would light up one cigarette after another.

Mitch had made his bones with the Rangers and the Cubs before coming to Philly via free agency in 1991. He recorded his most consistent season for the '91 club with a 2.34 ERA, along with 30 saves and a 12-5 record. The Phils unloaded him after the sad conclusion to the '93 season. Mitch would throw with limited success for three different teams through 1997, and retire from the Royals at age 32. Not being able to stay out of baseball for long, Mitch joined the Atlantic City Surf of the Independent League, pitching for them from 2001 to 2003. He has since joined the Phillies broadcast team and makes appearances with the MLB network as a studio analyst.

The Setup Men

Mitch Williams was backed up by the perfect righty-lefty combination of David West and Larry Andersen. West, like many of the others on this club, experienced a resurgence in his career in 1993. Allowing only 60 hits in 86 innings, he struck out 80 and locked in with a 2.92 ERA. West pitched two more strong seasons in Philly, starting 14 games for the '94 club, where he compiled a 3.35 ERA. He was granted free agency at the end of the '96 season, after his talents began to deteriorate. West attempted a comeback in 1998, managed to make the Red Sox, but after only two innings of play, he was given unconditional release.

Right-handed Larry Andersen matched West's ERA with a 2.92, while striking out 67 in his 61 innings. Known for his humor and easy manner, Andersen was one of the players who could keep a clubhouse lively. One of the biggest jokes he ever played, however, was on the Red Sox. After arguably the best mound work of his career for the '86 to '89 Astros, he was traded to the Bosox for youngster Jeff Bagwell. While Andersen appeared in 15 games for Boston, Bagwell went on to become a legend in Houston, winning Rookie of the Year in 1991, MVP in '94, with a good chance of making the Hall of Fame.

Andersen retired after the '94 season at age 41. He joined the Phillies broadcast team in 1998 and has continued to enjoy great success and popularity in the role. In fact, when Larry Bowa asked him to step down from the booth to join him on the field as a coach, Andersen declined. He was having too much fun, and the job security was better.

And the Rest

Shoring up the bullpen was Roger Mason, who, despite an ERA of 4.89, always took the mound with confidence. In fact, he's best remembered by Phillies fans as being the man in complete control of the last game of the 1993 World Series. Many speculate that if Jim Fregosi had kept him in, the results of this season would have been different. You know that I'm going to have to go into this in excruciating detail in just a bit. Why on earth should I force myself to relive it twice?

Phillies Memory

John Andelfinger, Philadelphia Musician

I was nine, they were Gods, then they played Toronto. Nine-year-olds don't understand, until they're older and can look back, that those guys were one of the purest sports teams to ever play. I don't mean pure as in 'roids. Lord knows, half of them, at least, were on something. They were pure in the sense that they played because they loved it. I wanted them to win so badly. Then they lost, then the strike, then I didn't watch baseball for a while. As a youth, it was hard to digest, those two together. But my love for those players and that team has never died. To me, they're still Gods.

Worst part, though, I went to the SkyDome in 2001, and the tour guide asked if anyone from Philadelphia wanted to see the trophy. I almost fought a security guard in a "foreign" country in high school. I had forgotten my D-cell batteries at home, or else I would've been throwing.

The Season

The 1993 Phillies were a club that would dominate the season from pillar to post. Behind Curt Schilling, they won on Opening Day and never looked back. Well, okay, they looked back a little bit—just a little, but I'll get to that in a minute. The point is that they never fell out of first. Each time they met adversity, they pulled together as a family and turned the tide quickly.

Take, for instance, the game in late April against the San Francisco Giants. The Phillies trailed 8-0 in the bottom of the sixth. It happens. Some nights, things just get away from you. You take your lumps, you take your shower, and you live to play another day. And then along came reliever Bryan Hickerson, who, after helping to record a hard out at first, slammed the ball to the turf in celebration. What the hell was that? In our own house, we had to watch some 8.71 ERA mid-reliever rejoice in some meaningless out during a wipeout? That's freaking insulting.

The Phils began assaulting the baseball with as much hostility as one would a piñata. They ended up taking the game 9-8 in 10 innings, and slammed the ball down in victory after the contest. Just a few days later, they cemented this fortitude when, leading 5-3 in the bottom of the eighth, the San Diego Padres loaded the bases with two outs. Larry Andersen stepped in, in relief of Danny Jackson, and proceeded to serve one up to catcher Bobby Geren, who blasted the ball way out to left. It looked like more than trouble, it looked over. But out of nowhere, Milt Thompson sprinted to the wall, and barely looking back, extended himself up and over, robbing Geren of the grand slammer that would have given the Padres a late-inning lead.

It was just a fun season to be a Phillies fan. They played the most enjoyable doubleheader in Phillies history on July 2. After several rain delays, the Phils battled back from a 5-0 deficit in game two against the San Diego Padres to tie the contest in the bottom of the eighth. Still tied in the bottom of the 10th, the Phillies found themselves coming to bat at 4:41 a.m. With runners on first and third and no one else left on the bench, Fregosi had to allow Mitch Williams to take bat in hand and face off against none other than Trevor Hoffman, the best reliever of all time. Williams would strike a soft liner over short to win the game. It would be his only at-bat all year. A 1.000 average.

Things were riding high in the old town for a quite a while that summer. When Danny Jackson destroyed the hapless Reds 12 to zip on August 29, they moved ahead of the second-place Cardinals by 10, and $10^1/2$ on the third-place Expos. It was in the bag. This team had such gumption and gristle that there was no chance that they could fall apart like their counterparts of 1964. But, you know, you get so caught up in the frenzy sometimes that you forget that you live in Philadelphia. Nothing's easy. Ever. After dropping three tight games in a row to the Cubbies, their lead fell to six and a half within the next week.

Leading by only five on the second-place Expos, the Phils traveled to Montreal for a three-game series on September 17. These Expos were a formidable ballclub. They sported the likes of Dennis Martinez (15-9; 3.85), Jeff Fassero (12-5, 2.29), John Wetteland (9-3, 1.37, 43 saves), Marquis Grissom (.298, 95 RBI), Moises Alou (.286, 85 RBI), and Larry Walker (22 HR, 86 RBI). Playing in Montreal, they were well off the radar. This team didn't recognize pressure and didn't seem disturbed that our club looked positioned to win a bar fight.

In game one, the Phils looked like they had it pretty much in hand. After rallying for seven runs in the sixth to take a 7-3 lead, they watched helplessly as the Expos tied it up one frame later. Then, in the bottom of the 12th, with The Wild Thing on the mound, Marquis Grissom doubled to lead it off, stole third, and came home to score on a sacrifice fly by Delino Deshields. The lead was now four.

The Phils took a 5-1 lead into the eighth the next night, only to see those Expos rally for another three runs to bring themselves within one. With Williams on the mound again in the ninth, Larry Walker earned a one-out walk. Williams picked him cleanly off first in the next moment, but Krukker couldn't hold onto the ball, sending Walker to second. On the very next pitch, Walker moved to third, and everyone held their breath. But Williams found a way to pull it together, striking out Mike Lansing, then coaxing Sean Berry to fly out to end the game. Lead back to five. Why wasn't it ever easy?

The Phils built up an early lead again the next night, making it 5-2 behind Danny Jackson in the fifth, but those old Expos just wouldn't go away. They fought back to 5-4, taking the game into the bottom of the ninth, when Fregosi trotted out The Wild Thing to the mound once more. With one out and runners on first and second base, Larry Walker hit a slow roller to first that Kruk again misplayed to load up the bases. One out later, Wilson Cordero smashed a fastball over short to bring two runs in and give the Expos another come-from-behind victory that pulled them within four once more.

It was September 19. There were 13 games to go. No one was laughing now. No one was strutting now. This was getting scary. We were able to put those fears aside soon enough, however, as we went on to sweep the Marlins in the next series. After winning our opening game against the Braves, we extended our lead to a comfortable six games with nine to play.

It took six more games, but the Phils finally cemented that Division Championship with a 5-0 win over the Pirates. The great thing about the victory was that no one seemed relieved, they felt empowered. They had stood up to adversity again, and now were ready to take on the Atlanta Braves.

THE 1993 NATIONAL LEAGUE CHAMPIONSHIP SERIES

The Atlanta team might well be called the clean-cut Braves, the Indomitable Braves. They were the National League champs the last two years running, and they sported one of the greatest pitching staffs that has ever taken the field with Greg Maddox (20-10, 2.36), Tom Glavine (22-6, 3.20), Steve Avery (18-6, 2.94), and John Smoltz (15-11, 3.62). Their offensive power came from David "There is No" Justice (40 homers, 120 RBI), Ron Gant (36 homers, 117 RBI), and Terry Pendleton (17 homers, 84 RBI). Jeff Blauser (.305, 110 runs, 16 SB) and Otis Nixon (47 steals) provided the speed at the top of the order.

The Braves were as precise and certain as the Phils were unkempt and blustery. It was the equivalent of pitting the IRS against a tornado. That tornado might be able to do some damage, perhaps some very significant damage, but when things calmed down, the IRS would assess it and make sure all accounts were paid...in full. We'd done fairly well against them during the season, splitting our 12 games, and only being outscored by a run, 65-64. Still, it was clear that they looked at us as a stepping-stone for their earned right to revisit the World Series, while we looked at them like Clubber Lang looked at Rocky Balboa.

Game One

Wednesday, October 6 (Veterans Stadium)

We gave the ball to Curt Schilling to make our mark on this series, and Schilling did so early, striking out the first five batters he faced. Lenny Dykstra announced our offensive arrival in the series with a leadoff double against Braves starter Steve Avery, then came around to score on a grounder from John Kruk. The Braves would march right back to take the lead with single runs in the third and fourth, but Pete Incaviglia would tie it up with a solo shot in the fourth, and Kruk would give us back the lead in the sixth, when he came around to score on an Avery wild pitch.

Schilling retired after pitching eight and striking out 10, leaving the game to Mitch Williams. Schilling donned the towel, Fregosi lit a cigarette, and the top of the ninth inning commenced. In a typical move, Mitch immediately walked the tying run to first, then induced Mark Lemke into what looked like a tailor-made double play to Kim Batiste at third. Batiste, in as a defensive replacement for Dave Hollins, made a throwing error to put runners on first and third with no outs. Otis Nixon grounded in the tying run, and the game went into extra innings. After Williams got out of a second and third jam in the 10th inning, Kim Batiste earned his redemption with a game-winning double that scored Krukker in the bottom to give the Phils a tough first victory.

Game Two

Thursday, October 7 (Veterans Stadium)

The Braves took Tommy Greene out of this contest early, building an 8-0 lead by the third inning. It was a laugher, especially with Braves starter Greg Maddox allowing only five hits in his seven innings of work. Behind homers by Fred McGriff, Jeff Blauser, Demon Berryhill, and Terry Pendleton, the Braves crushed the Phils, 14-3, to tie the series. God, it sucks when you lose at home. It sucks worse when you're never even in it.

Game Three

Saturday, October 9 (Atlanta-Fulton County Stadium)

Our first game in Atlanta looked to be going well enough at the start. While Terry Mulholland held the Braves scoreless through five, we plated a run in the fourth on back-to-back triples from Mariano Duncan and John Kruk, then another in the sixth on a solo shot by Krukker. Then the dam broke.

The Braves scored five in the sixth inning to knock Terry Mulholland out of the game, then scored another four in the seventh to make game three another laugher. And those Atlanta fans kept making their signature tomahawk chops as the Braves scored a 9-4 victory to take a 2-1 lead in the series.

Game Four

Sunday, October 10 (Atlanta-Fulton County Stadium)

For the first time all season, the Phils were behind. They'd been in the driver's seat from day one, and now they were being tested. Oddly enough, they seemed to enjoy it. Danny Jackson put on a gutsy performance, allowing nine hits but only one run in his seven-plus innings. His only blemish came on a Mark Lemke RBI double in the second. Mark Lemke was kind enough to give us the run back with interest in the fourth inning, when he misplayed a grounder from Darren Daulton that led to two unearned runs on runs batted in from Kevin Stocker and Danny Jackson himself. Mitch Williams came in with runners on first and second in the eighth, and put the Braves down easily. He allowed only one weak hit in the ninth, but the save went down with uncommon simplicity. It was odd. Phils fans were confused. Was something wrong with Mitch?

Game Five

Monday, October 11 (Atlanta-Fulton County Stadium)

Finally, there appeared to be a game that looked like a lock. Curt Schilling, completely in his element, took a 3-0 shutout into the bottom of the ninth. The Phils had broken through early against Braves starter Steve Avery when John Kruk doubled down the right field line in the first to score Mariano Duncan. They added another in the fourth, when Pete Incaviglia drove one to right that Ron Gant completely misplayed, turning what should have been an easy out into a three-base error. Wes Chamberlain drove him in with a followup fly to center. We then added an insurance run in the ninth, when Darren Daulton led off with a homer.

Meanwhile, Curt was just breezing. In fact, Schilling had only one scare during the game. In the first inning with two outs and a runner on first, Fred McGriff hit a screamer long into right field that looked like it was going to leave the park. Chamberlain flew back, extended, but couldn't get to the ball. Jeff Blauser tore around second base as the ball bounded inches from the top of the fence. As Blauser turned the third-base corner, Wes beaded the ball to Stocker at short, and he threaded it to Daulton for a bang-bang out at home. End of inning.

Curt then found his game, entering the ninth having allowed only two more hits since. The last frame didn't start that well for him, however, as he walked the leadoff hitter. Then, reminiscent of game one, a tailor-made double-play ball was driven right to Kim Batiste, again serving as defensive replacement for Little Davey Hollins. Batiste booted the ball, and runners went to first and second with no one out.

Fregosi had seen enough. Schilling was tiring, and on came The Wild Thing. This time, Mitch wasn't up to the task. Fred Mc-Griff singled to bring in one run; David Justice sacrificed to bring in another; and Francisco Cabrera singled to tie the game. For a moment, it looked like the Braves would win when Mark Lemke sent a blast to left that just slipped foul. For some reason, this provided a wake-up call for Mitch, who struck out Lemke and then retired Bill Pecota to send the game into extra innings. Schilling kept the towel on.

You would think that the Phils would be deflated. Any other Phillies squad would have been. Not so this team. They seemed to thrive on adversity. Lenny Dykstra calmly lofted a round-trip-per with one out in the 10th to give our boys the lead that this time they would not give back. Larry Andersen held down the fort in the bottom, striking out the last two batters, and giving the Phils a hard-fought victory. I don't know when Schilling removed the towel.

The Phils had taken two of three in Atlanta-Fulton County Stadium, and would return home with a lead of three games to two. Yes, they were going to have go up against the likes of Greg Maddux in their next game, but you could just smell the World Series.

Game Six

Wednesday, October 13 (Veterans Stadium)

Mickey Morandini made quick work of Greg Maddux when he smacked a line drive off the ace pitcher's leg that left him limping off the mound. Maddux walked off the injury, but clearly labored from that point on. The Phils took advantage with a two-run double by Lenny Dykstra in the third, a two-run homer by Little Davey Hollins in the fifth, and a two-run triple by Mickey Morandini in the sixth that finally chased Greg from the game.

The Phils coasted the rest of the way behind a strong performance from Tommy Greene, who allowed five hits and three runs, two coming on a two-run blast by Jeff Blauser in the seventh. David West bridged the club into the ninth, and then, with the Philly fans offering their own mocking version of the toma-hawk chop, we watched Jim Fregosi light up another cigarette and Mitch Williams take the mound in the bottom of the ninth to try to hold down a 6-3 lead. Dear God, not again. This time, though, Williams muscled through the heart of the order easily, striking out two and giving the Fightin's their first World Series berth in 10 years.

It's impossible to underestimate the glory of that moment. The stadium erupted and so did the players. This had been a love affair all season, and everyone wanted to celebrate to-gether. The team did not surrender themselves immediately to their clubhouse and champagne. They stayed out on the field to take in the moment with the fans. And as Danny Jackson flexed those pecs from the pitcher's mound, we howled in glory along with him.

Philadelphia was reborn. We were not the also-rans. We were not a collection of the set-aside, forgotten, and unfulfilled promises. We'd overcome Tourette's; we'd blown through in-juries; we'd returned from early retirement; we'd leapt, bounded, bordered, and conquered. We'd taken over the ship now and were sailing to the World Series. Sure, that ship didn't look like the master of its fleet. No one ever bothered to batten down the hatches, no one had made certain to clean the sails, no one scraped the barnacles off the hull. And no one cared. They were going full steam ahead. And they didn't have to tuck in their shirts.

The Phils had just one more team to get through—the Toronto Blue Jays, the very club that had beaten the Braves in the World Series the year before. That was okay. If we were go-ing to win, we wanted to take the crown away from the Champs. Bring it on.

THE 1993 WORLD SERIES

The Blue Jays were a much different caliber of opponent than the Braves. I'm not talking about talent. They were good. Hell, they were great. We just didn't hate them. They were a nice bunch of guys from Canada. That actually took a lot of the fla-vor out of it for the Philadelphia fan. Sure, it's fun to win. And it's huge to win a championship. But Toronto? They were running as many articles in their main papers about how much fun it was to watch the Phillies as they did about their own team. What was that about?

I went up to one of the games in Toronto, brazenly wearing my Phillies colors. After they'd beaten us, more than a handful of fans came up to me to apologize and to assure me that my team wasn't out of it yet. Gawd! I wanted to scream. That's not how you should treat your opponent. You're supposed to accost them for wearing the opponent's colors. You're supposed to berate them every time their team gets an out, and then ridicule them hideously after your club takes them to task. One of the Toronto fans even hugged me. Another bought me a beer. Another told me how much he wanted to visit Philly this winter. I liked them! It was so unfair.

And the Blue Jays were strong. Four of their starters hit over .300 as they claimed the top three spots in the American League: John Olerud (.363), Paul Molitor (.332), and Roberto Alomar (.326) finished 1-2-3, respectively, while Tony Fernandez (.306) finished just outside the top 10. Another four finished in the top in runs scored: Molitor at number two with 121 and Devon White at number three with 116, with Alomar and Olerud tied for number eight with 109. Molitor (211) and Olerud (200) finished first and second in hits; Olerud (54) and White (42) finished first and second in doubles. Joe Carter led the team with 121 RBI (third) and 32 homers (sixth). Toronto had a solid but not dominant starting staff, led by Juan Guzman (14-3, 3.99, 198 K), followed by Pat Hentgen (19-9, 3.87, 122 K), Todd Stottlemyre (11-12, 4.84), and Dave Stewart (12-8, 4.44). Duane Ward (2.14, 35 saves) anchored the pen, while Danny Cox (3.12) and Mark Eichorn (2.72) served as setup men.

The Blue Jays had been in a dogfight most of the season with the Yankees and the Orioles, but they began to pull away after September 9, going 17-4 the rest of the way to win the division by seven games. They then pushed aside the Chicago White Sox in the American League Championship Series in six games. Manager Cito Gaston, now in his fourth season, had led them now to three straight division titles and was looking forward to his second consecutive World Championship. Move over, Yankees. The Blue Jays were here. But so were the Phillies.

Game One

Saturday, October 16 (Sky Dome)

The staff aces faced each other in Curt Schilling and Juan Guzman, and fans prepared themselves for a tight pitcher's duel. That was not to happen, however, as Guzman was wild and Schilling uncertain. The Phils struck quickly in the first inning, when Lenny Dykstra led off with a walk, stole second, and scored on a one-out single by John Kruk to left. Darren Daulton roped a single to right center to score Kruk, and the 1993 Series was off to a good start. A great start. The game would more resemble a ping-pong match for a while, as the Jays tied it with two in the second, the Phils went ahead with a run in the third, the Jays tied it with another in the bottom, the Phils reclaimed the lead in the fifth, and the Jays tied it in the bottom.

Things began to turn against our boys in the sixth. They missed their opportunity to take advantage of a couple of hits and a walk when Krukker struck out with the bases loaded. The Blue Jays were quick to take advantage in the bottom when John Olerud hit a solo homer to put Toronto on top for the first time and for good. The Jays scored three in the bottom of the seventh, finally chasing Schilling and taking a commanding 8-4 lead. Jim Eisenreich would get one back in the ninth on a two-out RBI single that brought home Kruk, but it was too little, too—well, it was too little. The Phils had dropped Game One, 8-5. But there was something different about this club. They didn't bow their heads as they walked off. They looked angry.

Game Two

Sunday, October 17 (Sky Dome)

The Phils jumped out early in Game Two, and didn't spend much time looking back as they rocked Blue Jays starter Dave Stewart for five runs in the third, the big smack coming from a Jim Eisenreich three-run dinger. The Jays finally touched Phils starter Terry Mulholland in the fourth, when Joe Carter hit a two-run shot, then chased him in the sixth, when Tony Fernandez doubled to left center to score Roberto Alomar, bringing the Jays within two. Lenny Dykstra gave us one back in the seventh with a rounder into the right field bleachers to make the score

6-4, but no lead was comfortable in this World Series. You just had to hold on.

The Blue Jays mounted their last threat in the eighth inning, when Mitch Williams came on with no outs and Paul Molitor on second. Never one to hold runners on that well, Mitch allowed Molitor to third and then home on an Olerud flyout. Mitch then walked Roberto Alomar to bring the tying run to the plate. Alomar then proceeded to steal second, then took off for third, and was gunned out by Darren Daulton.

The Jays again brought the tying run to the plate in the ninth, when Mitch walked Fernandez to start the inning, and then Ed Sprague hit a tailor-made double play to defensive replacement Kim Batiste at third. You've read that sentence before, twice actually, in the NLCS section. Batiste, who had entered the game as a ninth-inning defensive replacement for Little Davey Hollins, couldn't field the ball cleanly, and the Phils had to settle for a one-out force. The next batter hit another tailor-made double play, but this time avoided Batiste, thank God, allowing Kevin Stocker to turn it to end the inning and the ballgame. We had managed to steal a game in Toronto and were heading back to Philly.

Game Three

Tuesday, October 19 (Veterans Stadium)

Cito Gaston had a tough decision to make prior to the outset of Game Three. It would be the first time this season that his club had to go without a designated hitter. Paul Molitor had taken DH duties during the course of the year, and Gaston was reluctant to sit his hot hand. He sent Molitor out to first, taking the bat from the hands of John Olerud, who had led the Americans in batting average with a .362. Molitor silenced the critics by going three for four, igniting the attack that took Phils starter Danny Jackson for three runs in the top of the first, and the wind out of the Phillies' sails.

Blue Jays starter Pat Hentgen was in constant trouble through his six innings of work, allowing five hits and three walks, but the Phils could only touch him for a run. The Jays walked away with a 10-3 victory, and had stolen a win in Veterans Stadium. We felt bad, but not nearly as bad as we would in just 24 hours.

Game Four

Wednesday, October 20 (Veterans Stadium)

In Game Four, the Phils mauled the Blue Jays' pitching, scoring 14 runs on 14 hits. Lenny Dykstra crushed another two homers, Darren Daulton one of his own. Milt Thompson had five runs batted in. Three Phils had three hits in the game. We scored four in the first inning, five in the fifth, had a five-run lead in the eighth. And we lost. There. I wanted to get that out of the way. Now, if you want to continue to read the following report, you may, but at least it won't be as painful. You already know what's coming. For some it makes it easier.

The Blue Jays were on Tommy Greene right from the start, scoring three runs in the top of the first, then chasing him from the mound with a four-spot in the third. The Phils were on an offensive tear of their own, however, scoring four in their half of the first, thanks to a bases-clearing triple from Milt Thompson, then two two-run dingers from Dykstra, one in the second and another in the fifth; Daulton hit a two-runner in the fifth as well. By the time the dust settled around the top of the eighth, we led 14-9, and (gulp) were sending out the secure arm of Larry Andersen. Larry lasted only an out. With the score 14-10 and runners on second and third, Fregosi signaled for another cigarette and (gulp) Mitchie Pooh. The Wild Thing immediately let up a run-scoring single to Tony Fernandez, then walked the bases loaded, and then...well, then death threats began to pour in at Veterans Stadium. Seriously. People wanted to kill Mitch Williams. And he hadn't even lost the game yet. Philadelphians take their baseball very, very seriously.

Mitch struck out pinch hitter Ed Sprague for the second out of the inning, before a two-run single from Ricky Henderson made it a one-run game. For some reason, Mitch remained on the mound to pitch to Devon White, who couldn't have been happier to see that fastball over the fat part of the plate. He walloped a line drive triple to deep right center, to clear the bases and give the Blue Jays the lead, 15-14. And for the first time all season, the Phillies looked defeated. They fell in order in the eighth and ninth innings, and fell behind in the Series, 3-1. The city seemed empty that night. No one walked the streets, no one spoke to each other in the bars, and if anyone slept, they did so fitfully.

Game Five

Thursday, October 21 (Veterans Stadium)

Riding on the subway to the game the next day felt dismal. I've attended funerals that were livelier. When people spoke, they did so in whispers. When people locked eyes, they did so with silent acknowledgment of shared pain. No one wanted to see the end of this incredible season. But you had to see it. It deserved to be observed. Only Curt Schilling felt differently. He was pissed, and he took it out on the Blue Jays with every single pitch. I don't think he even blinked during the game. He threw a complete game, five-hit shutout, only allowing runners to reach second base twice during the contest. It was only the second time all season that the Blue Jays had failed to score.

The Phils scored all they needed in the first inning, when Lenny Dykstra walked, stole second, advanced to third on a throwing error by catcher Pat Borders, then scored on a John Kruk groundout. No hits, one run. They'd get another in the second inning, when Kevin Stocker doubled in Darren Daulton, but Schilling didn't need it. In fact, it looked like he felt insulted by it.

The strange thing was that no one really cheered until the very end of the game. We all sat with our stomachs clenched in a slick, wet fist until the final pop of Dykstra's mitt off a Paul Molitor line drive signaled the end of the game. No Mitch. No towels. No comeback. This would be the last playoff game ever played in Veterans Stadium.

Game Six

Saturday, October 23 (Sky Dome)

You can find this game on many of the "All-Time Greatest Games" lists. In fact, I recently looked over my TV schedule to find that ESPN was playing it...again. Football was season over. Spring Training was coming. Nothing much to do. I allowed my eyes to gaze upon it for a bit, happy to see the familiar red-and-white uniforms of our boys, watching Daulton and Company back in action. But I couldn't stay too long. No Philadelphian could, unless he (or she) is some kind of connoisseur of pain.

The game didn't start well when Toronto jumped all over starter Terry Mulholland for three in the first. The only saving grace was that, if you're going to lose, you might as well lose early. It's like pulling a bandage off quickly. By the seventh inning, the Jays had built a 5-1 lead, with starter Dave Stewart easing along with a two-hitter. But the Phils, who hadn't quit all season, weren't about to quit here either. After Kevin Stocker and Mickey Morandini worked their way onto the bases, Dykstra hit his sixth homer of the Series to bring the Phils within one and chase Stewart from the mound.

Mariano Duncan started the rally afresh with a line drive single against reliever Danny Cox, promptly stole second to put the tying run into scoring position, and then came around to knot the contest at five. Cox ended up leaving the game with one out and the bases loaded. When Pete Incaviglia hit a long fly to give the Phils the lead, Philadelphia felt vindicated. Suddenly that 15-14 loss didn't seem so bad. The Blue Jays might have pulled off the nearly impossible in that context, but we'd gotten them right back. And we'd done it with our backs to the wall. Take that! Besides, we had a man on the mound who looked in total control of his game.

Roger Mason had been in since the sixth inning and had allowed only one hit, no walks, and no runs while striking out two. However, after retiring the first batter in the eighth, Mason was summarily removed for the traditional setup tandem of David West and Larry Andersen. Two walks and a hit batsman later, Andersen coaxed Pat Borders into a pop to Mickey Morandini to end the inning and put some air back into our lungs.

We'd just dodged a bullet. But we all knew the gunfight was far from over, because none other than Mitch Williams began to warm up in the bullpen. It was a curious move. Hadn't Jim Fregosi seen how Williams had been pitching lately? Hadn't he watched him blow up in the eighth inning just the other day? I know Fregosi always followed the philosophy that if you fall off the horse, you've got to get right back on and, yes, it's a sound philosophy. But this was the sixth game of the World Series for God's sake.

To cheers from the crowd (and they weren't Phillies fans), Mitch Williams ran onto the field for the bottom of the ninth and immediately served up a walk to leadoff hitter Ricky Henderson. Devon White followed with a long, long fly to deep left that Milt Thompson managed to catch up to for the first out. But Paul

Molitor stroked a line drive single to center and then Joe Carter stepped up to the plate.

The rest is history. Williams. Fastball. Carter. Swing. Carter. Contact. Ball. Gone. Long gone. Series over. It truly was a remarkable game with a remarkable conclusion right out of the storybooks. I can see why ESPN keeps playing it again and again. It's just that these kinds of storybooks don't read so well to the kids of Philadelphia.

THE AFTERMATH

Before the 1994 season began, the Phillies would unload poor Mitch Williams to Houston, then send Terry Mulholland to the Yanks. Despite a record of only 54-61 in '94, the Phils would remain National League Champions through the '94 season, thanks to a players strike that canceled the World Series for the first time since 1904. When the strike was finally settled, John Kruk was gone, as were Danny Jackson and Milt Thompson. The Phils would finish 21 games out of first and only three out of last. Little Davey Hollins would go to Boston in the middle of the campaign, and Tommy Greene would retire.

The Phils would finish in last in 1996, resulting in the termination of Jim Fregosi. Lenny Dykstra would retire soon afterward. Pete Incaviglia would go to the Orioles, and Jim Eisenreich would be granted free agency. Curt Schilling would stick around the longest, languishing with the also-ran Phillies into the middle of the 2000 season, when his trade demands were finally met. The erstwhile group of forgotten players who managed to find the resiliency to give us one of the greatest seasons in Phillies history had finally gone.

THE SECOND
PHILASTIC
DYNASTY

Intermission: The Prelude

PART ONE: THE BOWA YEARS

After seven years in the mire of the National East cellars, Larry Bowa came to town to change things. He brought an attitude that Philadelphia respected. He wouldn't accept anyone who gave less than 100 percent, and he firmly believed that the club had the talent to be winners. Up until this time, Bowa had only a year and a half of experience as a manager, which he earned with the San Diego Padres in the late 1980s. His personality wasn't a good fit for the laid-back California club, and Larry was summarily dismissed midway through the '88 season.

Bowa left Philly at the end of the First Philastic Dynasty. At that time, the town breathed baseball, spoke baseball, felt baseball. On his return, he found our city remarkably changed. We'd become a football town pure and simple. Other than the aberration that was 1993, when Bowa served as the third base coach, Philadelphia had come to consider their baseball team as a bridge to get from the end of the football season to the beginning of training camp.

The Phils were only needed to provide escapist entertainment from April through July. It's not that long a time, and yet they couldn't live up to it. We'd suffered losing seasons 13 out of the last 14 years. If you sat in the stadium, people would talk mostly about who they thought the Eagles should draft and why they believed that this was going to be the year we finally took the Super Bowl. Now and again, you would hear them erupt in a cheer, but it would most likely be the E-A-G-L-E-S chant.

The year before Bowa arrived had been a particularly awful one. Our record of 65-97 was the worst in the majors. We scored the fewest runs, hit the lowest number of homers, and our pitching staff ranked below the median in every category. Clearly something had to change. The ownership assured us of this. They understood our pain and, as a result, they decided to make two dramatic moves going into 2001: They would hire Bowa, and they would cut the payroll by 3.5 million dollars. They then tried to convince us that the Phillies were a middle-market team and the players had to accept the payroll of a middle-market team. They assured us that money doesn't buy championships, that it's good old-fashioned baseball knowledge…yada yada yada. You couldn't blame the fans for chanting E-A-G-L-E-S during this commentary.

Larry Bowa certainly didn't listen, not to the palaver of the owners and not to the dismissal by the fans. In his very first season, he brought the team that had changed very little from 2000, from the depths of the professional baseball world, to second place. We finished only two games behind the Braves, having been in first as late as September 1. Bowa would win Manager of the Year for his efforts. His club won 86 games in both 2003 and 2004, but his fire and brimstone attitude had begun to lose favor as the team matured. At the end of the '04 season, the Phils decided to go with a more nurturing manager in Charlie Manuel. No one can argue the choice. In fact, it was an inspired one. However, no one can argue the fact that without Larry Bowa, the team wouldn't have begun to carry themselves with the sense of poise and purpose that would give us what we have today: the Second Philastic Dynasty.

PART TWO: UNCLE CHARLIE, THE EARLY YEARS

Charlie Manuel was not the fans' choice for manager. Of the managers who interviewed for the job, the overwhelming fan favorite was Jim Leyland, who had managed the Pirates to so many successful seasons in the '90s, and the Marlins to a World Series title in '98. Leyland had been candid in his Phillies interview and with the press. He said exactly what the fans had been saying for years. The team had "too many strikes" in its lineup and some significant changes had to be made, both offensively and defensively. And it was going to cost money.

Charlie Manuel, on the other hand, didn't confront the brass and he didn't offer anything alarming in his interviews with ownership or the press. And it wasn't surprising. After all, Charlie was "one of them." He'd been serving as a special assistant to the general manager since he stepped down as manager of the Cleveland Indians in 2002. No one was surprised when he got the job. In fact, it seemed a "typical" choice. The ownership never wanted to hear the truth. They felt more comfortable with someone already familiar with the organization, someone who thought that the Phils were doing "just peachy, thanks." The Philly fans didn't like Charlie's rural Virginia accent. He sounded like a "good ol' boy." Maybe that kind of thing could fly in Minnesota or Cleveland, where he'd earned his chops, but it just didn't belong in Philadelphia.

The 2005 Season

We gave Charlie little credit for the team's playoff run in 2005. As far as we were concerned, this was Larry Bowa's club, the one that ran to an 88-74 record, only two games from the first-place Braves and only a game behind the Astros for the Wild Card. When we spoke of Charlie, it was to crucify him for any and every managerial decision that went even slightly wrong. He had a tough time transitioning from the American to the National League. It was a helluva learning curve, if the guy was even learning at all. Bowa or Leyland wouldn't have brought Billy Wagner into a game in the eighth inning; Bowa or Leyland would have known how to handle the double switch; Bowa or Leyland would have pulled Randy Wolf earlier, would have pinch-hit for Myers, would have...blah blah blah. Charlie Manuel couldn't win for winning.

The 2006 Season

Charlie's team made another hell of a run in 2006. Though they would finish as a distant second to the Mets, they would stand only three games back from the Wild Card-winning Dodgers. That was close enough for us to blame everything, once again, on the manager. After all, it certainly wasn't the players' fault.

Ryan Howard belted 58 home runs—a franchise record; Chase Utley started in the All-Star Game; Cole Hamels enjoyed a winning rookie year; Jimmy Rollins landed as a clear triple threat. If the ownership would just wake up, they'd recognize that all we had to do was find a manager who could take us to the next level that we seemed so capable of reaching.

The 2007 Season

Things got even uglier for Charlie when the Fightin's trundled off to another slow start in '07. After a particularly bad 8-1 loss to the New York Mets on April 17, WIP host Howard Eskin repeatedly put our manager on his heels, demanding to know why he didn't challenge the players more, why he didn't confront them, why he didn't do what Bowa or Leyland would have done, and on and on. When Eskin took his war to the airwaves, the fans were more than willing to join in the attack. Still, ownership did nothing, and Charlie didn't seem bothered by our cries for change. What's worse is that the Phils seemed poised to treat us cruelly. By the time September 12 rolled around, the Phils trailed the Eastern Division-leading Mets by seven games, so at least the division was out of the question. But the damn thing was, we were only two and a half games behind the Wild Card.

It was dreadful. If we could just go on a quick losing snap, the pain would be over. Why did the Phils have to linger for so long? About the only thing we could look forward to was the weekend of September 14, when we would travel up to Shea Stadium for a three-game spot. The bandage could be torn off, the season would be over—and so would the pain—and we could start the healing process.

But something odd happened. We swept the Mets, and then—stranger still—we continued on to a six-game winning streak. Meanwhile, those New Yorkers went and dropped five in a row. By the morning of September 19, we were a game and a half behind the Mets for the Eastern title. There were only 11 games remaining.

Going into the last game of the season, we'd pulled even with the Mets, but anything could happen. We were still a game behind the Padres for the Wild Card, tied with the Rockies. There was still the definite possibility that we could finish in second in the East, like we'd done so many times in recent years. (Who cares if we were one game out or two at this point?) And we could actually finish as far as third in the Wild Card.

(We'd been there before, too.) But even before we took the field for that last game, the news of the Mets' first inning flashed across our scoreboards. The Florida Marlins had shelled Mets starter Tom Glavine for seven runs in only a third of an inning. Jesus. All we had to do was take this game and we would have the greatest comeback since 1964—only we'd be at the other end of the collapse this time.

Jimmy Rollins, on his way to winning the MVP, let everyone know how this scenario was going to play out. He hit a line single to center to start the game. He then proceeded to steal second, steal third, and come around to score when Chase Utley lofted one to right field. We never looked back, winning the game 6-1 behind a superb performance by Jamie Moyer, who nailed down his team-leading 14th of the year. We'd taken the division for the first time in 14 years and were playoff-bound.

Phillies Memory

John Cunningham, Philadelphia Author

On the final day of the 2007 regular season, gone was our memory of the 10,000th loss in Phillies history that we'd witnessed in July. The Mets' wide margin had vanished. The Phillies and the Mets were now tied for first place. As my 34-year-old son, Michael, and I walked into Citizens Bank Park, the waving white towels were everywhere. So was the electricity. I fought away the tears of joy for what might actually happen. For the Phillies. And for Michael. We'd waited 14 years. We could wait a little longer.

Before the Phillies even batted, a loud collective roar erupted. The out-of-town scoreboard showed the Mets were losing 7-0 to the Florida Marlins in the first inning. Mike flashed an inerasable smile. Although Jamie Moyer was hitting the corners and J-Roll was performing like an MVP, we felt tortured only by time. Finally, in the ninth inning with the Phils up 6-1 over the Washington Nationals, Brett Myers struck out the last batter and the atmosphere was engulfed with screaming fans, ringing bells, and exploding fireworks. As Mike and I hugged each other, I could let the tears of happiness flow for the both of us.

The Phillies dropped their division series in three straight losses to the Rockies that season, but none of us cared. We'd arrived. We'd gotten our taste, and now we just had to keep moving forward.

And, oh yeah—we never complained about Charlie, now Uncle Charlie, ever again.

8

2008: The End of the Drought

2008 National League Standings

Team	Wins	Losses	Ties	WP	GB
Philadelphia Phillies	92	70	0	.568	—
New York Mets	89	73	0	.549	3
Florida Marlins	84	77	0	.522	7.5
Atlanta Braves	72	90	0	.444	20
Washington Nationals	59	102	0	.366	32.5

NLDS:
PHILLIES 3; MILWAUKEE BREWERS 1
NLCS:
PHILLIES 4; LOS ANGELES DODGERS 1
WORLD SERIES:
PHILLIES 4; TAMPA BAY RAYS 1

I read Bernard Malamud's *The Natural* when I was 11 years old. It was truly a learning experience. And not a good one. I knew the reality of life as well as any other 11-year-old kid. Life was filled with sunshine, cotton candy, swimming pools, and late-summer barbecues. Evil always got defeated in the end, the Prince married the Princess, and your mom made you a brown-bag lunch before she kissed you and sent you off to school. So when I ventured forth into *The Natural* during that beamish summer of 1972, I did so with the cocky confidence of one who knows the shape of the world, all its contours, and every possible avenue of joy. The book is a good one, but not an easy read for a kid. It's full of mature subjects, contemplative thought, and erratic rhythms. It took me all summer to read it, but I knew it would be worth the ride.

So when Roy Hobbs stepped up to the plate in the bottom of the ninth, with two outs and two runners on, grasping Wonderboy in his powerful hands, I read with ease and confidence. Strike one. Nice buildup in the suspense. Strike two. Predictable, but necessary. You don't hit the game-winning home run with only one strike against you. Then the long foul ball, and then the world began to turn upside down.

Roy Hobbs turned back to the plate to find Wonderboy broken in half. That wasn't supposed to happen. He carved that bat when he was a boy. It carried the weight of his father. It carried the weight of his dreams. It carried the weight of a young boy's confidence that everything in the world would turn out right in the end. Then, nervously gripping a new bat for the first time in many a long year, Roy Hobbs swung and missed at the next pitch. The game was over. Roy had lost. The Knights had lost. I had lost. I remember the book falling to my side as I leaned up on an elbow to watch my friends leaping into the pool at Mermaid Lake. They were laughing effortlessly, still young kids with confidence and dreams. But I had turned into something else. I had found out that sometimes, at the very end, there was a chance you could strike out.

This knowledge proved prophetic in my Phillies fandom experience. I loved seeing Mike Schmidt smoke the ball, Steve Carlton groove another across the plate, Scott Rolen effortlessly go from first to third on a single, Lenny Dykstra will a ball over the left field wall. But like any Phillies fan, I knew the eventual outcome of the season. A gut-wrenching defeat made only slightly more palatable in that you knew, after all, that it would be gut wrenching and, therefore, you could prepare.

And then 2008 happened. A great deal of talent. A great deal of hope. A great deal of promise. Yeah. Been there, heard that.

Grab me another beer and let me steel my nerves. Then, with the contest tied in game one of the division series, Brett Myers, the weakest-hitting pitcher on the Phils squad (perhaps on any Phils squad), stepped in against the hottest pitcher in the National League, CC Sabathia. There were two outs and two on. That was okay. Myers would strike out certainly, but it would set the Phillies up to begin the next inning with their leadoff hitter.

Then Myers did something uncanny. He fought off 11 pitches from Sabathia, finally drawing a walk to load the bases for Shane Victorino. That wasn't supposed to happen. Every Phillies fan knew that wasn't supposed to happen. And I was suddenly brought back to the 1978 movie theater where I parked my reluctant butt next to Claudia Ericson to take in Barry Levinson's *The Natural*. I didn't want to see that film. Hell, I'd already lived through the book once. Who am I kidding? I lived through that book again and again and again since that time. I did not want to see it again. But Claudia was adamant. It was opening night of the movie, and Claudia loved opening nights. I, for one, loved Claudia Ericson, so I was down for it. I took a deep breath, dipped my hand into the popcorn, and then sat stunned as Roy Hobbs lifted that two-strike fastball over the right field fence, winning the game and the season for the New York Knights. With one pitch, my entire youth had been redeemed. My entire faith in humanity and in human outcomes had been redeemed.

So when Shane Victorino strode to the plate, I suddenly questioned everything that I thought I knew about the Phillies. And when Shane launched that grand slam to right center, effectively winning the game for the Phils, you could feel the writing on the wall. Despite the entire history of the franchise, you really could. The Phils were going to win it. They'd won it with a two-out walk in the third inning of the division series. They had wrestled the pen from the poisoned hand of fate and begun to apply their own words to the page. The words echoed those of Dave Cash so many years before: "Yes we can!" And the Second Philastic Dynasty had been born.

Preseason

The 2008 season began in November 2007, and it didn't begin well. It was the old pleasure-pain scenario. First the pleasure: the Phillies finally signed a bona fide closer, picking up Brad

Lidge from the Houston Astros. In 2005, the man pulled in 42 saves with a 2.29 ERA. Of course, the reason he'd been made available is that, after allowing a game-winning home run to Albert Pujols in the '05 National League Championship Series, he lost his confidence, his ERA ballooned to 5.28, and he lost his closer's job.

Still, on paper it looked good. We didn't actually have a closer on our team. Sure, Brett Myers had the mentality and had racked up 21 saves in 2007, but losing him from our starting staff had weakened that area considerably. Signing Lidge actually gave us two players: a needed closer and a needed starter. And then Lidge showed up to the press conference on crutches. Not a good sign. We were told not to worry. And we didn't. When you've only won one championship in 126 years, you don't go around concerned that you might lose another one this coming year. Lidge, they said, would be ready by Spring Training. And indeed he was. The only problem was that his Spring Training didn't last long. In his first game, he twisted his ankle and would have to sit for the remainder of the Grapefruit League. We were told not to worry. Yeah, right.

The Manager

Uncle Charlie, as we have come to know him, bears the name well—a kind, genial, warm and gracious man. He'll never berate a player to the press, instead electing to chastise him only in private, and will support his players at all levels. Charlie Manuel is a man who takes care of his boys. It seems a little shocking that this man, who made his bones while playing in Japan in the '70s, was best known as Aka-Oni, or The Red Devil. Charlie was one of the most magnificent American exports that ever hit the country.

A massive power hitter who consistently hit 40 homers and 100 RBI per season, Charlie was a force to be reckoned with. He led the Yakult Swallows to their first pennant in 1978; then, playing for the Kintetsu Buffaloes in '79, Charlie was on pace to break the monthly home run record. Most Japanese considered it an insult for a foreigner to hold such a record, and, not surprisingly, Charlie was beaned with a fastball so viciously that he was in the hospital for six weeks. He was told to sit out the rest of the season, but instead returned to belt 37 homers and 94

RBI, leading the Buffaloes to their first pennant and winning the MVP at the same time.

Manuel returned to the U.S. to manage in the minor league systems of the Twins and Indians until he took over the helm of the Indians' major league club in 2000. He led them to a second-place finish his first season, a first-place finish in his second, and left the team in a contract dispute during his third. Very shortly after, he joined the Phillies organization as a special assistant to the general manager and became the manager of the club itself in 2005. The rest, as they say, is a warm and genial history.

The Lineup

Leading Off:

Shortstop Jimmy "J-Roll" Rollins, .277, 47 SB, 9 Triples

Jimmy Rollins was just coming off his MVP year, when he'd led the Phillies by force of personality and drive to steal a division championship from the defending Mets on the very last day of the season. The only person who stood unsurprised was Rollins himself. As he'd claimed in the 2007 preseason, "The Mets had a chance to win the World Series last year. Last year is over. I think we are the team to beat in the NL East, finally."

Jimmy Rollins enjoyed being a leader; he enjoyed playing ball, and thanks to his style of play, the 2008 Phils seemed infected with his easy-going, let's-enjoy-the-hell-out-of-this-game nature. I can't remember how many times I sat tense and nervous before the game, only to turn to the dugout to see the laughing face of Jimmy Rollins keeping everyone loose on the bench, reminding all that this is supposed to be a game and it's supposed to be fun.

Batting Second:

Center Fielder "The Flyin' Hawaiian" Shane Victorino, .293, 36 SB, 102 R

My favorite memory of Shane Victorino came in a tense 2008 NLCS contest against the Los Angeles Dodgers. With the game on the line, Casey Blake lifted a long, long fly to deepest center field. Shane maneuvered back on the fly, and as he stretched out to full extension against the wall, he was smiling. When he pulled the ball down safely, he was laughing. Like J-Roll before him, Shane knows the game is supposed to be fun, and he enjoys the hell out of it. He doesn't appear to get nervous by growing tension; he appears to get inspired by it.

Victorino reminds one of a young Pete Rose, who, during possibly the greatest World Series ever played—against the Boston Red Sox in 1975—in possibly the most tension-filled game ever played, Game Six, stepped up in extra innings with the winning run on base, and paused to say to catcher Carlton Fisk, "God, this is a helluva game, isn't it?"

It's as if Shane is a fan first and a player second. He's one of us out there, cheering as loudly as we are. Shane first broke into the Phillies everyday lineup when Bobby Abreu was traded midway through the 2006 season. He impressed through '06 and '07, but really turned up his game in '08, when he hit .292, stole 36 bases (sixth), racked up eight triples (fifth), and scored 102 times.

Batting Third:
Second Baseman Chase Utley, .292, 33 HR, 113 R, 104 RBI

Chase Utley had been a phenom since his first day of pro ball in 2003, when he launched a grand slam. He became the Phillies' starting second baseman in '06, had a 35-game hitting streak, led the league in runs with 131, and made his first All-Star team. He didn't slow down in '07, hitting .332 (third in the league) while collecting 103 RBI and scoring 104 runs. It seemed a tall order for the 29-year-old to keep getting better, but Utley cracked a career-best 33 homers (ninth) in 2008, along with 41 doubles (10th), 78 extra base hits (fifth), and 177 total hits (10th), while scoring 113 times (fifth). Just for good measure, he also led all second basemen in putouts (340) and assists (463).

Batting Cleanup:
First Baseman Ryan Howard, .251, 48 HR, 146 RBI, 105 R, 199 K

Three years removed from Rookie-of-the-Year honors and two from MVP, Ryan Howard put on an offensive display in 2008 that rivaled any other season of his young career. He led the league in homers (48) and RBI (146), was fourth in total bases (331), fifth in extra base hits (78), seventh in slugging percentage (.543), and ninth in runs scored (105). It was good enough for the 28-year-old to finish second in the MVP race.

Known for his slow starts (indeed, he hit only .172 in April of '08), Ryan carried the team in September. As Rich Hoffman of the *Philadelphia Daily News* put it, "Howard's power numbers are real and his impact on this team is enormous. It is hard to shrug off when you see it every night. At the time of the year when it matters the most, it is hard to get hung up on strikeouts or on-base percentage when you see another ball launched into the September night."

The most impressive thing about Howard, however, is his quiet calm. You're reminded of a lion quietly waiting in the deep grasses beside the water hole. Waiting, waiting, waiting to pounce. Perhaps he was waiting in April. Quietly. Silently. Because when he does pounce at the end, with one of those mammoth shots that electrify the early-fall nights, it's as if the sky has ripped open.

Batting Fifth:
Left Fielder Pat "The Bat" Burrell, .250, 33 HR, 86 RBI, 102 BB

People loved him. People cheered for him. People hated him. People jeered him. They stood and called his name. Some in hate, some in adoration. One thing no one felt during the reign of Pat Burrell was apathy. Pat broke into the Phillies lineup in 2000, earned fourth place in the voting for Rookie of the Year, and by 2002 had a season that earned him a six-year, $50 million contract as the pride of Larry Bowa's new Fightin' Phils. And then 2003 happened. Pat hit .209. The scary thing is how the fans reacted. Pat received terrific ovations each time he came to the plate. No one knew what was wrong with our new golden boy. And he didn't seem to get it either.

Pat wasn't like Mike Schmidt, who would stand elusive and cold; he wasn't like Lenny Dykstra, who seemed to taunt each pitch that came in. He seemed to understand as little as we did about the fortunes that befell Philadelphia. It was like he was going through his own Black Friday, a whole freaking season of it. We wanted him to know we could relate.

Pat gave back to us the next season, gathering 19 homers by the All-Star Break, then going on a tear in September that brought us close to the division title. But something happened along the way: the fans began to boo. Pat had begun to bristle against the ownership, who had tried to trade him earlier in the year, and against Larry Bowa, his manager, and the long love of the Philly fans. After Burrell hit a game-winning homer one night, he actually snubbed Bowa, who'd come out to congratulate him. You don't do that to a member of our family.

In 2007, Pat's tumultuous saga continued. Hitting .201 in June, his mind seemed so far away from the field that after a called strike three, he didn't look like he was trying to figure out where that last pitch had gone, but rather like he was trying to remember who his third grade teacher was. Then, in July, something clicked. It wasn't like a hot streak either. It was like Burrell had figured something out. He became a freaking monster. Pat hit .435 in July with a .768 slugging percentage; he then hit 10 homers with a .650 SLG in August. His clutch hitting in September helped the Phils topple those New York Mets for the division title. The fans began to cheer again.

Pat produced one of his most consistent seasons in 2008, hitting 33 homers and gathering 86 RBI, as the Phillies took their first World Series in 28 years. Nonetheless, the brass did not seem eager to renew Burrell's contract at the end of the season. Pat didn't seem too interested either. He wouldn't even discuss the money offered him and was quick to shop his services on the free agent market. Some fans were happy, some fans were angry; some blasted the ownership, and some quickly dismissed his legend. No one sat in apathy.

Batting Sixth:
Right Fielder Jayson Werth, .273, 24 HR, 73 R, 20 SB

Who the hell was Jayson Werth? I thought our right fielder was supposed to be that guy Jenkins that we got from Milwaukee. Werth? Wasn't he the guy who hit a whopping nothing in 2006, following a whopping .234 in '05? Most fans didn't take much notice when Werth would saunter out to right from time to time in 2007. Charlie Manuel liked to give all his players some time in the field; he didn't want them to get rusty when he needed a pinch hitter. The thing was, this Jayson Werth guy looked pretty damn good. At one point he'd gotten nine hits in nine consecutive at-bats, breaking Pete Rose's 8-8 stretch in 1979.

When center fielder Shane Victorino went on the injured list in the early part of the 2008 season, Jayson started to see a lot more playing time. He announced his arrival as a star one warm May evening when he rapped three homers, including a grand slam. Before much longer, Werth's play had relegated Geoff Jenkins to a pinch-hitting role. And not much longer after that, he was one of the most feared batsmen of the National League. His influence, however, has gone much further than his bat.

Jayson Werth knew beyond a doubt that the Phils would win. I distinctly remember one game where we trailed by four in the bottom of the ninth. The Phils got a runner on first with two outs, and the camera panned to the dugout. Jayson could be seen bobbing and weaving behind the players. I figured he must have been looking for a good vantage point to watch the play. After the game, he revealed that he'd wanted to find the best location from which to launch himself onto the field to congratulate the teammate whose winning run he felt certain would come in. The Phils lost that game, but it didn't deter Jayson. In the next game, he was back there bobbing and weaving again. He simply never had a doubt as to the outcome.

Batting Seventh:
Third Baseman Pedro Feliz, .249, 14 HR, 58 RBI

The slick-fielding Pedro Feliz came up as a utility player for the Giants, filling in at first, second, third, short, right, left, and catcher. He whacked 20 or more homers for four consecutive years, from 2004 to 2007, then asked for a three-year contract extension. The Giants didn't exactly refuse him, but they didn't seem terribly excited about it either. After Feliz made himself available on the open market, San Francisco upped their offer, but by that time Pedro no longer felt welcome. He joined the Phillies in '08, and though back problems limited his power, he gave the club the best glove at third since Mike Schmidt helmed the hot corner.

Batting Eighth:
Catcher Carlos "Chooch" Ruiz, .219, 14 Doubles

Of Panamanian descent, Carlos Ruiz broke into the Phillies lineup in 2006; by 2007 he had become a fan favorite. An excellent field general, Ruiz made only two errors in 744 chances in

'07, while throwing out 26 base runners (fifth). He handled his pitchers effortlessly, and proved equally able to set up for Brad Lidge's out pitches without telegraphing and to talk down the flamboyant Brett Myers. With such a young staff, the club needed someone with Chooch's calm and cool discipline to help ease them into the playoffs, and then to help keep them focused and controlled throughout.

The Bench

Charlie Manuel had a healthy arsenal of weapons to turn to in 2008. For power there was Geoff Jenkins, who had consistently hit over 20 homers for the previous nine seasons in Milwaukee. A starter until the '08 season, Jenkins could spell in the outfield as well. For average there was Greg Dobbs (.301), who had proven himself one of the premier pinch hitters in the game. A jack of all trades, Dobbs filled in at first, second, third, right and left. Right fielder Matt Stairs may have gotten only 17 regular season at-bats since being acquired from the Blue Jays at the trade deadline, but he will forever live in the hearts of Phillies fans, thanks to a gargantuan home run he blasted in the championship series against the Dodgers.

Two years removed from his season as the game's oldest rookie, catcher Chris Coste spelled Ruiz on afternoon and Sunday games. A well-liked player, Coste wrote a best-selling book about his life and baseball times that only increased his popularity. Outfielder So Taguchi, a platoon starter in his past three years in St. Louis, came in as a late-inning defensive replacement, while Eric Bruntlett served the same role in the infield.

The Starting Staff

The Ace:
Left-Hander Cole Hamels, 14-10, 3.09, 196 K

Cole Hamels had always shown great promise in a career that has been studded with incredible games, heroic performances, and bitter injuries. He won the Paul Owens Award for the best pitcher in the Phillies minor league system in 2003, but he had to sit most of the 2004 season due an elbow injury. He came to the majors in 2006 and made the All-Star team the next year.

Hamels looked on his way to a huge season, throwing his first complete game against the Reds in late April, then carrying a perfect game into the seventh inning against the Brewers a few weeks later. But as the Phils prepared an assault on the Mets, he succumbed to the disabled list once more, this time with an elbow strain. Hamels would turn in a fine season in 2008, with career bests in ERA (3.09), strikeouts (196), shutouts (2, third in the league), and innings pitched (227, second). As everyone knows, Cole saved his best for the playoffs, where he would go from a promising young pitcher to a household name.

Second in the Order:
Right-Hander Brett Myers, 10-13, 4.55, 163 K

A stalwart minor league pitcher in the early 2000s, Brett Myers had once been considered the jewel of the organization. In his first full season in the majors, he earned 14 wins while striking out 143. By 2005, he lowered his ERA to a 3.72, while passing the 200 mark in innings pitched (215) and upping his strikeouts to 208 (third in the league). The Philadelphia fan base was justifiably high on Myers going into 2006, but the world was about to turn, and so were the fans. Brett pitched exceedingly well for us that season, leading the club in wins, ERA, and strikeouts, but on a sad night in Boston, witnesses saw him punching his wife. Although charges were eventually dropped, the incident clearly showed Myers' abusive nature, and the critics began to come out in droves. It didn't help that the Phillies front office refused to penalize him for his actions. They noted that the assault wasn't a baseball incident, but since neither the law nor the MLB was willing to take a stand against Myers, the fans took it upon themselves. And they did a fine job.

Myers' already turbulent career didn't let up in 2008. After earning the Opening Day start for the club, he became ineffective. During the months of May and June, Brett was able to notch only one victory; his control left him and his ERA shotgunned to 5.46. He agreed to a minor league assignment in July. Many speculated that Myers would never return to the team, that he had not only lost his mojo, but also his talent and, what's worse, his strike zone. No one could have seen that Brett Myers would return with a vengeance, throwing his best baseball in years in the second half of the season when he went 7-2 with a 1.80 ERA. Even fewer could have predicted what he would do with the bat in the playoffs.

Third in the Order:
Left-Hander Jamie Moyer, 16-7, 3.71

Jamie Moyer has played in four decades, from 1986 through 2010; along the way this cut-fastball and change-up pitcher has amassed 267 victories. He's the oldest man to ever throw a shutout, when at 47 he tossed a complete game two-hitter against the Atlanta Braves. It's surprising, then, that Moyer didn't become an effective starter until his mid-30s.

A journeyman pitcher from 1986 to 1995, Moyer played for five teams and compiled only a 59-76 record. He'd bounced back and forth to the minors—from the bench to the rotation, from regular to spot starter—until he was traded to the Seattle Mariners in the middle of the 1996 season. Finally, at the age of 33, Jamie Moyer had found a home. After pitching 10 stellar years for the Mariners (a full career for most pitchers), Moyer joined the Phillies for their 2006 pennant run. He notched 14 wins in 2007, including the pennant winner against the Washington Nationals on the last day of the season. After leading the 2007 team in games started and innings pitched, Moyer went out at 45 years of age to lead the club in wins (16), winning percentage (.696), and starts (33) in 2008. Someone had given this man a drink from the fountain of youth, one that he didn't consume until he was in his 40s.

Fourth in the Order:
Right-Hander Kyle Kendrick, 11-9, 5.49

Kyle Kendrick worked his way through a thoroughly unimpressive minor league career where he went 32-61. In 2007, however, Kyle posted a 10-4 record in the majors, the best winning percentage he had at any level of baseball. What was that all about? Kendrick had his problems with consistency in 2008. Although he pulled in 11 wins, third highest on the squad, his ERA bulged to 5.49. He returned a couple of times to assist in instrumental games, but was left off the postseason roster.

Fifth in the Order:
Right-Hander Joe Blanton, 4-0, 4.20

The Phils picked up ace Oakland pitcher Joe Blanton to fill in for the collapse of Adam Eaton during an Athletics fire sale. Blanton had come up through the A's organization, winning 12 with a 3.54 ERA in his rookie year of 2005. He won 30 more games over his next two seasons, leading the league in starts in 2007 with 34. Joe quickly made his presence known in Philadelphia, never losing a game in his 13 starts. Posting a 4-0 regular season record, Joe was just setting the table for what was to come in the playoffs.

The Closer:
Right-Hander Brad "Lights Out" Lidge, 1.95, 41 Saves

Sometimes Brad Lidge needed the fine glove of Jimmy Rollins or Chase Utley to steal a hit with runners in scoring position, but you can't argue with perfection. And that's what Lidge had in 2008. Given 41 save opportunities during the regular season, he saved 41, striking out 95 in only 69 innings. Lidge finished fourth in the Cy Young balloting and eighth in the vote for Most Valuable Player.

Brad Lidge was a gorgeous thing to watch, especially when he'd get that slider going for him, which picks up speed as it moves down and away. It's a perfect complement to his four-seam fastball, which clocks in at 92 miles per hour. Carlos Ruiz is able to play the pitches perfectly, never telegraphing that he might soon have to be scrambling for that outside slider. Lidge never seems disturbed, even under the most trying of circumstances, perhaps because he learned how to deal with adversity from the beginning. Coming up with the Houston Astros in 2002, he proceeded to miss all or part of each of his first four seasons, due to a torn rotator cuff, a broken arm, and a strained rib cage.

Lidge became a closer in 2004, and earned his nickname "Lights Out" when he set a National League record for relievers with 157 strikeouts. And then disaster struck. The Astros were coasting in their National League Championship Series against the St. Louis Cardinals, leading the series 3-1, and the game was 4-2 in the ninth. The Houston fans were all on their feet, expecting to see the team's first-ever World Series appearance. The anticipation only grew wilder as Lidge recorded the first two outs, then the first two strikes on David Eckstein. But Eckstein stroked a single, and Jim Edmonds followed with a walk. Lidge then served up a fastball to Albert Pujols, who smashed the pitch off the roof of Minute Maid Park. The Cardinals won the game, and Brad lost some of his confidence. Make that a lot of his confidence. His 2006 ERA skyrocketed to 5.28. The Astros delegated him to middle relief in 2007, and traded him to Philadelphia for Michael Bourn at season's end. Lidge responded with one of the most dominant seasons ever for a relief pitcher, winning Comeback Player of the Year, the DHL Delivery Man of the Year, the Philadelphia Sports Writers Association's Outstanding Athlete of the Year, and—oh, yeah—the World Series.

And the Rest

Right-hander Ryan Madson, who had been touted as one of the best arms in the organization since 2004, finally found his home in 2008 as the eighth-inning bridge to Brad Lidge. With his place in the order solidified, Madson actually saw his fastball increase in speed, now jacking up to 97 m.p.h., a nice complement to his out pitch: the change-up. His 3.05 ERA of this season is among his best.

Right-hander Chad Durbin (5-4, 2.87) provided middle and long relief for the club. A journeyman reliever who had fared poorly in his last few years, Chad made quite an impact on the squad when picked up as a free agent for the 2008 season. Turning in the best season of his career, Durbin became one of the go-to guys on the squad.

Left-hander J.C. Romero had been languishing on the verge of retirement when the Phils signed the 31-year-old on as a free agent in 2007. Romero then lifted the Phils pen with an impeccable 1.24 ERA that year, and proceeded to lead the '08 team with 81 appearances, while collecting a 2.75 ERA.

Phillies Memory

Stef Bingham, Philadelphia Special Studies Teacher

My family and I are huge Philadelphia sports fans. Looking back at the 2008 season, there is one memory that stands out the most. There were five people living in the Bingham household: my father and mother (both 53), my brother (20), my grandmother (83), and me (22). We would often gather during the regular season to watch the games and cheer on our team. I remember as the Phils got closer to clinching the division and then finally gained the playoffs, our hearts would pound more and more each game.

When the Phillies started the championship series, my family and I started watching the games out on the deck together. We developed a ritual during game one of the championship series. We all had white rally towels that we would wave in the air while screaming at the television. We watched every game together with our towels. We, as a family, had such a wonderful and exciting time watching the Phillies take control and finally win the World Series that year. It brought our family closer together and gave us such wonderful memories.

The Season

The Phils had played miraculously well the last several years, especially down the stretch. But it was no secret that they'd been slow from the starting gate for a very long time. The last time they'd had a winning record in April was back in 2003 in the days of Omar Daal and Larry Bowa. Since then, they'd gone 10-11 (2004), 10-14 (2005), 10-14 (2006), and 11-14 (2007). Shane Victorino and Jimmy Rollins both went down to injury, but Pat "The Bat" Burrell came out alive, chasing 25 RBI, and Chase Utley led the league in homers with 11 while hitting at a .360 clip on his way to winning Player of the Month. More importantly, the team went 15-13, tied with the Mets, only a half game behind the first-place Marlins. I know it might not sound like the record is that awesome, but for this very reason, the Phils did not have to claw their way back into the race as they usually did; for this reason, they had more in the tank for the playoffs; for this reason alone, perhaps, they became champions of the world for only the second time in their long history.

Utley cooled off in May, but Jayson Werth stepped up to command a starter's assignment. Ryan Howard picked himself up out of an early slump, while J-Roll and Victorino returned from injury. The Phils paced the Marlins with a 17-10 May, remaining a half game out while the Mets, at .500, sat four games back. The Phils' 12-14 June does not quite reveal the turbulent nature of the club's play. Though they opened the month well, going 9-3, they lost 11 of their last 14 games. It was the month that saw Brett Myers fall back to the minor leagues; it was the month that saw Adam Eaton fall from any possibility of grace, and a month that saw a team-high six-game losing streak. Somehow through all of this, the Phillies claimed first place, finishing June half a game ahead of the Marlins and three and a half games ahead of the rival Mets, who had fallen to two games below .500.

The Phils righted the ship by the All-Star Break, but the Mets had caught fire, chasing us down to within half a game. On July 17, with our rotation hurting, we traded for Oakland ace Joe Blanton. Joe made his mark immediately by starting the Phils' only victory in a three-game series with the Mets that concluded with the New Yorkers reclaiming first place in the National League East. We had worked back into a one-game lead over the Mets by the end of the month, a game and a half over the Marlins, thanks to a fine 15-10 July record. But we all knew this one was again going to go down to the wire.

The Phillies bookended their 16-13 August with four-game sweeps involving the Los Angeles Dodgers. We were swept by them when the Phils visited LA at the outset of the month, and then we returned the favor when we hosted the Dodgers at the end. August ended with the Phils a full game behind our New York rivals—the Marlins by this time a distant seven back, barely a game over .500. This was going to be the usual two-team race.

After the Phils dropped a series to the Marlins, ending on September 10, they looked up to see that their slow start in the final month had left them three and a half games behind the red-hot Mets. But we rallied for seven straight victories, including a four-game sweep of the Brewers and a three-game sweep of the Braves. Waking up on September 26, the Phils found themselves in a position to clinch the division, leading by two games with two games to play.

It was a historic game in many respects. Clinging to a 4-2 lead in the top of the ninth, the Phils trotted Brad Lidge out to the mound. We all dreaded this moment. In so many ways, we had wished that Brad would have blown a save earlier in the year, say in the month of May or June when it wouldn't have merited even a footnote. We'd known throughout the season that the man couldn't remain perfect. He played for Philly, after all. We had hoped that that first blown save wouldn't come in some crucial game—like this one.

With one out, Brad allowed a ground ball single through to right field, then walked the next batter to put the tying runs on base. Nationals second baseman Anderson Hernandez then hit a short fly that fell between The Flyin' Hawaiian and Jayson Werth to bring a runner around. One out. Runners on first and second: 4-3 Phils. Lidge looking for perfection. When shortstop Cristian Guzman ripped a single to center, it seemed all but over, but Shane Victorino fielded cleanly, held the runner at third, and kept the game knotted. Still, we all knew what would happen next. We'd known it all year. Brad just didn't have it today. He'd faced five batters; four had gotten on, and the powerful Ryan Zimmerman was striding to the plate.

When Zimmerman ripped the next pitch up the middle, it was a relief of sorts. Perfection was over. Now we'd all be more at ease in the playoffs when Lidge would take the mound. Then, just as I was formulating my rationalization, out of nowhere Jimmy Rollins dove, gloved the ball, and flipped it quickly to Utley on second; he turned it to Howard to complete the double play. And the victory. And the save. And perfection. And the division title. For the second year in a row.

As for the Mets, they'd drop two of their last three games to lose the Wild Card to the Milwaukee Brewers. They would have to sit at home for the playoffs again, which, as any Phillies fan knows, is just as triumphant an outcome as winning the division ourselves.

THE 2008 NATIONAL LEAGUE DIVISION SERIES

The Milwaukee Brewers were advancing to the playoffs for the first time since 1982 when they lost the World Series to the St. Louis Cardinals. Only two weeks prior, the Brewers had just done something historic. With 12 games remaining, they sat atop the Wild Card standings, second in their division, and they fired their manager. Ned Yost was suddenly out of a job. Visions of Pat Corrales, fired as manager of the 1983 Phillies when they themselves were in first, wafted through the mind. Dale Sveum took over, led the Brew Club to a 7-5 finish, and took the Wild Card over the Mets.

This wasn't the biggest "Brew move" of the season, however. That had come on July 7, when they traded with the Indians for CC Sabathia. Sabathia turned the team from a contender to a force, going 11-2 with a 1.65 ERA, enough to get him recognized in both the Cy Young and MVP voting, even though he played less than half his games in the National League. The left-handed Sabathia was complemented by right-handed Ben Sheets (13-9, 3.09). Their power came from Prince Fielder (34 HR, 102 RBI) and Ryan Braun (37 HR, 106 RBI). They had plenty of speed as well with Corey Hart (23 SB), Rickie Weeks (19 SB), and Mike Cameron (17 SB).

Game One

Wednesday, October 1 (Citizens Bank Park)

Cole Hamels started his historic playoff run with eight innings of two-hit shutout ball, while the Phillies scored all of their three runs in the third inning—two unearned. After an error by Brewers second baseman Rickie Weeks put runners on first and second, Chase Utley hit a two-out, two-run double, then scored on a bases-loaded walk to Shane Victorino. Brad Lidge continued to walk the tightrope in the ninth inning. After wild pitching runners to second and third with one out, he managed to strike out both Prince Fielder and Corey Hart to end the game. And with that the Phils had taken their first playoff game since 1993.

Game Two

Thursday, October 2 (Citizens Bank Park)

This was the game that cemented the Phils as a team of destiny. Facing the powerful CC Sabathia, they knew they would have to scrape and clutch for every hit they could muster. And if a run crossed (perhaps two), they would consider themselves lucky and hope that their pitching, in the Jekyll-and-Hyde form of Brett Myers, would shine. One thing going for us was the fact that CC's start had been pushed up a day. This was only a Best-of-Five series after all, and Dale Sveum didn't want to fall behind 2-0. Sabathia had proven very effective on three days' rest many times before, but you had to begin questioning how much endurance the man could muster. He'd started three times in the last eight games of the Brewers' stretch run. This would mark

CC's fourth start in their last 10 games. The strain began to show early.

In the second inning, with the Brewers ahead 1-0, Sabathia allowed back-to-back doubles to Jayson Werth and Pedro Feliz to tie the game. Then after recording the second out of the inning, he faced off against Brett Myers. Even for a pitcher, Myers was a poor hitter. He'd hit only .069 in 2008, which was actually an improvement over the season before, when he'd managed to hit a spectacular zero. Sabathia looked to be out of the inning with minimal damage.

After getting ahead of Myers 1-2, however, something very strange happened. Brett Myers turned into the reincarnation of one Ty Cobb. Myers proceeded to foul off pitch after pitch after pitch. Sabathia would lace one fastball after a curve after a fastball after a curve, but Myers was tenacious. He worked an 11-pitch walk that clearly unnerved the dominating left-hander. After that, Sabathia walked Jimmy Rollins to load the bases, then hung one up to Shane Victorino that he took out of the park for the Phillies' first grand slam in their postseason history. The Phils had suddenly gone from a scrappy club fighting for each run they could earn, and even unearn, to a team that had just crushed the most dominant pitcher in the game. And all thanks to the unlikely bat of one Brett Myers.

The Fightin's wouldn't score another run in this game, but they wouldn't need to. Myers went seven strong, allowing only two more hits the rest of the way. And this time, with a 5-2 ninth-inning lead, Brad Lidge retired the Brewers in order. It was his second save in as many games.

Game Three
Saturday, October 4 (Miller Park)

With their back to the wall, the Brew Crew pushed across two first-inning runs against Jamie Moyer. The Phils, meanwhile, could do little against Brewers starter Dave Bush. Trailing 4-1, they managed to put a little scare into Milwaukee when they loaded the bases with no one out, but Salmon Torres coaxed Pedro Feliz into a groundout double play, then caused Carlos Ruiz to ground to the mound.

Game Four

Sunday, October 5 (Miller Park)

With CC Sabathia waiting in the wings for game five, the Brewers sent out Jeff Suppan (10-10, 4.96) to try to keep their season alive. Jimmy Rollins wanted nothing to do with that, and made it known in only the sixth pitch of the ballgame, which he skyrocketed into the bleacher seats. The Phils never looked back. Pat Burrell hit a three-run homer in the fourth, followed by a solo shot from Jayson Werth to give our boys a 5-0 lead. Burrell then capped the scoring with his second homer of the game, this one a solo shot in the eighth.

Joe Blanton continued his unbeaten streak in Philadelphia, nailing down his first postseason win for the club, his fifth overall, as he went six innings of one-run work. Brad Lidge came into the ninth inning in a non-save situation to nail down the victory. The Phils had triumphed against a strong opponent. They'd gotten their first taste of playoff victory and clearly wanted more. For that, though, they'd have to face the surging Los Angeles Dodgers.

THE 2008 NATIONAL LEAGUE CHAMPIONSHIP SERIES

On July 31, the Dodgers were only playing .500 ball and sitting in second place in the National League West. They knew they had to do something to kick the team into gear, and something is what they did. A major something. They picked up Manny Ramirez in a three-team deal with the Red Sox and the Pirates. Then, behind him, they began setting the baseball world on fire. In just two months of play, Manny hit .396 for his new club, while bringing in 56 RBI, and slugging 17 homers and 14 doubles. He had an on-base percentage of .489 and a slugging average of .743. Despite the fact that Ramirez played in less than half of the National League season, he ended up fourth in the voting for MVP honors as he led the team to the National League West title by two games over the Diamondbacks, and then a series sweep over the much-vaunted Cubs.

The Dodgers also featured the power of James Loney (90 RBI) and André Ethier (20 home runs), to go along with the speed of Juan Pierre (.283, 40 SB) and Matt Kemp (.290, 35 SB, 93 R). Their pitching staff was led by Derek Lowe (14-11, 3.24) and Chad Billingsley (16-10, 3.14), while the tandem of Takashi Saito (2.49, 18 saves) and Jonathan Broxton (3.13, 14 saves) closed their games. The Phils and Dodgers had split their season series, each team sweeping a four-game set at home. The Phils, however, would get the home field advantage, thanks to a better overall record (92 wins to 84). This would be the first postseason meeting for these clubs since the Phils had edged them 3-1 in the NLCS of 1983.

Game One

Thursday, October 9 (Citizens Bank Park)

Manny Ramirez came out bombing in the first inning, barely missing a home run to dead center, the ball bounding off the top of the wall; his double, however, scored the first run of the game against starter Cole Hamels. Meanwhile Dodger ace Derek Lowe looked on top of his game, coasting into the bottom of the sixth with a four-hit shutout, the Dodgers leading 2-0. After an error by shortstop Rafael Furcal put Shane Victorino on first, Chase Utley powered a two-run homer to tie the game. One out later Pat Burrell smacked a line drive over the left field fence to give the Phils a lead of 3-2. Brad Lidge came on into the ninth for an oddly uneventful 1-2-3 inning to give the Phils the game-one victory. It was his third save of the postseason, and the second win for Cole Hamels in as many tries.

Game Two

Friday, October 10 (Citizens Bank Park)

The second game looked ominous right from the start. Just before the outset, manager Charlie Manuel learned that his mother had passed away. Just after that, Shane Victorino learned that his grandmother had done the same. The Phils were quick to dispel these demons, however, as they knocked Dodger starter Chad Billingsley off the mound in the third inning, batting around in the second and third while scoring four runs apiece in each frame. The surprising offensive star was again Bret Myers, who went three for three, with three runs batted in.

Manny Ramirez tried single-handedly to power the Dodgers back into it when he clubbed a three-run shot in the fourth to make the score 8-5. Casey Blake nearly did the same in the seventh when he launched a gargantuan shot that would have tied the game, if Shane Victorino had not made a spectacular catch, smiling the entire way. The Phils again turned to Brad Lidge to hold down the save in the ninth. It only became a save situation after he walked the tying run to the plate. Still, he'd now saved his fourth of the Phils' five victories in the playoffs and had not yet allowed a run. It was long past eerie.

Game Three

Sunday, October 12 (Dodger Stadium)

The Dodgers torched Phils starter Jamie Moyer for five runs in the first inning, then knocked him out with another in the second for a 6-0 lead. Not all the fireworks came from the Dodger bats, however. One very significant one came from a Hiroki Kuroda fastball thrown over the head of Shane Victorino in the third inning. This was apparently in retaliation for the several times that Phillies pitchers had either thrown too close or hit Dodger batters. The benches cleared. No punches were thrown, however, and play resumed without anyone being tossed out of the game. Still, both teams had been alerted. This was no longer a series; this was a war. The Dodgers took the game easily, 7-2, and stood within a game of tying the Phils in the series.

Game Four

Monday, October 13 (Dodger Stadium)

This was the game that would make journeyman Matt Stairs, who had only accumulated 19 regular season at-bats for the Phils, into a household name. The clubs traded runs, chasing starters Joe Blanton and Derek Lowe from the mound, to take the game tied 3-3 into the bottom of the sixth. Then, thanks to a Casey Blake homer and a Ryan Howard error, the Dodgers plated two to grasp a 5-3 advantage. When they loaded the bases with one out against Scott Eyre, they looked to blow the game wide open.

Catcher Russell Martin then hit a screaming line drive off reliever Ryan Madson that looked like it would go through the middle to score at least two more. However, at full extension, Chase Utley made an unbelievable catch, and then, barely keeping his balance, he stumbled over to second to make the unassisted double play. Even though the Phils still trailed by two, the momentum had clearly shifted. Shane Victorino served notice of that fact with a two-run line drive homer that barely cleared the wall in left to tie the game. One out later, with another runner on first, Matt Stairs took a Jonathan Broxton fastball long into the night. The ball was gone half a moment after it touched the bat, as Stairs hit the most dramatic home run of his career to give the Phils a come-from-behind 7-5 lead.

Charlie Manuel went to his closer with two outs in the eighth to face Manny Ramirez. No runners were on, but Ramirez was lethal, and if you're going to face their best, you had to send in your own. Ramirez won the battle with a double to center. Brad Lidge struck out Russell Martin to follow, which should have ended the inning, but the pitch got away from Carlos Ruiz, sending Martin scampering to first and Ramirez to third. The tying runs were on. The save was once more in jeopardy. Lidge didn't blink, however. After coaxing James Loney to pop out to left to end the inning, he went through the ninth with relative ease to give the Phils a come-from-behind victory and a 3-1 lead in the series.

Game Five

Wednesday, October 15 (Dodger Stadium)

The Phils took the Dodgerland fans immediately out of the game when Jimmy Rollins led off the contest with a home run. Philly would score two more in the third inning to chase Dodger starter Chad Billingsley from the mound, and add another two in the fifth, thanks in large part to three errors by Dodger shortstop Rafael Furcal. Series MVP Cole Hamels didn't need as many as that, as he went seven innings to nail down his second win of the NLCS. His only mishap was to allow a tremendous solo shot from Manny Ramirez in the seventh. But you gotta forgive that. Brad Lidge naturally came on in the ninth to retire the Dodgers and give the Phillies their first World Series berth in 15 years.

Phillies Memory

Henry Hunt, Lifetime Fan of 31 Years

It was hard having your favorite team, your home team, be the laughingstock of major league baseball most of your life. We did have that magical 1993 season that was quickly forgotten when that ball went over that left field wall. For the most part it was losing season after losing season. Then the diehards like myself really had something to talk about in '06 and '07. "This team has got some great young talent. They are going to be NL East contenders next year."

Once '08 got started, you knew there was something about this group of guys. They were electric! It seemed as though every week they were doing something magical. Whether it was a ninth-inning rally or dominant pitching from your homegrown (Hamels) or hometown boy (Moyer).

That magic never stopped once the Fall Classic got here. I can still remember running through a crowd of fans looking for a friend to celebrate Shane's grand slam against the almighty CC. The only time I ever worried that fall was in the Dodgers series when they were trailing late in the game. Thankfully, another small-time guy (Stairs) came through and hit a ball that I'm not sure has even landed yet. I don't think there is a Phillies fan on the planet that wouldn't buy Matt Stairs a beer if they saw him out on the town.

My most memorable moment of the season came at Game Five of the World Series; I knew that night was the night. If Blanton is hitting home runs in the World Series, your team is destined to win. I just wanted to be down there to finally storm up Broad Street after 28 years of losing. The line for McFadden's was about 10,000 deep. No shot my fiancée and I were getting in there.

Then all of a sudden, as we are walking back to the car to go somewhere else, I feel a guy grab my arm. He asked if I had tickets and I said, "Nah, sorry!" He then asked if I'd like to go to the game. I asked, "How much?" I was thinking he would have some insane price that I couldn't afford.

He replied. "Free!" Of course like any other Philadelphian, I snickered and said, "Yeah, right. Free!" Turns out he was a businessman from New York and his clients bailed on him. He ended up walking us through the gates with his tickets. I grabbed my fiancée in a hug of excitement once we got through the gates. I turned to thank this stranger only to find that he was gone.

As we all know, the magic continued. Charlie kept calling all the right numbers. The runs scored and we were ahead. It was time to put the 'lights out' on these Rays. Lidge threw that nasty sinker and that golden voice of Harry Kalas let all of Philadelphia know that "The Philadelphia Phillies are the 2008 World Champions of Baseball!"

THE 2008 WORLD SERIES

Let's not kid ourselves here. We may have won our league, but Tampa was the nation's darling. The Rays had finished in last every season but one of their entire existence. The season before, the club threw a party because they had managed to win 66 games. The 2008 squad, however, miraculously won the American League East title in a seesaw battle with the Yankees and the Red Sox. They would have to defeat the Sox again in the ALCS in a blisteringly hard-fought 4-3 series.

The Rays had it all this year. Their power came from Carlos Peña (31 HR, 102 RBI) and Evan Longoria (27 HR, 85 RBI); their speed from BJ Upton (44 SB, 85 R), Carl Crawford (25 SB), and Jason Bartlett (20 SB). Their staff featured the likes of James Shields (14-8, 3.56), Andy Sonnanstine (13-9, 4.38), Matt Garza (11-9, 3.70), Edwin Jackson (14-11, 3.42), and their only starting lefty, Scott Kazmir (12-8, 3.49). They worked a few closers during the year, in Troy Percival (4.53, 28 saves) and Dan Wheeler (3.12, 13 saves), but of late they had been turning to late-season callup David Price (1.90). The Rays would receive home field advantage since the American League had won the All-Star Game this season, 4-3.

Game One

Wednesday, October 22 (Tropicana Field)

The opener at Tropicana Field would pit the Phillies' emergent superstar, Cole Hamels, against the Rays' Scott Kazmir. Philly jumped on Kazmir early, when Chase Utley hit a one-out homer in the top of the first inning. When we loaded the bases in the top of the second with only one out, things looked even more hopeful, especially with our man-in-the-clutch, Jimmy Rollins, at the plate. However, Rollins lofted a medium fly to center, which Shane Victorino decided to try to score on, only to be thrown out at the plate.

After Carlos Ruiz grounded home Victorino in the fourth to make the score 3-0, the Rays began to claw their way back. Adding single runs—in the fourth on a Carl Crawford solo homer and in the fifth on an Akinori Iwamura double—they pulled to within a digit. The Phils tried to give Cole Hamels some insurance, but left a runner on in the sixth, two in the seventh, and runners on second and third in the ninth. And then on came Lights Out Lidge, who quite simply turned the lights out: strike out, strike out, pop foul to third.

Game One was over, and we'd already stolen one in Tampa. Cole Hamels (4-0, 1.55) had already tied a record for the most wins ever for a pitcher in a postseason performance, and Brad Lidge—well, people were starting to think that maybe he was, in a word, perfect.

Game Two

Thursday, October 23 (Tropicana Field)

The Dr. Brett and Mr. Myers show came to Tampa for Game Two. And the Rays were glad to have front row seats. They took Myers for two runs in the first, another in the second, and another in the fourth to give them a healthy 4-0 lead behind hot hand starter James Shields. It's not that they were hitting Myers hard. Three of the four runs scored on groundouts. However, Myers kept allowing those pesky lead runners to get on, and, with the speed of those young Rays, they were quick to take advantage of any ball hit in the infield.

The Phils were unable to score until the eighth inning, when none other than Eric Bruntlett hit a solo shot. After Carlos Ruiz came around to score in the ninth, the Phils brought the tying run to the plate with only one out. With Chase Utley and Ryan Howard due to come up and fate clearly moving into the Phillies clubhouse, the faithful thought that maybe...just maybe. But David Price struck out Utley, then got Howard to ground out to end the inning and the ballgame. Destiny forestalled. Still, we had to consider ourselves more than lucky. We would be coming home to Philly with the Series tied at one.

Game Three

Saturday, October 25 (Citizens Bank Park)

The rains bucketed down on Philadelphia over the weekend, delaying Game Three for an hour and a half before country singer Tim McGraw, the son of the Tugger, walked onto the field to spread his father's ashes on the pitcher's mound. It was a great tribute to a great man, the last to stand on the mound when the Phils won their only World Series. The fans desperately hoped he would be here now for another.

Jamie Moyer, who had allowed six runs in just over an inning in his only outing in the NLCS, took the mound for the Phillies against the Rays' Matt Garza, who had won Most Valuable Player in the ALCS with a 2-0 record and a 1.38 ERA. The temperamental Garza seemed to react poorly to the lusty Philadelphia crowd and, like Burt Hooton many years before, got a little wild in response. After allowing a hit to Jimmy Rollins, he walked Jayson Werth and then threw a wild pitch to put runners into scoring position. Utley then grounded in the Phils' first run of the game.

After the Rays tied the game in the top of the second, thanks to a double by Carl Crawford, the Phillies bounced right back on the wings of Mr. October himself, Carlos Ruiz, who crushed a fastball from Garza out of the park. The Phils added two more in the sixth when Chase Utley and Ryan Howard started the inning with back-to-back homers, and suddenly we'd pulled ahead, 4-1. Things looked stellar. But the Rays would chase Moyer from the mound in the seventh, when they scored two runs on two hits. They would tie the game in the eighth inning, when BJ Upton singled off Ryan Madson, then proceeded to steal second and third, scoring when Ruiz overthrew an attempted pickoff.

The game tied at four, the Series tied at one. It was the bottom of the ninth, and you would think the Phils were spending the day at the beach. Jimmy Rollins looked like he'd just come into a surprise party. Shane Victorino was laughing in the dugout. Jayson Werth was trying to find the best vantage point to mob the winning runner as he crossed the plate. After Eric

Bruntlett coaxed a walk to lead off the inning, he proceeded to second on a wild pitch, then to third on a throwing error. No outs. Any ball hit out of the infield could win us the game. Rays reliever Grant Balfour had no choice but to set up the force, and so he intentionally walked Shane Victorino and Greg Dobbs to load the bases.

The Rays maneuvered in Ben Zobrist from right field to act as a fifth infielder as Grant Balfour set to face Carlos Ruiz. Balfour came in with a fastball, Ruiz swung with all his might, and got barely none of it. The ball went about 45 feet on a short pop. Third baseman Evan Longoria rushed in, stabbed at the ball barehanded, brought it up as it bounded off the turf, and tried to wing it home in one motion, but the ball would have none of it. Carlos Ruiz had hit the first walkoff single in World Series history, and the Phils had taken a 2-1 lead.

Game Four

Sunday, October 26 (Citizens Bank Park)

Later that same day, the Phillies and Rays came out under the threatening Philadelphia skies for a pivotal Game Four. This time, it really wasn't much of a contest. The Phils crushed the Rays 10-2 behind Ryan Howard, who hit two home runs (a three-runner in the fourth and a two-runner in the eighth), and Jayson Werth, who crushed a two-run homer himself in the eighth. For Joe Blanton, it was a historic day. He not only notched his sixth win against no defeats as a Phillie (2-0 in the playoffs), but hit a solo shot in the bottom of the fifth. It was the first home run by a pitcher since Ken Holtzman achieved the feat for the Oakland A's back in 1974. It was Blanton's first home run since high school. As the game concluded, putting the Phils within one game of winning their first World Series in 28 years, the rains began to fall, offering a portent of things to come.

Game Five, Part One

Monday, October 27 (Citizens Bank Park)

A good friend of mine, Brian LaTroy, had enjoyed one of the best summers of his life in 2008. He and his nine-year-old son Jerry had grown exceptionally close through the tried-and-true, time-honored experience of baseball. They traveled to Citizens Bank Park 22 times during the course of the season, little Jerry thrilling to each impossible victory, agonizing at every loss, and hoping with the wide-open eyes of youth. Jerry wore the same beat-up cap his father bought him for Christmas to every game. He put it on at breakfast, and grudgingly took it off every night. He knew for a fact that the Phillies couldn't possibly win if he didn't have it on. And now the Phils were on the doorstep, just like he knew they would be. They had a 3-1 lead in the Series and were bringing the unbeatable Cole Hamels to the mound. Even better than that, Dad had tickets to the game.

Lightning like this doesn't strike twice. Every boy gets one nine-year-old summer. Every boy gets one summer when he experiences the game with his dad for the first time. And if he's lucky, he might just see the Phils do well. If he's very lucky, he might just see them make a run at the pennant. If the stars just happen to be in the right alignment, which apparently only happens in Philadelphia twice every 126 years, he might even see the Phillies win a World Series.

This just happened to be the year when everything went right, save for Jerry, who went to bed feeling rather ill on the 26th, and when he woke, laid claim to a 104-degree fever, a bad cough, and the shakes. Unlike most nine-year-old boys, however, Jerry leapt out of bed, got dressed, and tried to dash out of the house to the bus before his mom could tell he was sick. There was no way he was going to miss this game. There was also no way that a mother could miss this kind of sickness. She pulled him back before he even got to the door, felt his forehead, and sent him to bed. Dad called in sick himself to sit beside his boy. He gave him something for the fever, let him sleep, and hoped that he'd be better in time for the game. When Jerry woke at noon, he felt a little better. He could go, he said. It didn't matter that the late-October temperature was dropping steadily. It didn't matter that the weathermen were calling for a chillingly cold rain. He was fine. He could do this.

Such thoughts were ridiculous and the dad knew it. Sure, they could keep that fever under control if Jerry stayed home. But if he went to the park, he might just end up going to the hospital. The one summer that every nine-year-old gets was over. And so was the chance that those stars that have aligned only twice in franchise history were indeed aligning for him. Jerry insisted that his dad go to the game. He wanted a program, some souvenir to say that somehow he'd been a part of this event. So, with a heavy heart and an extra ticket that he refused to use, Dad set off to see Game Five of the 2008 World Series.

With the skies overcast and rain threatening, the two clubs considered postponing the game, but with the Philly forecast calling for extended days of rain, and neither club particularly wanting to play baseball in November, the game got under way at 8:30 p.m. Scott Kazmir took the mound for the Rays. If he could throw the kind of gem he'd grown accustomed to through his young career, he could change this momentum around, and bring the Series back to Tropicana Field. The Phillies didn't seem intimidated, though, and for the third time in as many games, they jumped ahead in the very first inning. Kazmir was atypically wild, walking the bases loaded with two outs, before Shane Victorino lined a single to left that brought home Jayson Werth and Chase Utley.

Most of Philadelphia figured that this should have been enough. Hell, we had Cole Hamels on the mound. It was doubtful the guy even needed two runs. It seemed, at least for a while, that we were right. Hamels went through the first three innings, the only blemish coming on a ground ball single. He seemed totally on top of his game, until the rains began to come down...heavily. The umpires were reluctant to call the game. It's not as if play could be resumed when the skies cleared up later that evening. It was just going to get worse. So they decided, much as they did in Game Four of the 1977 World Series, to let the game play out.

Cole Hamels began to have trouble gripping the ball, and any bouncer to the turf led to a water polo event. In the fourth inning, still trailing 2-0, Rays first baseman Carlos Peña lofted a one-out double, his first hit of the Series. Evan Longoria squirted a grounder that sprayed its way past Utley and Rollins to bring Peña sloshing into home for the first Rays run of the game. It marked Longoria's first hit of the Series as well.

Going into the top of the sixth, the Phils still clung to that 2-1 lead, but the storm was starting to get out of hand. The infield a pool. The outfield a sea. The ball as difficult to grasp as a seal.

But still the game went on. Hamels swept the rainwater from his eyes and managed the first two outs of the inning, but then BJ Upton pounded a ball into the depths of the infield. Rollins couldn't quite dog-paddle over to make the play, leaving the tying run on first. And then it got rather comical. Upton stole second in such a blinding storm that when he slid, you couldn't even see the play through the wave that his spikes kicked up.

Carlos Peña tied the game with a line drive single into the tsunami, and everyone started to get scared. The lights were barely cutting their way through the flood. People feared that a rogue wave could sweep them away at any time. Hamels reared back and hurled a ball toward home that someone must have seen, but certainly not the batter and certainly not Carlos Ruiz. The ball squirted to the backstop while Peña alerted to second with the go-ahead run.

When Evan Longoria mercifully flied out to center to end the inning, the umpires called it. They didn't pause for a rain delay. They simply suspended the game. They didn't have any choice. Utley told reporters afterward that "the infield was basically underwater." It was the first World Series game in history that had ever been suspended. And in the middle of the night, Jerry's fever finally broke. In two days' time, he felt well enough to attend the rest of Game Five.

Game Five, Part Two
Wednesday, October 29 (Citizens Bank Park)

The rains receded in a couple of days, allowing play to resume in the bottom of the sixth, and Phillies fans felt nervous. We had believed the Series was in the bag on Monday, what with Cole Hamels and the momentum, what with a quick lead and the home crowd behind us. But then the rains came and now—well, we just figured things might go wrong. But Geoff Jenkins, pinch-hitting for Hamels to lead off the second half of the game, roped a double to center off Rays reliever Grant Balfour. Jimmy Rollins sacrificed him over to third, and Jayson Werth singled him home to (just that quickly) put the Phils back in the driver's seat. We couldn't hold that lead for long, however. In the top of the seventh, Rays right fielder Rocco Baldelli smoked a solo shot off Phils reliever Ryan Madson to tie the game.

Going into the bottom of the seventh, with the game remaining tied, Pat Burrell took a few swings from the batter's circle. Pat, as we all know, had been through the ups and downs of many a Philly player before him. He'd endured the wrath and the praise, the despair and the fulfillment. This postseason had displayed these swings in miniature. He'd led the team with homers and runs batted in during the NLDS, led the team in average with a .333 during the NLCS, but was having a miserable World Series. He'd come up to bat 13 times and gotten exactly no hits. In addition, we all knew that this at-bat would more than likely be Pat's last. He was in the final season of his contract, and even though the Phils would have the opportunity to sign him in the off-season, talks had broken off long ago. Good ol' Pat would be taking his very last swing in his nine-year Phillies career.

Facing Rays reliever J.P. Howell, Pat stung a fastball that immediately sent the cameras popping. It lifted high into the right field lights, over the outstretched glove of Rocco Baldelli, and banged up against the top of the right field wall. Pat Burrell stood proudly on second as the potential winning run of the World Series. Eric Bruntlett came out to pinch-run for Burrell, who jogged off the field, received a couple of claps on the back, a high five or three, before he took a seat on the bench. His career as a Phillie was over, but not before single-handedly, here in the seventh inning, taking us to the doorstep of victory. One out later, Pedro Feliz roped a single to right to score Bruntlett (and Pat) to put the boys back ahead, 5-4. And, by the way, that was Feliz's last at-bat for the Phils as well.

Uncle Charlie would turn to none other than Lights Out Lidge for the ninth. You could hear the stadium explode in cheers, but in the back of any superstitious fan came the additional rumble of "Oh, shit!" Lidge had saved 41 games in 41 opportunities during the regular season. He'd gotten two chances in the NLDS and done the same; three more in the NLCS, and he had saved one thus far in the World Series. Right now, Lights Out came into the ninth inning with a perfect 47 for 47.

The inning started tamely enough as Brad coaxed Evan Longoria to pop out Chase Utley, ending Longoria's series at a miserable 1 for 20 (a .050 batting average). He tossed his helmet away and groaned back to the dugout. Rays catcher Dioner

Navarro was determined not to let things end so meekly, how-ever, as he punched a single into right. Fernando Perez replaced the slow-of-foot Navarro at first and promptly stole second to put the tying run, the streak-ending run, into scoring position. It's just never easy, is it?

Ben Zobrist came on to pinch-hit for Rocco Baldelli, and promptly smacked a sinking liner to Jayson Werth. Werth stabbed the ball out of the air and threw to second on a rope to keep the tying run 120 feet from the plate. Two outs. And then Lidge was set against pinch hitter Eric Hinske. A starter for much of the season, Hinske had only gotten one at-bat in the World Series. It just so happened to be a home run off Joe Blan-ton in Game Five. Lidge bore down on Hinske, getting two quick strikes; then, with Perez taunting off second, Hinske lifted the bat to his shoulder, Carlos Ruiz set up low and outside, and Brad Lidge let fly his sinker—the one that had struck out 92 batters in the regular season, another 11 in the post. Hinske swung hard just as the ball broke down and in, grabbing at the dirt. Ruiz gloved it. Strike three. Lidge fell down on his knees, and the players flew toward him.

We'd won the World Series. The 2008 World Series. And we'd done it behind a perfect season by Brad Lidge, a heroic last bat from Pat Burrell, and a coming-of-age star turn by Cole Hamels. But all of that paled before what was going on in Sec-tion 224, seats 132 and 130, where a father and a son who'd been through the entire season together, leapt into each other's arms, relishing in a moment that comes just once in a lifetime—and only when the stars align just perfectly for a boy in his ninth year of life.

Phillies Memory

Frank Paul "The Ball" Petrash, Shortstop

The Phillies wrapped up their three-day, series-winning game on Wednesday, October 29, 2008; the ensuing 72 hours were the best in my life. For me it began at Tavern on Broad; I ran out of the bar quicker than Chooch ran into the arms of Brad Lidge. That night, everyone in Philadelphia was best friends. After innumerable, emphatic embraces I had with fellow anonymous Philly denizens, I watched as cars were turned over, dumpsters set on fire, and trees pulled out of the ground. Yes, trees pulled out of the ground. I enjoyed every moment of what people would describe as an "overwhelmingly scary" riot. But at the time I was high on happiness; nothing was going to faze me. It was all smiles.

Two days later was the parade, Halloween, and an unseasonably warm day in Philadelphia; a perfect storm, a trifecta of awesomeness, a recipe for a day that will be remembered forever (besides where alcohol blurs the memory). If I had to pick one moment of the day that stands out above all others, it would have to be seeing Pat Burrell come inching down Broad, beer in hand, on a Budweiser chariot pulled by two Clydesdales. I think it was at this moment where I shed my first tear, something I'll never be embarrassed to admit. Those 72 hours we were all champions, world fucking champions.

2009: World Series, Part Deux

2009 National League Eastern Division Standings

Team	Wins	Losses	Ties	WP	GB
Philadelphia Phillies	93	69	0	.574	—
Florida Marlins	87	75	0	.537	6
Atlanta Braves	86	76	0	.531	7
New York Mets	70	92	0	.432	23
Washington Nationals	59	103	0	.364	34

NLDS: PHILLIES 3; COLORADO ROCKIES 1

NLCS: PHILLIES 4; LOS ANGELES DODGERS 1

WORLD SERIES: NEW YORK YANKEES 4; PHILLIES 2

Preseason

As would be expected, the basic composition of the World Champions remained the same from 2008 to 2009. The biggest change would come in general manager, with Pat Gillick stepping down after guiding our club to the promised land. Stepping in would be former Phillies batboy and outfielder Rubén Amaro Jr. Longtime Philly Pat "The Bat" Burrell had moved on to Tampa, to be replaced by Raul Ibañez, offensive star of the Mariners.

The Manager

Charlie Manuel returned this season as a hero. Just a few scant years ago, people had openly ridiculed his accent, his learning process, and his demeanor on the field. Charlie had earned more than everyone's respect; he'd earned their love. That's a great deal harder to achieve in Philadelphia. Just ask Mike Schmidt.

The Lineup

Leading Off:
Shortstop Jimmy "J-Roll" Rollins, .250, 100 R, 77 RBI, 21 HR, 31 SB

Usually known for fast starts, Jimmy Rollins' flight took off so poorly that Charlie Manuel ended up putting him on the bench, hoping to clear the man's head. Nearing the end of June, Rollins was hitting .195, with an on-base percentage of .237. As the season broke into July, he had the lowest batting average in the entire major leagues. No one knew what was going on. Had J-Roll suddenly lost his abilities?

But suddenly something clicked. Rollins began to light fire in the second half, upping his average by 78 points, moving into 10th in extra base hits with 69, while finishing fourth in doubles (43) and stolen bases (30). His defense remained consistent throughout as he nailed down another Gold Glove, his third consecutive one, and came in second in fielding percentage with a .990.

Batting Second:
Center Fielder Shane "The Flyin' Hawaiian" Victorino, .292, 102 R, 13 Triples, 25 SB

Shane Victorino's fine offensive numbers mirrored the ones he put up in 2008. His 13 triples led the league, while his 181 hits placed him in fifth. He finished seventh in runs (102), ninth in doubles (39), and ninth in stolen bases (25). Shane's performance earned him his first All-Star appearance, becoming the very first Hawaiian to make the squad.

Batting Third:
Second Baseman Chase Utley, .292, 31 HR, 112 R, 93RBI

Chase Utley battled back from a midseason injury to put together another superb offensive season. After lighting the baseball world on fire in the month of April, Utley looked like he was going to make a run at becoming the Phillies' third MVP winner in the last four years. Playing in pain for most the second half, his contribution slowed, but not his game. Chase earned his fourth straight All-Star appearance and won his fourth straight Silver Slugger.

Batting Fourth:
First Baseman Ryan Howard, .279, 45 HR, 105 R, 141RBI

Ryan Howard dominated the power rankings of the MLB again in 2009. On his way to becoming the quickest player ever to reach 200 home runs (658 games), he smoked three grand slams, the last traveling 475 feet at Citizens Bank Park. He finished first in runs batted in (141), second in extra base hits (86), third in home runs (45), third in total bases (352), fourth in slugging percentage (.571), and fifth in runs scored (105). Still, Ryan suffered in two areas of his game: he led the league in errors by a first baseman, and he came in second in strikeouts with 186 of them.

Batting Fifth:
Right Fielder Jayson Werth, .268, 36 HR, 98 R, 99 RBI, 20 SB

Jayson Werth proved that 2008 was certainly no fluke as this multi-tooled player continued to flourish. Though his batting average dipped, his on-base percentage rose to a .373, and he scored a personal best in homers with 36. Always patient at the plate, Werth led the majors in pitches-per-at-bat with a 4.50. On May 12, he made the league stand up and take notice when he stole second, then stole third, and just for the hell of it, stole home as well. In all, Werth stole four bases on the day. Move over, Rickey Henderson. Jayson made his first All-Star team this season when Charlie Manuel selected him after Carlos Beltran could not report. Although some suggestions of nepotism were whispered about, you really couldn't argue with Werth's statistics.

Batting Sixth:
Left Fielder Raul Ibañez, .272, 34 HR, 93 R, 93 RBI

Raul Ibañez, known for his power in Seattle, won the fans over immediately in Philadelphia. For the first few months, the guy seemed like the next coming of Roy Hobbs. At the All-Star Break, he was hitting .314 with 60 RBI. And then he went down with a groin injury. When Ibañez returned, he had trouble getting his swing back. His average dipped, his power declined, and he had difficulty maneuvering in left field. He started pressing, which only made things worse. Raul finally came around in time for the playoffs, where he lit up as wildly as when he first joined the team, hitting seven doubles, a pair of homers, and 13 RBI.

Batting Seventh:
Third Baseman Pedro Feliz, .266, 83 RBI

Pedro Feliz improved in nearly every category from 2008 and, thanks to a few key hits, he helped propel the Phillies into the World Series. Despite his stellar work, both offensively and defensively, the Phils would grant Feliz free agency at the end of the season to make room for the return of Placido Polanco in 2010.

Batting Eighth:
Catcher Carlos Ruiz, .255, 9 HR, 43 RBI

Carlos Ruiz game reached a new level in 2009. His average went up 36 points, his home run total 5, his RBI 12, and his slugging percentage 125. Ruiz had a .996 fielding percentage (second in the league), while nabbing 23 base runners (second). And these weren't even his important contributions. Carlos simply knows how to run a ballgame. His communication with the pitchers is so impeccable that there is rarely a pitch shaken off. He can set up for Lidge's outside sliders with the same ease of motion as for one of Hamels' curves. In many ways, Carlos Ruiz proved to be our Most Valuable Player in 2009.

The Pines

Charlie Manuel could again look to Greg Dobbs to come off the bench for pinch hitting and defensive replacement duties. However, Dobbs saw his average dip 54 points to .247, his RBI total fell 50 percent, from 40 to 20, his home run total from nine to five, and his doubles from 14 to six.

Matt Stairs added some pop off the bench, and though the 41-year-old would hit just .194 with a .379 slugging percentage, the fans cheered lustily for the man every time he approached the plate. That championship series home run had gone a long way. It always will.

Eric Bruntlett continued to impress as a defensive replacement, but his average fell to a .171, the lowest of his seven-year career. Even Bobby Wine would have thought such a season was a little off. The Phils granted him free agency at the end of the campaign. He has since been picked up and released by both the Washington Nationals and the New York Yankees without seeing any major league playing time.

Ben Francisco joined the team along with pitcher Cliff Lee in a late-season trade. Francisco served as a pinch hitter and utility outfielder. The 27-year-old had a fine glove, could hit for average, and had some good power.

John Mayberry finally broke into the majors after a stellar minor league career. He only hit .211, but had some impressive shots and always looked good with the glove.

The Starting Staff

The Ace:
Left-Hander Cliff Lee, 7-4, 3.39

It seems kind of strange placing a man who got only 12 starts for his club in the role of ace. But it is nonetheless true. Cliff Lee made such an incredible impact on this team and its fans that he simply vaulted into the hearts of Philadelphians. The fact that he loved us right back and chose to sign with the Phils, instead of taking bigger offers from the Yankees and the Rangers, just made him greater in our eyes. Hey, the man could come here and tank, and we'd still love him. Wouldn't we?

Lee came into his own as a starting pitcher for the 2004 Cleveland Indians when he went 14-8. He came in fourth in the Cy Young Award voting the next season when he posted an 18-5 record. After capturing another 14 in 2006, he appeared destined for greatness. But 2009 proved disastrous for Cliff. After suffering from a groin injury in Spring Training, he was sidelined for a month. When he returned, he was not the same. Struggling to 5-8 with a 6.29 ERA, Lee got himself into trouble with his teammates and the fans. When he beaned Rangers right fielder Sammy Sosa on a night when the Rangers were honoring Sosa's 600 homers, his own catcher and he had words, followed by a closed-door meeting with his teammates after the game. No one left happy. In late July, when the Boston Red Sox knocked Lee around, the hometown crowd jeered him. Cliff mockingly doffed his cap and was sent to the minors the next day. And they say Philly is a tough town. No wonder he was so amazed at the camaraderie of the Phillies clubhouse and the unbridled love of the fans.

Lee returned in 2008 to have the greatest season of his career, when he won the Cy Young Award with a record of 22-3 (first), to go along with an ERA of 2.54 (first) and 170 strikeouts (ninth). With free agency looming, he was traded to the Phils just before the deadline. Cliff proceeded to win his first five games while posting a 0.68 ERA. The fact that he went only 2-4 for the rest of the season isn't even a blip on the radar. And if you don't already understand why, just read ahead to the play-off section of this chapter.

Second in the Order:
Left-Hander Cole Hamels, 10-11, 4.32

After the incredible postseason that Cole Hamels put together in 2008, the man was expected to win 40 games in the following year, together with an ERA of negative seven. And that wasn't just in the eyes of Philadelphia. He'd become the darling of baseball.

Hamels did not respond well. Having the most trying season of his young career, Cole's ERA rose by more than a full run, while his opponent batting average on balls-in-play rose from .275 to .325. Some speculated that his troubles were due to an injury he suffered in Spring Training, or that his mind just wasn't on the game. Others said that he partied too much during the off-season, or that the opposition had figured out a way to steal his signs. And finally Cole said some things to the press that got misconstrued and even the fans turned against him...for a while.

Third in the Order:
Right-Hander Joe Blanton, 12-8, 4.05

Joe Blanton's undefeated Phillies career (he was 6-0, including the playoffs, in 2008) ended on April 16 when the Nationals batted him around for three runs in the first inning on their way to winning the contest, 8-2. But Joe picked his head up and went on to win 12 games for the club. No Phillie won more. Blanton anchored the team in a season that saw many question marks regarding their starting rotation, and produced one of the most consistent seasons of his career.

Fourth in the Order:
Left-Hander Jamie Moyer, 12-10, 4.94

At a remarkable 46, Jamie Moyer finally began showing signs of age in his 24th season of baseball. Though he claimed his 256th victory, enough to become number 41 among the winningest pitchers in baseball history, Jamie's ERA ballooned to the point where Charlie Manuel had no choice but to send him to the bullpen.

Moyer and his replacement, Pedro Martinez, became a good complement to one another. On August 18, in relief of Martinez, Moyer threw six scoreless innings for win number 11. Then on August 28, he threw four scoreless innings in relief of Martinez for his 12th. Moyer's season ended in pain, however, as he had to be helped from the field on September 29, after tearing muscles in his groin. The forever-young Moyer vowed he'd be back on the mound in time for Opening Day 2010.

Fifth in the Order:
Left-Hander J.A. Happ, 12-4, 2.93

J.A. Happ lost the Spring Training contest for the fifth starter's position to Chan Ho Park, but after Park struggled, Happ came in to claim his place in the baseball world. His terrific rookie season won him the *Sporting News* Rookie of the Year award and the Players Choice for Outstanding Rookie. Because of the jumble of starting pitchers the Phils had in the postseason, Happ got to start only one game of the nine in which he appeared.

Sixth in the Order:
Right-Hander Brett Myers, 4-3, 4.84

After taking the Opening Day starter's role for the 2009 Phillies, Brett Myers struggled through the first two months of the season until finally leaving the mound on May 27, complaining of muscle soreness. It ended up that he required surgery on his hip, which sidelined him into mid-August. Once ready to return, Brett promptly injured his eye and was forced to miss another two weeks. Myers reclaimed his spot on the roster in September, but only in a supporting role. He got less than two innings of postseason work and was granted free agency at the end of the year.

Seventh in the Order:
Right-Hander Pedro Martinez, 5-1, 3.63

After losing Brett Myers to injury and being forced to relegate both Jamie Moyer and Chan Ho Park to the bullpen, the Phillies went on the market for a starting pitcher. They eventually lured the legendary Pedro Martinez out of retirement in mid-July. After a storied career, Pedro had been granted free agency by the New York Mets after a subpar 2008 campaign (5-6, 5.61). No team sought him out for 2009, so Pedro took his game to the World Baseball Classic, pitching six scoreless innings for the Dominican Republic in order to showcase his still-viable talents. But there were no takers.

    With their back to the wall, the Phils put Martinez through a couple of simulated games and signed him to a one-year contract. Pedro assumed he would be playing a backup position, but soon found himself the number-three starter. He won his first five decisions, including a shutout of his former Mets in a game where he threw 130 pitches. Pedro thought that he had rekindled his career, but no MLB club sought him out for 2010, not even the Phils.

The Relief Core

The Closer:
Right-Hander Brad "Lights Out" Lidge, 0-8, 7.21, 31 Saves

What the hell happened? Brad Lidge went from a perfect 2008 to the worst season ever thrown by a reliever earning 20 or more saves. When Lidge went down due to injury in June, people thought that perhaps the nagging problems of his right knee and elbow had been the issue all along. However, Brad's work didn't improve on his return. He blew 11 saves during the course of the season, couldn't buy a win, and posted an astronomical 7.21 ERA.

Fans still loved the guy. He'd basically handed us our World Championship the year before, but some began calling for a change. Uncle Charlie, however, stood by his man for as long as he could. Finally, when Lidge showed no signs of snaking out of the mess, Manuel began testing other arms, only to find that they didn't have the stuff either. When asked how he felt about having to turn away from Lidge, Uncle Charlie told the press, "Baseball is bigger than my heart." He would be forced to go with Lidge for the playoffs and, to Brad's credit, he took the ball with strength and focus. He didn't seem at all disturbed by his own statistics. The man with the damaged psyche that we'd been worked up about in his St. Louis days made no appearance here.

Setup Man:
Right-Hander Chan Ho Park, 3-3, 4.43

The first South Korean ever to play professional baseball, Chan Ho Park broke into the majors in 1994 for the Los Angeles Dodgers. From 1997 through 2001, he won at least 13 games for the Dodgers, his best season being 2000 when he went 18-10 with a 3.27 ERA. He made his only appearance in the All-Star Game the next season.

Park played with the Rangers and Padres from 2002 to 2006, but was hampered by injuries. Bouncing around between the minors and his own Korean league, he made brief appearances with the Dodgers and the Angels, before the Phils took a chance on him in 2009. He won the fifth starter's job out of Spring Training, but pitched poorly. When Park was converted to a reliever, his star really rose. Suddenly, his fastball returned, as did the movement on his slider. Apparently, he had given up a lot of his velocity in order to have the energy to go longer into games. He had a 2.52 ERA as a reliever and was signed to the Yankees after the season. Unfortunately, Chan Ho Park could not hold his job in the MLB in 2010, and is now playing for the Orix Buffaloes in the Nippon Professional Baseball organization.

Setup Man:
Right-Hander Ryan Madson, 5-5, 3.26, 10 Saves

Ryan Madson continued to excel as the setup man for the Phillies in 2009—so much so that fans began to call for him to take Lidge's place as the closer. In September, Charlie Manuel finally answered the call and went to Madson to test his closer's psyche. Ryan didn't pass the test, and the Phils again reverted to Lidge. Part of the reason might have been that Madson appeared in more games this year than any other prior season (79), and was clearly exhausted at times while out on that mound. Once better rested, he turned in a fine postseason.

And the Rest

Charlie Manuel had many consistent arms to turn to in the pen, such as right-hander Chad Durbin, who put in another good year with a 4.39 in 59 appearances; right-hander Clay Condrey, who posted a 3.00 ERA in 45 games; and lefty Scott Eyre, in his last season of baseball, going out with a 1.50 ERA in 42 games.

In terms of long relief, Charlie could go to right-hander Kyle Kendrick (3-1, 3.42) and left-hander Antonio Bastardo, who looked good in the five starts he got during the season. Left-hander J.C. Romero saw limited action due a suspension at the start of the season because of a performance-enhancing drug dispute and an injury when he returned.

Spring Training

The Phils were naturally upbeat as they started workouts. Chase Utley showed his own strength of conviction, returning early from late-November hip surgery to begin actively playing in games on March 15. Pedro Feliz, who had surgery the same day as Utley, his for a herniated disc, returned the same day.

Cole Hamels gave us quite a scare in two major instances. First he was featured on the February 23 cover of *Sports Illustrated*, which reportedly is considered bad luck. Second, he left Spring Training early, complaining of elbow soreness. MRIs proved negative, but did throw him back a few days, thus preventing him from starting on Opening Day.

Jimmy Rollins, Shane Victorino, and Matt Stairs reported late to Spring Training due to their involvement in the World Baseball Classic. All three hoped that the activity wouldn't throw off their game, even though it admittedly threw off their regimen. Usually a slow starter and a strong finisher, Ryan Howard sent an alert to the entire MLB as he led the Grapefruit League in homers with 10. It looked like it was going to be one hell of a season.

The Season

The Phils took a casual stroll through their opening month, finishing 11-9, a game and a half behind the leading Marlins. The biggest news coming from the team in April was the death of beloved broadcaster Harry Kalas on Monday, April 13. It was a loss that every Philadelphian felt, sending the team and the city into mourning. The team wore black HK armbands for the remainder of the season.

Phillies Memory

Matt Wells, Longtime Fan

I don't think I'll ever forget the day Harry the K died. He was my voice of spring and I felt lucky to have had him call my team for that many years. I loved him so much that it was as if he were a close personal friend when in reality we had never met. At that time, the Phillies were in Washington to play the Nats and I was at work in a warehouse in Hatfield, PA. I had heard earlier in the day that something was wrong with Harry and he wouldn't be calling today's game.

It wasn't until we all turned on the radio to listen to the game that we heard the news of his death. I didn't really know how to feel at that moment. After all, I never knew the guy, but after being a fan for so long and inviting him into my living room or workplace every day at game time, I guess I was more attached than I realized. The game was in Washington but the stands were mainly filled with Phillie fans. I remember they had a moment of silence for him there and one of the Phillie fans yelled, "We love you, Harry." I lost it. I cried. It was the worst day of work I had ever had. Nobody talked. I only wish I could have been around to hear Harry and Whitey together.

Ryan Howard and Raul Ibañez carried the team through May, hitting 10 homers apiece as the Phillies put together a 17-11 record to finish the month in first, but just half a game better than the Mets. Jamie Moyer, though pitching inconsistently at best, nailed down his 250th victory. Though June would initially see the Phils continue their hot streak of 16 wins out of 20, dating back to May 15, it would include their coldest streak as well. They fared rather poorly in interleague play, going 6-12, including a six-game losing streak against the American League. The cold spell made it harder to dismiss the dismal start by "No Longer Lights Out" Lidge. Blowing saves on two consecutive nights against our 2008 NLCS rivals, the Los Angeles Dodgers, it was beginning to look like this was not just a slow start. Antonio Bastardo, who took the place of the struggling Jamie Moyer, had two strong outings to add some bright promise to the month.

Even though the Phillies' record in June was a weak 11-15, they actually increased their lead to a game and a half over the Marlins and four over the Mets. After sweeping the Mets in an Independence Weekend series, the Phils cruised into the All-Star Break with a 48-38 record, good enough for a four-game lead over the Marlins and six and a half over the Mets. Chase Utley and Raul Ibañez were selected as starters for the Nationals, while Ryan Howard, Shane Victorino, and Jayson Werth would serve as backups.

The Phils' July proved to be their greatest month since May 2001, as they went 20-11, rattling off 10 straight at one point. Still, we were looking to improve our rotation, and it looked like we were going to make a deal for Roy Halladay at the last minute. The problem was that the Blue Jays wanted us to throw J.A. Happ into the deal. Happ, however, had started this rookie season of his at 7-0 and was proving to be our most dependable starter. Instead, the Phils would make one of the greatest trades in franchise history when they picked up Cliff Lee on July 29.

Still looking to bolster the starting staff, the club picked up Pedro Martinez in August. Both Martinez and Lee would win their first five outings. Cliff would sport an ERA of just 1.35, only once allowing as many as two runs in an outing. The club would go 16-11 during the month of August to increase their Eastern Division lead to eight games on both the Braves and the Marlins. The Mets, meanwhile, had fallen to a dismal 59-72, a full 17$\frac{1}{2}$ games behind. The Phils looked like a pretty safe bet.

Atlanta would win 17 of their first 21 games in September to pull within four. They would run out of gas at the last lap, however, dropping each of their last six contests. The Phils were able to clinch with four games remaining—early enough for them to set their rotation for the playoffs. And as the champagne poured for the National League Eastern Division winners, the dulcet tones of Harry the K singing "High Hopes" rang out through the stadium.

Phillies Memory

Simon Ceferatti, Future Phillies Broadcaster
(as told to his mother, Maria)

Harry Kalas. Just writing his name, I can hear his voice in my head. His voice narrated the soundtrack of my childhood growing up in South Philly. Just blocks away from Veterans Stadium, on warm spring and humid summer evenings, with every window open on the block, Harry's voice could be heard with its strong but tender satisfying lilt, causing the abrupt abandonment of games of "hide and seek" and "jailbreak." If the Phillies were in a slump, Harry's tone coaxed us to be patient, and if they were on a winning streak, Harry was jumping up and down right next to us in the 700 level. For some reason, I thought of Harry as a grandfather figure—wise, stoic, and always there.

My nine-year-old son, Simon, is a Phillies fan, and he, too, was taken by Harry's voice, but for him the reasons were a bit different. My son has been blind since birth, and he has spent many hours listening to the Phillies on the radio and on TV. He can readily imitate the voices of Larry Anderson and Scott Franzke, and takes particular pride in his rendition of Harry Kalas' famous "This ball is outttta herrrre!"

We were all very saddened when Harry passed away, and my son was no exception. About two weeks after Harry died, the choir in which my son sings was invited to perform the National Anthem at Citizens Bank Park. I contacted the Phillies office ahead of time, and they graciously arranged for my son to meet Larry and Scott in the radio booth. Not only did they greet Simon with such kindness and enthusiasm, but they let him sit at the booth with them and placed a pair of headphones on him so that he could listen in on the broadcast.

Although it would have been Simon's dream to meet Harry during his fourth-inning broadcasts in that booth, we felt like the spirit of Harry was still there, in the chair where Simon sat, in the energy on the field, and in the heart of every Phillies fan—young or old, sighted or blind. I'm glad that my son and I both share a special love for Harry, and we know that we can still hear his encouraging, grandfatherly voice in our memories whenever we need some high hopes.

THE 2009 NATIONAL LEAGUE DIVISION SERIES

The Colorado Rockies had been in the hunt for the Western Division title right up to the end as they had gotten red-hot during the month of September. They won the Wild Card by four over the Giants, five over the Marlins. Their staff was led by Ubaldo Jimenez (15-12, 3.47), Jason Marquis (15-13, 4.04), and Jorge de la Rosa (16-9, 4.38). Huston Street (3.06, 35 saves) served as their closer. Their power came from Troy Tulowitzki (.297, 32 HR, 92 RBI), Ian Stewart (25 HR), and Clint Barnes (23 HR). Their speed came from Dexter Fowler (27 SB), while Seth Smith (.293) and Brad Hawpe (.285) were their high average men. In short, this was a very well-rounded team.

Game One

Wednesday, October 7 (Citizens Bank Park)

Cliff Lee shrugged off September, when he'd gone 2-4 with a 6.66 ERA, to close down the Rockies with a complete game six-hitter. At one point, Lee had retired 16 straight batters, from the second through the seventh. He didn't lose his shutout until two outs in the ninth inning, when Troy Tulowitzki drilled a line drive, RBI double. Rockies starter Ubaldo Jimenez had gone toe-to-toe with him, hurling goose eggs into the bottom of the fifth, when Raul Ibañez doubled in Jayson Werth, then came along to score on a Carlos Ruiz single. We would add another three in the sixth on runs batted in from Ryan Howard, and again Werth and Ibañez.

Game Two

Thursday, October 8 (Citizens Bank Park)

Cole Hamels took the mound for game two, but it was clear right from the start that this wasn't the same Cole Hamels as in 2008. Perhaps it was because his wife was nine months pregnant and was due at any moment. He misplayed a first-inning grounder up the first-base line to allow the Rockies their first run; then he allowed a fourth-inning, two-run homer to catcher Yorvit Torrealba, who hadn't hit a round-tripper since early May. He left after five innings, with the Rockies leading 4-0, and immediately went to the hospital to see the birth of his child.

The Phils mounted a bit of a comeback in the sixth, when Ryan Howard doubled home Shane Victorino and Raul Ibañez singled home two more to make the score 4-3. Charlie Manuel brought both Joe Blanton and J.A. Happ in for relief of Hamels, thus limiting his mound choices for the rest of the series. Happ would only throw four pitches before a line drive off his leg took him out of the game. The Rockies rallied for an insurance run in the seventh. Although we'd pull within one again on a Jayson Werth solo shot in the eighth, we would get no closer, giving the game to the Rockies, 5-4.

Game Three

Sunday, October 11 (Coors Field)

This game proved to be a battle of endurance. Originally scheduled for Saturday, October 10, the contest had to be delayed because of a snowstorm. Temperatures were near zero and dropping fast come game time. It didn't help that the teams wound up playing a playoff record four-hour-and-six-minute contest.

Charlie Manuel surprised many by going with J.A. Happ instead of Pedro Martinez, figuring the snow delay had given him the extra rest needed. Happ didn't find his groove, however, allowing five hits and three runs in his three innings of play. Joe Blanton came on in relief, allowed a run of his own, as did Scott Eyre in relief of him. Those five runs, however, would not be enough to stymie the Phils. Chase Utley opened our scoring with a solo blast in the first off Rockies starter Jason Hamme. Then, trailing 3-1 in the fourth, the Phils posted a three-spot, thanks to runs batted in from Ryan Howard, Raul Ibañez, and Carlos Ruiz.

Entering the ninth inning with the game tied at five, the Phillies put together the rally that would send them over the top. Jimmy Rollins led off with a ground single up the middle against Rockies closer Houston Street. Shane Victorino then sacrificed him into scoring position, and Chase Utley grounded a ball past the pitcher for an infield hit that put runners at the corners with only one out. Ryan Howard pushed the run across with a sacrifice fly to center to give us a lead that, this time, we wouldn't give back. Brad Lidge came on to put the game away (but not before walking two batters) to give the Phils a 2-1 lead in the best-of-five.

Game Four

Monday, October 12 (Coors Field)

The starters from game one met again for this contest with the Phils standing behind Cliff Lee, and the Rockies behind Ubaldo Jimenez. The Phils got on the board quickly when Shane Victorino lined a first-inning homer into the frosty night. Jayson Werth added a solo shot in the sixth to give Cliff the usual two runs he needed to win. Lee, however, was having a tougher time of it than he had in game one. Colorado finally got to him in the sixth inning, when Troy Tulowitzki doubled home Todd Helton to make it a one-run game. Then they chased him from the mound with a three-spot in the eighth inning on runs batted in from Jason Giambi and Yorvit Torrealba.

Trailing 4-2 in the ninth, the Phils got to work. Ryan Howard calmly told his teammates to just "get me to the plate, boys." It was a tall order. He was three batters away and there was already an out recorded. Rollins got it started with a single over second, but Victorino followed it by grounding into a force for the second out of the inning.

Ryan Howard moved into the on-deck circle. He looked to be in a zone. He had all evening. Staring ahead as if in a trance, Ryan was entirely focused on a vision only he could see. After Chase Utley worked a walk to put the tying runs on base, Howard got to the plate, boys. He stared at the ball in the pitcher's hand, took a couple of practice swings, then waited. We all did—for the inevitable. It came on the fourth pitch. Howard bruised a fastball from Houston Street to the wall in right for a double that scored the tying runs of the game. Jayson Werth followed with a bloop to shallow right that fell in to give the Phils an improbable 5-4, ninth-inning lead.

The Rockies threatened again in the bottom of the ninth, when Brad Lidge was called on with runners on first and second, with two outs. Lidge had to face the Rockies' Troy Tulowitzki. After working him to a 2-2 count, Brad put him away with that nasty slider of his to give the Phils the game and the series. Lidge had done his job this time, and he walked confidently from the mound. Perhaps it was the dawn of a new season for him, a time to put away the mishaps of the regular season and start again. Only time would tell.

THE 2009 NATIONAL LEAGUE CHAMPIONSHIP SERIES

The Los Angeles Dodgers had another strong season in 2009, taking their division over Colorado by three games, then storming past the Central Division champion Cardinals in three. They had won more games than the Phils this season (95-93), and had taken the season series 4-3 to earn the home field advantage. The moundsmen were led by our old friend Randy Wolf (11-7, 3.23), Chad Billingsley (12-11, 4.03), Clayton Kershaw (8-8, 2.79), and Hiroki Kuroda (8-7, 3.76). Another familiar face had recently joined them—Vincente Padilla, recently cast off by the Texas Rangers. Padilla had turned in a trim 4-0 record in his brief stay with LA, along with a 3.20 ERA. Closer Jonathan Broxton (2.61, 36 saves) stood prepared for revenge after giving up the Matt Stairs homer in game four of the 2008 NLCS that had locked the series.

The Dodger offense had a fine mixture of power and speed. Manny Ramirez, having been suspended for steroid use earlier in the season, rebounded to have a fine, if unspectacular, year (.290, 19 homers, 63 RBI). André Ethier led the club with 31 round-trippers, Matt Kemp pounded out 26, while Casey Blake added another 18, and James Loney, 13. Three players stole more than 10: Matt Kemp (34), Rafael Furcal (12), and their catcher, Russell Martin (11). These Dodgers were going to be a tough nut to crack. And besides, they had the eyes of the nation on them. Fans wanted to see an old-fashioned Yankees–Dodgers series, especially one that would feature the return of Joe Torre, former manager of the Yanks, now with the Dodgers.

Game One

Thursday, October 15 (Dodger Stadium)

The Phillies staked Cole Hamels to an early 5-1 lead in game one, scoring all their runs off Dodger starter Clayton Kershaw in the fifth inning. Carlos "Mr. October" Ruiz had popped a three-run homer, shortly followed by a Ryan Howard two-run double. The problem was that Hamels gave most of it right back in the bottom of the inning, one run coming around on an André Ethier grounder, another two on a blast from the always-potent bat of Manny Ramirez.

Cole was forced out of the game in the sixth, after allowing back-to-back hits. He left with a 5-4 lead, having allowed eight hits in his 106-pitch outing. The Philly relief squad was able to put out the fires, but Hamels' second poor postseason outing gave cause for concern. Raul Ibañez hit a three-run homer in the eighth to give the Phils an 8-4 advantage, which should have been pretty safe. However, Ryan Madson allowed two right back in the bottom of the inning, and then Brad Lidge put two runners on before escaping with another save. We had taken a 1-0 lead in the series; we were 5-1 in the playoffs in total, but we weren't marching with the same assured confidence as in the season past.

Game Two

Friday, October 16 (Dodger Stadium)

The two starters of game two represented an unusual casting call for Major League Baseball. Neither the Phillies' Pedro Martinez nor the Dodgers' Vincente Padilla had been on the team rosters at the start of the season. Both had been cast off, forgotten until midseason. It says a great deal about the depletion of each pitching staff that these two had become the go-to men in one of the most pivotal games of the championship series. And it says a lot about the spirit of both men that they threw gems. Martinez was masterful, giving seven innings of shutout ball, while allowing only two hits and no walks. Meanwhile, Padilla had been touched only by a Ryan Howard solo homer shot in the fourth.

It wasn't until Chan Ho Park came in for Martinez in the eighth inning that things got ugly. With runners on first and third, catcher Russell Martin hit a sharp grounder to Pedro Feliz, who slung the ball quickly to Chase Utley for one, and then onto first—well, way off of first, actually. The first Dodger run came around to score, tying the game at one. Martin advanced into scoring position, and Park left the game. Our old friend Jim Thome hit a line single to right that put runners on first and third, and after a walk to Rafael Furcal to load the bases, Ryan Madson came in to walk André Ethier, forcing the leading run across the plate. The Dodgers had taken a 2-1 lead, with only one hard-hit ball all inning. Jonathan Broxton proudly stepped forward to take his first steps toward redemption by taking us down in order in the ninth inning. The game had gone to the Dodgers, 2-1, the series was tied at one game apiece, and we were heading back to Philly.

Game Three

Sunday, October 18 (Citizens Bank Park)

The Phillies made quick work of game three, knocking out Dodger starter Hiroki Kuroda with six runs through the first inning and a third. The big guns had come from a two-run triple from Ryan Howard, a two-run homer from Jayson Werth, and an RBI double from Jimmy Rollins. Over the course of the game, they went on to score five more, thanks in part to a three-run homer from The Flyin' Hawaiian. That's 11 runs in all! It ends up, however, that they really only needed one. Cliff Lee threw eight innings of three-hit shutout ball for another masterful performance, earning his second win of the playoffs.

Phillies Memory

Winter Favre, Age Nine

In the fall of 2009, I was at the championship game with my dad. I was very excited about it. I had never been to a championship game before. The Phillies really mean a lot to me. Every year I want them to win. The Phillies won that championship game we went to. We stayed in the stadium a half an hour after the game cheering for them. I was very happy for them.

Phillies Memory

Brian Favre, Cub Scout Leader

It was game four of the NCLS. This was the second time my daughter and I had ever been to a baseball game. She is a huge fan of the Phillies; as for myself, I followed them but did not call myself a fan. Little did I know that was all about to change.

It was an amazing game. The Phillies led most of the night until the Dodgers went ahead 4-2. Things were looking grim for the Phillies and my daughter kept on telling me how they were going to make a comeback, to just wait and see. It was getting late and she had school the next day. I thought about leaving early but she insisted we stay because, as she assured me again, they were going to win, and I didn't want to miss it.

It was the bottom of the ninth with two outs and she turned to me; I started to tell her it was not their night when Jimmy Rollins hit a two-run double to win the game. The stadium went crazy, I grabbed Winter, and we started dancing and screaming. It was amazing.

She yelled as loud as she could, "I told you." We did not want to go home; we just wanted to stay all night and cheer. It is one of my finest memories with her.

With that win the Phillies taught her to never give up; she also taught me never to doubt her; it was one of those bonding moments you always hear about but never experience. Well, I experienced it. I have since become a fan of the Phillies and enjoy watching them with my daughter. Baseball and the Phillies is our little special time together and it is something I will never forget.

Game Four

Monday, October 19 (Citizens Bank Park)

The Phillies welcomed back former staff ace Randy Wolf with a warm ovation and then a two-run, first-inning homer off the bat of Ryan Howard. It was Howard's eighth straight postseason game with an RBI, tying Lou Gehrig. Philly starter Joe Blanton, however, would have a tough time of it. The Dodgers would tie the game in the fourth inning, then move ahead on a solo shot from Matt Kemp in the fifth. After giving up another run to make the score 4-2 Dodgers in the sixth, Blanton's day was over.

Chase Utley would chase Randy Wolf from the mound with a run-scoring single to bring the Phillies back to within one, but the Dodgers' relievers would keep the Phils at bay until the ninth inning, when Jonathan Broxton sprung back to the mound to try to tie the series at two. After recording the first out, he had to face his old nemesis, Matt Stairs, who had hit that gargantuan homer in game four of 2008, which turned the tide against the Dodgers. Stairs didn't even have to lift the bat from his shoulder, as Broxton proceeded to offer him a four-pitch walk. Clearly unnerved, he then plunked Carlos Ruiz to put runners on first and second before inducing pinch hitter Greg Dobbs to line out to third. Two outs. There was light at the end of the tunnel.

Not much light, however. J-Roll ripped a 1-1 fastball into right center that rolled to the wall, scoring both runners and giving the Phils another come-from-behind victory over the Dodgers. Broxton was again at the wrong end of a late-inning blowup, and the Phillies were now a game away from their second World Series berth in as many years.

Game Five

Wednesday, October 21 (Citizens Bank Park)

Cole Hamels took his place on the mound to try to wrap up the series, and even though the Phillies staked him to six runs in the first four innings, he was unable to make it through five. After allowing solo homers to André Ethier in the first, James Loney in the second, and Orlando Hudson in the fifth, Hamels was removed from the championship series. It was a long walk to the dugout—for everyone. Even though we were in the driver's seat at the time, we had to question the fact that with Hamels tanking, and the only dependable starter was Cliff Lee. Still, we could worry about that another day. Right now, we could relish the fact that our offense had made quick work of Vincente Padilla with a three-run homer from Jayson Werth in the first, a solo shot by Pedro Feliz in the fifth, and an RBI double by Raul Ibañez in the fourth.

The Phils put the game away with a two-run homer from Shane Victorino in the sixth inning and a solo shot from Jayson Werth in the seventh. It was a 10-4 lashing, another 4-1 domination of the Dodgers in the NLCS, another World Series berth. But there remained concerns, the biggest being that outside of Cliff Lee, we didn't really have a consistent starter. At least our offense was working on all cylinders, especially Ryan Howard, who walked away with MVP honors for the series, having hit .333 with two homers, a double, a triple, and eight runs batted in. Now, if he could turn in a similar performance in the World Series.

THE 2009 WORLD SERIES

After a 59-year wait, the Phillies finally got a chance to get their revenge on the 4-0 lashing that the Bronx Bombers had given our Whiz Kids way back in 1950. None of the players, not even Jamie Moyer, had been alive to see that, but Philadelphians have a long memory. The two teams were both highly touted, posting between them 20 All-Stars, three former MVPs, and three former Cy Young winners. The only regular starter, on both teams combined, who didn't have at least 10 homers was Carlos Ruiz, who had nine.

With a 103-59 record, the New York Yankees sported the best winning percentage in all of baseball (.636), had won their division handily over the Red Sox by eight games, and outdistanced the 2008 champion Rays by 19. They'd swept the Twins in the American League Division Series, then put away the Angels, 4-2.

CC Sabathia got a shot at some revenge from his defeat in the 2008 National League Division Series when he threw for the Brewers. He'd gone 19-8 for the Yanks, with a 3.37 ERA, striking out 197 in the process. A.J. Burnett backed him up with a record of 13-9 and 4.04, while veteran Andy Pettitte sailed through the season with a 14-8, 4.16. Joe Girardi had been using just this three-man rotation thus far through the playoffs and made no plans for altering his strategy for the World Series. The always-fearsome Mariano Rivera took on the closing duties after putting together yet another impeccable season with 44 saves (third in the league) and a 1.76 ERA.

On offense, the Yankees had power enough to spare. Mark Teixeira led the club with 39 long balls, followed by Alex Rodriguez with 30, Nick Swisher with 29, Hideki Matsui with 28, Robinson Cano with 25, Johnny Damon with 24, and Jorgé Posada with 22. That's seven of their starting nine who belted over 20. Their speed came from Derek Jeter (30 SB, 107 R), Brett Gardner (26 SB), Johnny Damon (107 R), and Robinson Cano (103 R). If the Phils were going to get through these guys, they were going to have to jell, and quickly.

Game One

Wednesday, October 28 (Yankee Stadium)—The Cliff Lee Game

The Yankees hosted the first two games of the Series, thanks to the 4-3 victory by the Junior League in the All-Star Game this year. Game One would pit former Cleveland Indian teammates CC Sabathia and Cliff Lee against each other. Both were former Cy Young Award winners, and both were hotter than hell. Between the two this postseason, they sported a 5-0 record with an 0.96 ERA. Neither men disappointed. Sabathia went seven innings, allowing only four hits and two runs, both coming on solo shots from Chase Utley, while Lee was indomitable, striking out 10 in a complete game performance, allowing only six hits and no earned runs. Cliff had now gone four postseason games without ever giving up more than a run. This was the best start to any postseason career since Christy Mathewson during the period from 1905 to 1911.

Still, the game was more than a matter of Cliff Lee's pitching. He made two catches for the highlight reels, the first coming on a pop to the mound where he stuck out his glove in an offhand, "Who cares?" attitude. Lee basketed the ball as if it were tossed from his eight-year-old in the backyard. In fact, if he caught a ball like this against his son, the boy would probably get angry: "Dad! If you don't want to play, just say so!" Then there was the screaming grounder that he caught behind his back before nonchalantly flipping it to first for the out. At least Cliff smiled after he did that. With four late-inning runs, the Phils dominated the Yanks 6-1 in the opening game. Now we had to see if the rest of our pitchers would arrive for the The Show.

Game Two

Thursday, October 29 (Yankee Stadium)

Pedro Martinez took the mound for the Phillies in Game Two, facing the Yankees for the first time in the postseason since the historic 2004 NLCS when he'd helped the Bosox overthrow "The Evil Empire." The Phils broke through in the second inning when Raul Ibañez hit a ground-rule double, then came around to score on an RBI single from Matt Stairs. But that was all they could grab against Yankee starter A.J. Burnett, who turned in a masterful performance. Martinez threw a fine game as well, but there wasn't much room for error. His only two mistakes were costly ones, as he allowed a solo shot to Mark Teixeira in the fourth to tie it and another by Hideki Matsui in the sixth, which gave the Yanks their first lead in the Series.

Trailing 3-1 in the eighth inning, the Phils mounted one last rally. With two runners on and one out, the red-hot Chase Utley grounded into a controversial inning-ending double play. Replays show that first-base umpire Brian Gorman missed the call at first, his second blown call of the game.

The World Series now stood tied at one. The Phils had to be happy with stealing a game in New York City, but there was no disguising the fact that everyone held their breath in anticipation of what would happen in the Cole Hamels start on the club's return to Philly.

Game Three

Saturday, October 31 (Citizens Bank Park)—
The Halloween Game

For the third game in a row, the Phils scored first, taking Yankee starter Andy Pettitte for three in the second inning. Jayson Werth led it off with a solo shot, and Jimmy Rollins later coaxed out a bases-loaded walk, followed by a Shane Victorino sacrifice fly. Things couldn't have looked better for the Phils' return. The problem was that Cole Hamels once again couldn't even make it through five. With one out in the fourth inning, Cole walked Mark Teixeira and then allowed a long blast from Alex Rodriguez that smacked off a camera in right field and was ruled a ground-rule double. Play was stopped while, for the first time in a World Series, the umpires used instant replay to review the call. In the end, they reversed their decision, calling the play a two-run homer. They claimed that the camera was in the field of play and that the trajectory of the ball would have gone into the stands.

The Phillies protested, but to no avail. Meanwhile, the long delay had clearly unnerved Cole Hamels. In the top of the fifth, he managed to record only one out before letting up three runs, one on an RBI single from Andy Pettitte, no less (only his second hit in the past four years), and two more on a Johnny Damon double. Cole's postseason ERA ballooned to 7.58. He seemed a far cry from the champion we heralded in 2008.

The clubs traded solo shots in the sixth inning, Nick Swisher for the Yanks and Jayson Werth for the Phils, making the score 6-4. But the Yanks pulled away with single runs in the seventh and eighth, the last coming on a Hideki Matsui blast against Brett Myers, who was making his last' appearance as a Phillie. Carlos Ruiz crushed a ball from Phil Hughes in the ninth to bring the Phils within three, but Mariano Rivera closed out the game to give the Yanks an 8-5 victory, and a 2-1 lead in the Series.

Cole Hamels made the error of telling reporters after the contest, "I can't wait for the season to end." He was referring, of course, to his personal season, but the sound bite didn't play well, making it appear as if he were wishing away the Phils' dramatic season and their unparalleled run for a second consecutive World Series title.

Game Four

Sunday, November 1 (Citizens Bank Park)

Charlie Manuel had a difficult decision to make in the first-ever November World Series game. Should he bring Cliff Lee in for Game Four? Yankee skipper Joe Girardi, who had been going with a three-man rotation all through the postseason, had already given the nod to CC Sabathia. Cliff would be going on short rest, but as our most effective starter, it would assure him two possible starts in the remaining games. In the end, Manuel went with the well-rested Joe Blanton, who had a 4.89 ERA this postseason. Joe added kerosene to the controversy when he allowed two first-inning runs. He would soon get his game back, however, allowing only two hits and two more runs in his six-inning performance.

The Phils took advantage of the ill-rested Sabathia, scoring a run on back-to-back doubles from Shane Victorino and Chase Utley in the first inning, then tying the game on a Pedro Feliz RBI that scored Ryan Howard in the second. Instant replays show that Howard didn't touch home plate on the play, marking yet another botched call from the umpiring crew in this Series.

The Yankees moved ahead with a two-spot in the fifth inning on runs batted in from Derek Jeter and Johnny Damon. However, in this continuing seesaw battle, Utley would hit his third solo shot of the Series to end CC's day in the seventh, while Feliz would tie the game with a solo shot in the eighth.

Brad Lidge, who had thus far been perfect through the postseason, came on for the ninth inning and recorded the first two outs. He proceeded to lose an intense battle with Damon, who finally lined a single to left on the ninth pitch of the at-bat. After Damon stole second, the Phils put on the usual Mark Teixeira shift, pulling Feliz well off the bag. Seeing this, Johnny sprinted to third. The steal proved disastrous for the Phils. Fearing a wild pitch or passed ball which would score the leading run, Lidge resisted throwing his best pitch, the slider, for the rest of the inning. Being too fine instead, Lidge hit Teixeira to put runners at the corners, then let one across the plate that Alex Rodriguez lined for a double to plate two. Jorgé Posada capped the scoring with a line single to left that scored Rodriguez and put the Yankees ahead, 7-4.

The air then went out of the Phillies. Mariano Rivera came on to close out the game, but the game was already over. You didn't see Jayson vying for position in the dugout, you didn't see J-Roll laughing, and Ryan Howard wasn't requesting that all his boys had to do was give him the bat. The Yanks had taken a 3-1 lead.

Game Five

Monday, November 2 (Citizens Bank Park)

Game Five was a match between the pitching philosophies of Charlie Manuel and Joe Girardi. A well-rested Cliff Lee worked his way to his fourth postseason victory, tying Cole Hamels in the previous year, while A.J. Burnett, on just three days' rest, was clearly off his game.

After the Yankees had gotten on the board with a single run in the first inning, Chase Utley jumped all over a Burnett fastball, taking it out of the park for a three-run homer. The Phils knocked Burnett out of the game in the third inning when they put up another three, thanks to runs batted in from Jayson Werth, Raul Ibañez, and Carlos Ruiz. They'd add two more in the seventh, both on solo homers, one from Utley (his fifth in the Series, tying Reggie Jackson's mark) and another from Ibañez.

With an 8-2 eighth-inning lead for Cliff Lee, everything looked to be cozy and comfortable. Lee, however, didn't look like the Cliff Lee we'd been watching thus far this postseason. He allowed a single to Johnny Damon to lead off the eighth, then a double by Mark Teixeira, followed by a bases-clearing double from Alex Rodriguez that ended his day. Robinson Cano sacrificed home Rodriguez to cap the scoring for the inning and bring the Yankees to within three at 8-5.

Ryan Madson came on for the ninth in place of Brad Lidge, who had given up three ninth-inning runs the day before. Madson, who had battled ninth-inning demons all season, continued to battle here. Jorgé Posada led off the inning with a double, followed by a pinch-hit single from Hideki Matsui that put runners at the corners. Derek Jeter grounded into a double play to follow, scoring a run, but at least emptying the bases.

After Madson allowed a single to Damon to once again bring

the tying run to the plate, you had to wonder how long it would be before Charlie Manuel would call on Lidge one more time. But Madson managed to strike out Mark Teixeira to end the inning and give the Phils a victory through his first-ever World Series save, but it was an exhausting performance all around.

Game Six

Wednesday, November 4 (Yankee Stadium)

If the Phils could dispose of the ill-rested Andy Pettitte in Game Six, they would force a contest between Cole Hamels and CC Sabathia for the seventh game. Hamels made it a point to impress upon anyone who would listen that he was wildly eager to get the ball into his hands again and to help his team win the championship. The Yankees, however, were determined not to give him the opportunity. They opened the scoring in the second inning off of Phils starter Pedro Martinez when series MVP Hideki Matsui knocked a two-run blast. The Phillies would counter with a run in the third, much thanks to a triple from Carlos Ruiz, who came around to score on a fly from Jimmy Rollins.

The Yanks were relentless on this day, however, tallying another two in the bottom of the fourth, again thanks to Hideki Matsui, who hit a two-run single this time. They pulled away for well and good in the fifth inning, when Mark Teixeira singled home one run and Matsui doubled home another two. Six runs batted in on the day! That tied a World Series record set by the Yanks' Bobby Richardson in 1960.

Ryan Howard, who would strike out a record 13 times in the Series, hit a two-run homer in the sixth inning to bring the Phils a bit closer at 7-3, but that's where the score would stay and stand. Andy Pettitte had been openly questioned coming into this game, but he recorded his fourth victory of the postseason and set a record for the most all-time postseason victories with 18.

The Phils didn't walk to the dugout with their heads down as the Yankees poured onto the field in celebration. They knew that they had come close, and they knew why. They were one pitcher, perhaps two, shy of being not just a good team, not just a great team, but an immortal one. It would be up to Rubén Amaro to make that happen.

2010: A Dream Deferred

2010 National League Eastern Division Standings

Team	Wins	Losses	Ties	WP	GB
Philadelphia Phillies	97	65	0	.599	—
Atlanta Braves	91	71	0	.562	6
Florida Marlins	80	82	0	.494	17
New York Mets	79	83	0	.488	18
Washington Nationals	69	93	0	.426	28

NLDS: PHILLIES 3; CINCINNATI REDS 0
NLCS: SAN FRANCISCO GIANTS 4; PHILLIES 2

Preseason

In many ways, the 2010 Phillies represented possibly the best team we've ever put on the field. They were the first Phillies club to complete a season with the most wins in the major leagues. And they're the only team that had three aces going for them. Arguably, they are the first team that ever had even two aces going for them. In all of the Steve Carlton years, the club searched for a suitable number-two man. You had Larry Christensen (19-6) in 1977, Dick Ruthven (17-10) in 1980, and John Denny (19-6) in 1983. Nonetheless, you'd be hard put to call any of these clubs a two-ace team. Christensen had an ERA of 4.06; Ruthven sported a 3.55 (good but certainly not ace-like); and even though Denny won the Cy Young in 1983, Carlton had an off year (15-16).

If you travel back to 1915, you could certainly call Grover Cleveland Alexander an ace, and he did have Erskine Mayer (21-15, 2.36) to back him up. But this was at a time when the league ERA was 2.75. Back in 1950, Robin Roberts had Curt Simmons (17-8), but Simmons was removed from the game in early September to follow the call to service in the Korean War.

It seems to me that the best one-two punch we ever had was back in 1964, when we could put Jim Bunning (19-8, 2.63) and Chris Short (17-9, 2.20) back-to-back. The only thing was that we put them back-to-back too much, and they didn't even make the playoffs. The best overall staff would have to be in 1993, when we could put Curt Schilling (16-7, 4.02), Tommy Greene (16-4, 3.42), Terry Mulholland (12-9, 3.25), or Danny Jackson (12-11, 3.77) out there to join the party. Still, not one of them had a season that would mark them as an ace. What these teams all have in common, however, is that they are all members of the greatest Phillies teams of all time. So the formula seems pretty simple: put two great pitchers together and we can take it far.

General manager Rubén Amaro did us one better in 2010. He gave us three: Roy Halladay (21-10, 2.44, Cy Young), Cole Hamels (12-11, 3.06), and Roy Oswalt (7-1, 1.74). In fact, going down the stretch, all three pitchers were so uncanny that it could be said that Roy Halladay was the best pitcher in baseball, but sometimes only the third best on the team.

These weren't the only additions that Amaro would make to the team. After losing out in the World Series of 2009, he was not going to sit and simply watch the team grow older. His moves were bold and swift. He informed Brett Myers, who had started three Opening Days for the Phillies, that we would not pursue a new contract; he released one of the best third basemen we've had in recent history, Pedro Feliz; and he let living legend Pedro Martinez return to retirement. Rubén signed former Philly Placido Polanco to play third base and then, after he signed Halladay, the city was riding a high—for all of 20 minutes—until we were informed that Amaro made his most startling trade of 2010: he sent away Cliff Lee for a few no-name prospects. Say what you will, Rubén Amaro had a vision and the courage to see it through to its end. Everyone knew that whatever lay in store, this was going to be a season when you just had to strap yourself in: we were in for a helluva ride.

The Season

The Phillies' opening game provided a great clue as to makeup of the team. We mauled the Washington Nationals behind a stellar performance from Roy Halladay of 11-1. Sadly, our home opener a week later was very telling as well when Jimmy Rollins, who had gotten off to a blisteringly hot start, was scratched from the lineup due to a "calf strain." Losing our spark-plug starting shortstop and leadoff hitter was a big blow, but it was only a portent of larger things to come. In all, we lost 19 players to over 400 days of injury. Every regular player except Jayson Werth went down for a time.

Still, the Phils kept their heads above water, and kept themselves in the game. We would remain in first place until the end of May before being overcome by the Atlanta Braves. We would struggle from this point, falling behind by as many as seven games on July 20, while keeping above the .500 mark by only three. With the trade deadline looming, Rubén Amaro got to work and picked up the best pitcher on the market—Roy Oswalt of the Astros. A three-time All Star, Oswalt had won 20 games twice in his career and at 32 years of age, he was still in his prime. No matter how hard it was to give up one of our best young players (J.A. Happ), Oswalt rejuvenated the club. The Phils went 41-19 the rest of the way and took the division by a full six games. Our oft-injured offense somehow managed to score the second most runs in the National League. And what's more important, we entered the playoffs with a full and healthy roster, ready to do battle behind the finest moundsmen ever assembled in Philadelphia.

THE 2010 NATIONAL LEAGUE DIVISION SERIES

It all began brilliantly enough, with Roy Halladay throwing only the second postseason no-hitter in baseball history. It was a nice bookend to the perfect game he threw against the Marlins earlier in the season. After we took game two, thanks to a succession of Cincinnati errors, Cole Hamels nailed down the series with the Reds with a complete game shutout.

No question about it: our pitching looked amazing. The problem was that the offense never really clicked. After scoring four runs off Edinson Volquez in the first one and a third innings of play in game one, the Phillies went on to tally a whopping three earned runs in the remaining 23 and two-thirds innings. We hit just .212 as a team, with a grand total of one home run. It was a frightening omen of things to come.

THE 2010 NATIONAL LEAGUE CHAMPIONSHIP SERIES

The championship series against the eventual World Champion San Francisco Giants wasn't pretty to watch. We dropped game one, 4-3, watching helplessly as some late-season pickup named Cody Ross hit two solo shots against Roy Halladay. Ross would hit another shot in the second game, the only blemish on a masterful performance by Roy Oswalt, as our bats came to life. We won the game, 6-1, to tie the series at one game apiece.

Giants starter Matt Cain allowed only two hits in the next contest, shutting us out 3-0. Like Halladay in game one, Hamels had given us a fine start, but we couldn't capitalize on getting five runners into scoring position. Charlie Manuel ignited some controversy in game four when he pitched Joe Blanton, despite trailing the series two games to one. Our offense managed to explode for four runs in the fifth inning, but Blanton couldn't hang onto the lead. Eventually, Manuel would turn to Oswalt, who had just pitched three days before, to take the mound in the bottom of the ninth of a tie game. The Giants would make quick work of him, scoring a run on a Juan Uribe sacrifice and taking a 3-1 series lead. Things looked glum in Philly, but if ever a team had the arms to bring them three wins in a row, it was this club. Now if only our offense would show up to the park.

Roy Halladay brought us back to within a game the next day. Even though Halladay pulled a groin muscle in the second inning, he pitched with grit through six, enabling the Phils to take the game, 4-2. Game six would see the fabulous return of our offensive game—at least for the first inning. There would be a double, two singles, a sacrifice fly, a walk, and a wild pitch. But when the dust had cleared, we managed only two runs off Giants starter Jonathan Sanchez. "The O" would completely shut down after this, leaving 13 runners on base during a 3-2 loss. We would hit only .216 for the series with three home runs.

It was difficult to watch the young Giants celebrate the victory on our own home field. But there was also something else in the air. The 2010 Phils were a team transformed. They were a club that was not going to sit back, happy in their continued excellence. These Phillies had the courage to understand that excellence is only one step on the road to legendary. And to travel that road, we would have to set our sights on the seasons to come.

Phillies Memory

John Burns, Longtime Fan

My baseball memories for my daughter Claire and me started in 2007 when The Bank exploded after Brett Myers struck out the last Nationals batter to give us the division title over the Mets. I had to hold my then seven-year-old in my arms because she became overwhelmed by the storm of joy and noise that was swirling all around us. It was a What-Have-I-Done? moment.

I feared that rather than turning her into a fan, I had helped to push her away from the game. This sensation went away over the following day or so when, on our way to her school, she and her friend Kate (who was also at the game) would wave their rally towels out of our car windows while chanting, "Let's Go Phillies" to anyone in earshot.

For Claire and the rest of our family, the 2008 moment remains The Parade that followed a storm of a different kind.